America's Other Clan

THE UNITED STATES SUPREME COURT

First Edition

By Albert I. Slomovitz

Kennesaw State University

cognella®
academic publishing

Bassim Hamadeh, CEO and Publisher
Michael Simpson, Vice President of Acquisitions
Jamie Giganti, Managing Editor
Jess Busch, Graphic Design Supervisor
Zina Craft, Acquisitions Editor
Monika Dziamka, Project Editor
Natalie Lakosil, Licensing Manager
Miguel Macias, Interior Designer

First published in the United States of America in 2014 by Cognella, Inc.

Interior images:
1-2: Copyright © Castanea dentata (CC by 3.0) at http://commons.wikimedia.org/wiki/File:Triangle_trade.png.; 1.6: Copyright © Hotstreets (CC by 2.0) at http://commons.wikimedia.org/wiki/File:Northwest_territory.png.; 1-8: Copyright © Beyond My Ken (CC by 2.0) at http://commons.wikimedia.org/wiki/File:Marbury_v_Madison_John_Marshall_by_Swatjester_crop.jpg.; 5-10: Copyright © Jeromie Huffine (CC by 3.0) at http://commons.wikimedia.org/wiki/File:EdJohnson.jpg.; 6-3: Copyright © 1946 Associated Press; 6-7: Copyright © Rmhermen (CC by 3.0) at http://commons.wikimedia.org/wiki/File:Rosa_parks_bus.jpg.; 6-9: Copyright © AnonMoos (CC by 3.0) at http://commons.wikimedia.org/wiki/File:Educational_separation_in_the_US_prior_to_Brown_Map.svg. All other images: Copyright in the Public Domain.

Printed in the United States of America

ISBN: 978-1-62661-957-9 (pbk) / 978-1-62661-958-6 (br)

www.cognella.com   800-200-3908

Contents

This book is a summation of years of discussion, analyzing materials, and delving deep into very uncomfortable waters. I dedicate this research to those who have been wronged by prejudice and intolerance. My hope for our country is a future that is based on mutual respect and equality.

INTRODUCTION

By Albert I. Slomovitz

All Sergeant Isaac Woodard needed was a bathroom break. Up to that point, his day had been very memorable. That morning, he had received his honorable discharge from the U.S. Army after five years of service in World War II. During that time, he had earned a number of military medals. Still in uniform, he was heading home to North Carolina on a Greyhound bus, looking forward to reuniting with family and friends and moving on with his life.

At the next bus stop, Sergeant Woodard mentioned to the driver that he needed to use the restroom. The driver cursed at him and said, "No." Sergeant Woodard cursed back, walked off the bus, and used the bathroom. That seemingly ended the incident. But there was one fatal flaw that Woodard could not have foreseen. At the next bus stop in Batesburg, South Carolina, the driver contacted the local sheriff, Linwood Shull, about this black man who had the audacity to argue with him. The sheriff took the sergeant off the bus, brought him to a nearby alley, and with other police officers, beat Woodard unmercifully with their nightsticks.

Next, Sergeant Woodard was taken to the local jail and continually assaulted throughout the evening. He was attacked so severely, that by morning, he was blind in both eyes and suffered partial amnesia. He was brought to a local court, found guilty of "disorderly conduct," and fined. He did not receive medical treatment for two days. What a cruel fate, to have survived for five years in military service, but attacked by lawmen in your own country![1] [Intro.1]

As a 20-year military veteran, this brutal attack was especially troubling to me. What happened to our legal, moral, and social system that allowed this and thousands of similar incidents to occur? It is my contention that in many ways, Woodard had been abandoned by the keepers of the United States Constitution: the U.S. Supreme Court. From the earliest days of this country, all the way through the mid-1900s, the Supreme Court justices had accepted and promulgated the premise that people of color were not on the same political, economic, social, or personal level as whites.

---

1   http://theobamacrat.com, Blinding of Isaac Woodard, Jr.

In this regard, while the Ku Klux Klan attacked individuals and people who advocated tolerance and equality, the Court—or, as I call them, "America's Other Clan"—attacked people of color with legal weapons. The attacks of the Klan were premeditated, vicious, and local, whereas the findings of the Court were nationwide. The effects of their legal decisions were far more substantial and widespread than the actions of the Klan. It may be fair to surmise that the decisions of the Court "Clan" emboldened the actions of the other Klan. In my opinion, the attitudes of the justices led people such as the sheriff in Sergeant Woodard's case to believe that the law he swore to maintain would not hold him in any way responsible because a black man was savagely beaten. This attitude prevailed throughout much of American history.

While the scope of this book begins in colonial times and ends in 2014, a particularly significant period was after the Civil War. In case after case, the Court did not affirm the core values found in the three post–Civil War amendments to the Constitution: the Thirteenth, Fourteenth, and Fifteenth amendments. Clearly, the High Court ignored many laws such as the Civil Rights Act of 1875, which called explicitly for equal accommodations of all public forms of transportation. The Jim Crow era in America simply would not have been able to exist without the benign blessing of the justices.

This work is not an attempt to besmirch the High Court. I have the utmost respect for the Court and the role it plays in our thriving democracy. Rather, the role of this book is to shine the light of history upon the Court and its decisions, so that all citizens can better understand our past. Once we see the past with more clarity, then vision and insight can light our way forward.

Other scholars have written extensively in this area of history. One of the premier academics is Michael J. Klarman, who authored the encyclopedic book, *From Jim Crow to Civil Rights*. He makes this major point at the beginning of his work: "This book makes no claim about how judges *should* decide cases … Judges are part of contemporary culture and they rarely hold views that deviate far from dominant public opinion."

It is on this significant point that I respectfully disagree. It is my contention that the Supreme Court of the land helped create, sustain, and promote the contemporary values, mores, and standards of their own time. I believe that most Americans presumed that the primary role of the Court was to interpret the Constitution and to help promote the values of our country. As the Court ruled, so America followed.

Because the Court did not take a clear stance of the illegality or immorality of attacks on the rights of the black community, such assaults persisted over time. It is not adequate, in my opinion, to maintain that the Court followed the majority values in America. That led directly to lynchings. When Ed Johnson or Leo Frank were illegally hanged in the early 1900s, some governmental entity had to take ultimate responsibility for those events. That role belonged to the High Court, I believe, and not to people such as Thomas Watson, a purveyor of racism and prejudice.

This work has multiple goals. First, from a historical perspective, it attempts to rebalance the significance the Court played in shaping America for at least a century after the Civil War in the arena of civil rights. Most texts of American history give a few short references to the decisions of the Court. This is frustratingly inadequate. From an educational perspective, the reader will interact with the words of the justices and decide for themselves what these words mean and grapple with the real-world consequences of those decisions. These cases also hold within them fascinating items of American history such as the reality of the post–Civil War "Black Codes" and the courage of Josephine DeCuir, a woman whom I describe as the Rosa Parks of the 19th century.

A final theme of this work is the broader subject of race relations in America. This research affords us the opportunity to grasp the tenacity and persistence of prejudice that existed and still exists in our country. Through our awareness of those forces, if we are able, by our own actions, to make society more fair and equitable for everyone, then this book will be a success.

ALL MEN ARE NOT CREATED EQUALLY

U nfortunately, slavery has long been a component in the history of humankind. Mentioned
in biblical times and practiced in almost every
major ancient civilization, this institution rapidly
became part of the New World's society. Around
the year 1500, increased explorations by various
nations, more awareness of shipbuilding, naviga-
tion, and the invention of the printing press created
a new frontier of global discoveries. Spanish and
Portuguese ships traveled the globe searching for
items of trade, knowledge, and information. When
Portuguese explorers came to the mouth of the
Congo River in 1483, they discovered a number
of tribes and people who populated the region.
The contacts between the explorers and different
African tribes developed into a series of trade
propositions involving slaves. Other powers, such
as the French and Dutch, also came to Africa and
began developing such commerce. (See Figure 1-1.)

This slave trade was fueled by New World
economies that had begun cultivating sugar in Brazil
and later in the Caribbean islands. African slaves,
some already exposed to European diseases, were
preferred to Native Americans, who often died as
they came in contact with foreigners. Beginning in
the 1520s, Europeans began to import African slaves

1-1: African slaves found on a ship engaged in global slave-trading.

to work the sugar plantations in the New World.[1] This paradigm of using slaves in agricultural endeavors was duplicated in the American colonies in the 1600s. Initially, colonies such as Virginia used indentured servants to work in the tobacco fields. Immigrants from England signed contracts that pledged (indentured) themselves to work for a colonial employee in return for passage to America. A typical agreement stipulated a period of four to seven years without compensation to pay off the money owed.[2] At the end of the agreed period, these workers were given their

"freedom dues," usually three barrels of corn and a suit of clothes. For the most part, these servants were poor Englishmen seeking work and adventure. Many were orphans who had no special training or skills. Staying alive through the contracted period was a risk for all concerned. Among one group of 275 indentured men who arrived in Maryland in mid-century, 40 percent died before their servitude period ended.[3]

Within a short period, a transformation occurred regarding the type of individuals utilized to work the agricultural fields in the colonies. Throughout the 1670s, slave labor began to replace the system of indentured servants. This change was generated by developments in earlier decades from British-ruled Barbados. During the mid-1600s, sugarcane had created great wealth for the island planters. World demand for sugar was growing dramatically. By mid-century, annual sugar exports from the British Caribbean totaled almost 150,000 pounds. Exports reached almost 50 million pounds by the end of the century.[4]

To meet this demand, the sugar growers purchased thousands of African slaves. For these slaves, life was brutal, lonely, and all too brief. Planters continually purchased new slaves as replacements for those who died. As planters from the islands migrated to colonies such as South Carolina, they brought their slaves with them and began to use them in place of indentured servants. In the Chesapeake, Virginia, region, tobacco farmers were transitioning from indentured servants to slaves as well. For planters, slaves had some obvious advantages over those who were indentured. First, while the slaves cost more, they never attained their freedom and worked for the planter their whole lives. Second, whereas the indentured servants had legal rights, the slaves had none. While the indentured servants had the benefits of a legal contract, the slaves had no such protection. Children of indentured mothers were born free, whereas children of slaves inherited the slave status of their mother.

---

1   McNeill, *A History of the Human Community*, p. 441.
2   Roark, Johnson, et al., *The American Promise*, p. 49.
3   Ibid.
4   Ibid., p.61.

During these decades of transition from indentured servants to slaves, colonial laws gradually began depriving the slaves of any legal standing. In 1662, Virginia's General Assembly considered whether any child fathered "by an Englishmen upon a Negro woman should be slave or free." In this case, the laws reversed the long-standing English tradition that children inherited property based on their father's status. The legislature decided that children born in America shall be "held bond or free according to the condition of the mother."[5] Such laws ensured that the children born to slaves followed in the same footsteps. This rule helped create new generations of American-born slaves, thrust into lives of destitution and servitude.

Even those who accepted Christianity and wished to enter the established colonial society had this possibility legally closed. A Maryland law of 1664 made clear that the legal status of non-Christian slaves did not change if they experienced conversion. The commonwealth of Virginia agreed, and in 1667 stated, "The conferring of baptisme doth not alter the condition of the person as to his bondage."[6] Within a brief period of time, African slaves were stripped of any legal rights from which they might have benefited. Bereft of these protections, life became brutal. Corporal punishments such as whipping, torture, and mutilation were routinely employed against them. A Virginia law of 1680 reflected this situation: "if any Negro so much as raises a hand, even in self defense, against any Christian he shall receive thirty lashes, and if he absent himself … from his master's service against lawful apprehension, he may be killed."[7] Certainly, slaves were seen as chattel—the personal property of their owners to be bought and sold as if a commodity.

Slaves were part of a larger economic engine that generated enormous wealth in the colonies. Businessmen initiated cross-Atlantic trading opportunities that involved large amounts of goods, including tobacco, deerskin, cloth, muskets, rum, and slaves. The trading of slaves was one aspect of this elaborate transoceanic endeavor named the Triangle Trade. Countries such as England further developed this trade by initiatives like the chartering of the Royal African Company, which dispatched a steady flow of merchant ships to West Africa. The slave trade became so profitable that independent traders soon also participated. By the 1700s, a whole system of procuring slaves from tribes and locations deep within the African continent to be delivered to Europeans waiting in western African coastal areas had become well established. The numbers tell the story: Between 1700 and 1800 ship captains purchased more than 6.6 million Africans. Of these, nearly 800,000, or 12 percent, died during the passage from Africa. Therefore, just over 5.8 million captives survived the Atlantic crossing. Of these survivors, about 9 percent, or over half a million, were sent to North America during the 18th century."[8] (See Figure 1-2.)

Of course, the indignities of slavery began long before the arrival of the slaves in America. First came the initial entrapment by other Africans. This was followed by being trussed up to prevent any escape and for a transfer to an intermediate trader. After a forced march to the coast, captured slaves contended with hunger, fear, and fatigue. At this juncture, a European trader, acting as an agent for a large company, might purchase the Africans. Captives from small ports were carried by ship to major trading forts such as the one at Cape Coast Castle organized by the Royal African Company. As the captives were being taken out to larger ocean-crossing vessels,

---

5 Jones, Wood, et al., *Created Equal*, p. 121. While slaves were already considered property, colonial governments, by the end of the 18th century redefined slaves as personal rather than real property, which allowed them to be disposed of quicker and easier in a legal context. J. Oakes, M. McGerr, J. E. Lewis, N. Cullather, and J. Boydston, *Of the People*, 2011, p. 281.

6 Ibid.

7 Ibid.

8 Ibid., p. 130.

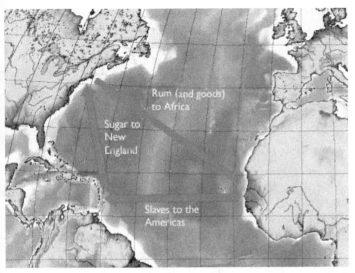

Rum (and goods)
to Africa

Sugar to
New
England

Slaves to the
Americas

1-2: Visual overview of the extensive transatlantic business endeavors involving slaves.

they often drowned by attempting to escape, even though their hands were tied behind their backs. Those who made it onto the larger ships had months of an uncertain voyage ahead. Onboard such ships, the captives, crowded into the lower holds of the ship, contended with horrible sanitation conditions, seasickness, loneliness, abuse from the crew, and more. Finally, if they survived this voyage—and many did not—they were subjected to "conditioning," where overseers were employed to "break" the slaves and force them to be compliant with their new reality and masters.[9] Certainly, many of these new slaves experienced what we now describe as post-traumatic stress syndrome. (Refer to Figure 1-3.)

Such conditions were reflected in the reality of slave life in the colonies. As the number of slaves increased in the colonies, given the brutal circumstances, many slaves attempted to escape. Laws passed in the 1700s mirrored the colonists' concern with this phenomenon. Virginia's Negro Act of 1705 mandated that white servants who were mistreated had the

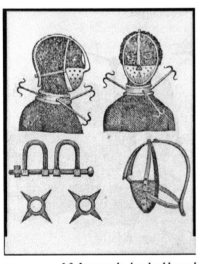

1-3: Iron masks, leg shackles and spurs used to imprison and degrade slaves.

right to sue their masters. African slaves had no such rights. Any enslaved person who tried to escape could be tortured and even dismembered in hopes of "terrifying others from the like practices." When masters or overseers killed a slave while inflicting punishment, they were automatically free of any felony charge, "as if no such accident had never happened."[10] Similar laws were passed in subsequent years. The Virginia legislature in 1723 provided the following law, "if any number of Negroes shall consult, advise, or conspire, to rebel or make insurrection … they shall suffer death."[11]

Despite such Draconian regulations, slaves yearned to taste freedom. In South Carolina, the Stono Rebellion occurred in September of 1739. On September 9th, a group of about 20 slaves gathered near the Stono River, about 20 miles from Charleston. They armed themselves and went to various homes, where they killed the owners and liberated the slaves and urged them to join their rebellion. By the afternoon, they had killed between 20 and 25 whites and had gathered together a group of about 50. That same day, these slaves were pursued by a posse of armed whites. Some of the slaves were killed or captured; a few managed to escape, only to be captured over the next month.[12]

---

9   Ibid., p. 133.

10   Ibid., p. 125.

11   Irons, *A People's History of the Supreme Court*, p. 14.

12   Jones, Wood, and Borstelmann, *Created Equal*, p. 138.

The legislature of South Carolina responded to this rebellion with an extensive law code regarding slaves entitled, "An Act for the better Ordering and Governing (of) Negroes and other Slaves in this Province." Following are samples of this code.

I. Be it enacted, that all negroes, Indians (free Indians in amity with this government, and negroes, mulatos and mestizos who are now free excepted) mulattos or mestizos who are now are or shall hereafter be in this Province, and all their issue and offspring born or to be born, shall be and they are hereby declared to be and remain forever hereafter absolute slave ...

V. If any slave who shall be out of the house or plantation where such slave shall live or shall be usually employed, or without some white person in company with such slave, shall refuse to submit or to undergo the examination of any white person, it shall be lawful for any such white Person to pursue, apprehend and moderately correct such slave; and if such slave shall assault and strike such white person, such slave may be lawfully killed.

XVI. Be it therefore enacted, that the several crimes and offences herein after particularly enumerated are hereby declared to be felony without the benefit of the clergy. That is to say, If any slave, free negroes, mulatto, Indian or mestizo shall willfully and maliciously burn or destroy any stack of rice, ... burn or destroy any tar kiln ... , take or carry away any slave, being the property of another, with intent to carry such slave out of this Province; or shall willfully and maliciously poison, or administer poison to any person, free man, woman, servant or slave ... shall suffer death as a felon.

XXXVII. And whereas cruelty is not only highly unbecoming those who profess themselves Christians, but is odious in the eyes of all men who have any sense or virtue or humanity; therefore to restrain and prevent barbarity being exercised toward slaves, be it enacted, That if any person or persons whosoever, shall willfully murder his own slave, or the slave of another person, every such person shall upon conviction thereof, forfeit the pay of 700 pounds current money ... And if any person shall on a sudden heat or passion, or by undue correction, kill his own slave or the slave of any person, he shall forfeit the sum of 350 pounds current money, And in case any person or persons shall willfully cut out the tongue, put out the eye, castrate or cruelly scald, burn, or deprive any slave of any limb or member, or shall inflict any other cruel punishment, other than by whipping or beating with a horsewhip, cow-skin, switch or small stick, or by outing irons on, or confining or imprisoning such slave; every such person shall for every such offense, forfeit the sum of 100 pounds current money.[13]

This brutality was not limited to the colonial South. Colonies such as New Jersey also had an active slave population. "In rejecting a proposed slave tariff in 1744, the Provincial Council declared that nothing would be permitted to interfere with the importation of Negroes. The council observed that slaves had become essential to the colonial economy, since most entrepreneurs could not afford to pay the high wages commanded by free workers."[14] Free blacks

---

13 Hall, Wiecek, and Finkelman, *American Legal History*, pp. 36–40.
14 slavenorth.com/newjersey

were barred by law from owning land in colonial New Jersey. In fact, from 1713 through 1768, the colony operated a separate court system to deal with slave crimes.[15] The colony had strict laws regarding slaves with the intention of avoiding slave revolts. Slaves could not assemble on their own or be in the streets at night. The punishment of being burned at the stake was used as well. "In 1735, a slave in Bergen County who attempted to set fire to a house was burned at the stake. Six years later, authorities in Hackensack burned at the stake two slaves who had set fire to barns."[16]

Similarly, across the Hudson River in New York City was the locale for an unbelievably brutal assault on people of color in 1741. A series of fires that plagued the city was blamed on a group of slaves. A mob captured the slaves and gave them quick trials. Thirteen blacks were convicted of treason and burned at the stake, 16 slaves were hanged for arson, along with four whites, and another 70 blacks were banished from the colony.[17]

As the decades of the 1700s grew closer to the time period of the Declaration of Independence and the rebellion against England, concerns such as the freedom of slaves were beginning to be expressed. For some, it seemed implausible to speak of freedom and notions such as "all men are created equal" and "unalienable rights" enjoyed by all citizens, while men and women of color were denied basic human rights. This attitude partially had its roots in the teachings of Quakers who resided in New Jersey and Pennsylvania. They argued that black bondage violated basic Christian concepts, especially the idea that all people are equal in the eyes of God. At the same time, slavery as an economic practice was much less an element in the economy of Northern society. By the 1780s, state governments in Pennsylvania and New England, as well as most Northern states, passed laws banning or abolishing slavery.[18]

In fact, the number of blacks living in America at this time is impressive. In 1774, on the eve of the Revolutionary war, blacks numbered 500,000 out of a total population of 2,600,000. This ratio of nearly 20 percent was maintained in 1790 when the first federal census was taken, the black population then numbering 757,181 out of a total count of 3,929,625.[19]

As Americans were addressing this issue, another topic of contemporary concern was the initial governing document of America, the Articles of Confederation. In 1787, many Americans had come to realize that the Articles were flawed in a number of ways. Under the Articles, the powers of government were concentrated in the legislature—a unicameral Congress—with the states having equal voting powers. It was apparent to most that this first attempt at a governing document for the new country needed revision.

In May 1787, urged by Alexander Hamilton and others who envisioned a strong national government, the Constitutional Convention was called to gather in Philadelphia. The task of these 55 men assembled in an atmosphere of secrecy was to create a new governing doctrine and document. Some of the topics discussed included the nature of the government, the power of the executive branch, and the balance of power between the states and the federal government.

One of the most passionately discussed topics was the nature of representation in the new government. If power in a future Congress was based solely on population, then the smaller states would lose much of their influence. In this regard, various governing strategies

---

15 Ibid.
16 Ibid.
17 Irons, *A People's History*, p. 14.
18 Ayers, Gould, et al., *American Passages*, p. 138.
19 *Ebony* Magazine, August 1975, "Black America at the Time of the Revolutionary War," Benjamin Quarles, p. 45.

were proposed, the Virginia and New Jersey plans. The former plan favored proportional representation, while the latter wanted each state to receive an equal vote, regardless of population. A committee led by Benjamin Franklin devised a Congress that included a Senate based on equal votes for the states and the House based on population. This understanding came to be called the Great Compromise.[20]

Linked to this question was a secondary, yet very significant, issue: How would slaves be counted in this new governmental system? As Peter Irons in his superb work on the Supreme Court notes, varying factions arose at the convention regarding how slaves fit into the

1-4: Gathering of the country's leaders at the signing of the U.S. Constitution, 1787.

framework of the new Constitution. Leaders such as James Madison were determined to find a viable solution to this issue. Political opinions regarding slaves and representation were varied. William Paterson from New Jersey, a future Supreme Court justice, believed that true gentlemen of good breeding were needed to govern. As far as slaves, Paterson's views were clear: "he would regard the Negro slaves in no light but property. They have no free agents, have no personal liberty, no faculty of acquiring property, but on the contrary are themselves property, and like other property entirely at the will of the master."[21] One of Paterson's goals was to prevent small Southern states with populations equal to that of small Northern states from being able to outvote Northern states based on any advantage they might have if they counted their slaves for purposes of representation. This topic was referred to a working group called the Committee of Eleven, which was not able to reach a resolution. (See Figure 1-4.)

At this stage, Hugh Williamson of South Carolina proposed a compromise: he moved that, "a census shall be taken of the free white inhabitants and three fifths of other descriptions and that representation be regulated accordingly."[22] This formulation had originally been devised by the Continental Congress in 1783, when that body was searching for a formula on how to apportion taxes of the states based on their populations, rather than their real estate holdings. Various percentages were proposed. Ultimately, James Madison recommended the three-fifths ratio, which was adopted by the 1787 Constitutional Convention.[23] While other delegates from South Carolina insisted that blacks be fully counted in the rule of representation, their view did not prevail. Madison found this idea objectionable on moral and practical grounds. Nevertheless, this new formula allowed Southern states to count slaves as three fifths of a person for direct taxes, House of Representative seats, and the electoral college.

This additional representational power allowed the Southern states with large numbers of slaves to acquire greater political power in the decades prior to the Civil War. The agreement ultimately became part of the new Constitution in the First Article, Second Section, and is the

20   Jones, Wood, and Borstelmann, *Created Equal*, p. 279.
21   Irons, *A People's History*, p. 30.
22   Ibid., p. 31.
23   Digital History.uh.edu, The Three-Fifth Compromise

first of many references in the Constitution that speaks obliquely—but never directly—about slaves or slavery.

> *Representatives and direct taxes shall be apportioned among the several States which may be included within this Union, according to their respective Numbers, which shall be deter-mined by adding to the whole Number of free persons, including those bound to Service for a term of Years, and excluding Indians not taxed, three fifths of all other persons.*

Within a few weeks of the Great Compromise, a new effort was made by some delegates to make a statement about slavery. Luther Martin of Maryland proposed that Congress be allowed to prohibit the future importation of slaves into America. Martin remarked that slavery "was inconsistent with the principles of the revolution and dishonorable to the American character to have such a feature in the Constitution."[24] Southerners such as John Rutledge of South Carolina threatened to leave the convention if the issue was considered: "The people of those states will never be such fools as to give up so important an interest."[25] As with the representation question, this topic was also referred to a committee. This group, unable to reach a definitive conclusion about slavery, devised a compromise position, which called for a period of 20 years prior to calling for a ban on the importation of slaves. James Madison cast the only vote against this proposal. He warned against the 20-year period. "So long a term will be more dishonorable to the national character than to say nothing about it in the Constitution."[26] This compromise was reflected in the Constitution's First Article, Ninth Section, first paragraph.

> *The Migration or Importation of such Persons as any of the States now existing shall think proper to admit, shall not be prohibited by the Congress prior to the year one thousand eight hundred and eight, but a Tax or duty may be imposed on such Importation, not exceeding ten dollars for each Person. (Refer to Figure 1-5.)*

One could surmise that, since the Southern representatives had agreed to a conclusion of the importation of slaves (albeit 20 years in the future), they now demanded something in return. This demand might have been the catalyst for the third reference about slaves in the Constitution, which reflected a situation that would not be resolved until the Civil War: the reality and status of runaway slaves. Led by delegates Butler and Pinckney of South Carolina, the convention voted on August 28 "to require fugitive slaves and servants to be delivered up like criminals."[27] The delegates agreed to this proposal by voice vote, and it is reflected somewhat obscurely in the Constitution, the Fourth Article, Section Two, the second paragraph,

> *No person held to Service or labor in one state, under the laws thereof, escaping into another, shall, in Consequence of any law or Regulation therein, be discharged from such Service or Labour, but shall be delivered up on Claim of the party to whom such Service or Labour may be due.*

---

24 Ibid., p. 34.
25 Ibid., p. 35.
26 Ibid.
27 Ibid., p. 34.

What this section seemed to enforce was the concept that slave owners or their agents had the legal right to track down, capture, and return escaped slaves to their places of confinement. The vagueness of this brief paragraph also raised many questions. Among those was one of authority: Was the enforcement of this part of the Constitution a federal or state requirement, and how would it be implemented on a practical basis? Were there consequences if state or local authorities chose not to detain a runaway? These topics were addressed, with Congress in 1793 passing the Fugitive Slave Act. "The 1793 act allowed masters or their agents who captured runaways to bring them to any magistrate, state or federal, to obtain a "certificate of removal," authorizing the claimants to take the runaway slaves out of the states where they were found, and back to the state where the slaves owed service."[28]

In addition to these three initial references to slavery in the Constitution, scholars point to other examples in the Constitution, which, upon reflection, indicate an acknowledgement of the institution of slavery. A case in point would be the Tenth Article of the First Ten Amendments to the Constitution. These well-known amendments, ratified in 1791, a few years after the acceptance of the Constitution, gave much legal weight to the authority of the states. Thus, when the Tenth Amendment states, "The powers not delegated to the United States by the Constitution, nor prohibited by it to the States, are reserved to the States respectively, or to the people," it seemed that the institution of slavery was a states' issue rather than a federal one.[29] Furthermore, the Constitution never addressed the topic of defining who a slave was and when or how they achieved their freedom. This lack of guidance, perhaps done deliberately, allowed local authorities to determine issues regarding slaves and slavery.

LANDING NEGROES AT JAMESTOWN FROM DUTCH MAN-OF-WAR, 1619

1-5: Based on the Constitution, slavery continued in the 1800s. This picture depicts slaves arriving in Virginia aboard a Dutch ship in an earlier time period.

28 Wiecek and Finkelman, *American Legal History*, p. 201.
29 Drobak, John N., Political Working Paper, Washington University, St. Louis.

1-7: In its early years, the High Court held its sessions in a chamber located in the U.S. Senate. The Supreme Court met in this facility until a new building was constructed in 1935.

States, shall be the supreme Law of the Land; and Judges in every State shall be bound thereby, any Thing in the Constitution or Laws of any State to the Contrary notwithstanding.

While the initial notion behind this article is the maintenance of some tension between the power of the states' judicial branches and that of the Supreme Court, the opposite would be the case. This change occurred because the Judiciary Act of 1789 provided for appeals from state courts to the federal judiciary, and finally to the Supreme Court of the United States. The result of this act and subsequent Supreme Court decisions gave the High Court, an agent of the federal government, the ultimate power to interpret the extent of state and national authority under the Constitution.[35]

The Judiciary Act of 1789 further created a number of new realities in American law. It established 13 legal districts around the newly formed country. Eleven of them were placed in three circuits ranging the length of the East Coast. Under this act, the Supreme Court was to have one chief justice and five associate justices. This number was modified to nine in 1837. The act also further defined the areas of authority for these new courts and the Supreme Court. District courts were to serve as trial courts hearing cases involving admiralty issues, forfeitures and penalties, petty federal crimes, and minor federal civil cases. The role of the Supreme Court was further defined in Section 25 of the act. It was a victory for those who favored the principle of national sovereignty. Appeals to the Supreme Court were provided based on the findings of the highest state courts. Appeals could be made if state courts ruled against a federal treaty or law, ruled in favor of a state law that seemed contradictory to the Constitution, or the state ruled against a privilege or right claimed under the Constitution or federal law. In effect, this meant that appeals would be taken in all instances where the state judiciary assuredly failed to give full recognition to the supremacy of the Constitution, or to the treaties and laws of the United States, as provided by Article VI of the Constitution.[36]

Despite the Judiciary Act, there were still some in Congress who felt that all three branches of governmental held equal responsibility to interpret the Constitution, especially the legislative branch. This debate was preempted by the Court in its groundbreaking decision of *Marbury v. Madison* in 1803. In his finding about the case, Chief Justice John Marshall promulgates some significant legal parameters for the Court. First, he concludes that the Constitution is the fundamental and paramount law of the land. Second, he affirms that it is the responsibility of the courts to interpret the law—to say what the law is. Marshall also determines that "the particular phraseology of the constitution of the United States confirms and strengthens the principle,

---

35   Kelly and Harbison, *The American Constitution*, p. 139. Another excellent reference to the early intellectual underpinning of the Constitution is found in Alexander Hamilton's *Federalist Essays* Number 78.
36   Ibid., p. 173.

supposed to be essential to all written constitutions, that a law repugnant to the constitution is void, and that the courts, as well as other departments, are bound by the instrument."[37] (Refer to Figure 1-8.)

This principle regarding the role of the Supreme Court is reiterated within a few years in a brief case entitled *Cohens v. Virginia*, decided in 1821. In this case, the High Court overturns a decision by the Virginia Supreme Court.

1-8: The supremacy of the High Court as the nation's utmost legal authority begins to be established at this time.

In a unanimous decision, the Court held that the Supreme Court had jurisdiction to review state criminal proceedings. Chief Justice Marshall wrote that the Court was bound to hear all cases that involved constitutional questions, and that this jurisdiction was not dependent on the identity of the parties in the cases. Marshall argued that state laws and constitutions, when repugnant to the Constitution and federal laws were "absolutely void."[38]

While the actual case was decided in the manner that the Virginia court had proscribed, the authority in reviewing any state's legal decision is reinforced by the nation's highest court.

These decisions in *Marbury* and in *Cohens* began a process which culminated decades later in the belief that it was the sole responsibility of the judicial branch—not the executive branch or the legislative—to interpret the constitutionality of a particular act or bill passed by Congress. While the president still had the power to veto legislation, the Supreme Court gradually became, according to the thinking of most Americans, the ultimate determining factor in the area of law.

This is a point that requires consideration and amplification. Once this principle of the Court being the final arbiter of the country's legal questions had been established in the minds of Americans, its position on contemporary questions became significant. While some of the questions decided were limited to specific or obscure legal points, others had the ability to change the course of people's lives. The author contends that the High Court's subsequent decisions regarding civil rights would be widely known and understood by most Americans. Considered to be the country's highest legal source, their decisions led to social degradation, economic deprivation, and even death for generations of African Americans. (See Figure.1-9.)

1-9: Despite legal challenges, slavery continued. Pictured here is a group of slaves handcuffed and with shackled feet passing through the nation's capital, ca. 1815.

As the new country began its existence, the long-standing issue of slavery and its many ramifications in the social, political, and legal fabric of America became apparent. In the early 1800s, as new states were organized, their choice of being a free or slave state affected the nation. For example, in 1818, the territory of Missouri petitioned Congress for statehood, with the intention of entering the Union as a slave state. In the next year, Maine applied for admission to statehood as a free state. Congress proposed

37   Ibid., p. 228.
38   http://oyez.org, *Cohens v. Virginia*.

that both territories enter as a slave state and free state, respectively, with an amendment offered by Senator Thomas of Illinois. This amendment prohibited slavery in any remaining portion of the Louisiana Purchase above the parallel of 36°30' north latitude. President James Monroe initially considered vetoing the Missouri Act (also known as the Missouri Compromise) as unconstitutional on the grounds that Congress had no authority to prohibit slavery in the territories, despite the fact that the Northwest Ordinance had done exactly that. Nevertheless, he ultimately signed it into law.[39]

Prior to full statehood, the proposed new state of Missouri submitted to Congress in 1820–1821 a new state constitution. It contained a clause that banned free blacks from entering the state. This provision generated controversy. Northern congressmen felt that the clause violated Article IV, Section 2 of the Constitution, which provides that "The Citizens of each state shall be entitled to all privileges and immunities of citizens in the several states." The congressmen also point out the incongruity that blacks, who were already citizens of some Northern states, would be denied entry into Missouri at all. This denial is, in their opinion, a clear violation of basic constitutional rights.[40] In reply, Southern legislators contend that those privileges were not meant to be extended to blacks and mulattos by the Constitution. Southern leaders felt that blacks could not be considered citizens, since they did not possess all the civil and political rights enjoyed by whites, even in the free states. Therefore, the privileges and immunities clause of the Constitution is not applicable to them. Eventually, this particular matter is settled with the intervention of Congressman Henry Clay, who devised a compromise wherein the state would be admitted for statehood with the promise that Missouri would not attempt to pass any law that barred the entry of a citizen from another state.[41]

Even at this early stage of America's existence, the issue of slavery and its growth or cessation was a topic that elicited strong emotions. Thomas Jefferson, in correspondence with U.S. senator John Holmes, speaks of his concern that the federal government was usurping too much power regarding the admission of Missouri as a new state. His words portray his sentiments regarding slavery,

> *But this momentous question, like a fire bell in the night, awakened and filled me with terror. I considered it at once the knell of the Union … we have the wolf by the ear, and we can neither hold him, nor safely let him go. Justice is in scale, and self-preservation in the other.*

> *I regret that I am now to die in the belief that the useless sacrifice of themselves, by the generation of [17]76 to acquire self government and happiness to their country, is to be thrown away by the unwise and unworthy passions of their sons, and that my only consolation is to be that I live not to weep over it. If they would but dispassionately weigh the blessings they will throw away against an abstract principle more likely to be effected by union than by scission, they would pause before they perpetrate this act of suicide on themselves and of treason against the hopes of the world.[42] (See Figure 1-10.)*

---

39   Kelly and Harbison, *American Constitution*, p. 265.
40   Ibid., p. 268.
41   Ibid., p. 269.
42   http://loc.gov.exhibits/Jefferson

Another quote, from Georgia representative Thomas W. Cobb in 1819, reflects the hardened emotions of the South: "If you persist, the Union will be dissolved. You have kindled a fire which all of the waters of the ocean cannot put out, which seas of blood can only extinguish."[43]

In many ways, the admission of Missouri represents one small instance of how the question of slavery dominated American history throughout the early decades of the 19th century. An ultimate resolution seemed impossible between those who called for the cessation of slavery and those who were equally determined to perpetuate the institution at almost any cost. Various events of the 1820s, 1830s, and 1840s reflected this ongoing controversy. Obviously, the slaves themselves, their actions as individuals and as a collective body, influenced this topic as well. In 1822, a free black man named Denmark Vesey organized a fairly ambitious rebellion among the house slaves and black artisans in Charleston. His plans were betrayed to white authorities who called out the militia, hunted down Vesey and his conspirators, and ultimately hanged them.[44] (Refer to Figure 1-11.)

This specter of a slave rebellion that was averted was not the case in Virginia a decade later, when Nat Turner in August of 1831 gathered followers and began moving from one white farmhouse to another, killing anyone found inside and gathering their horses and weapons. By night's end, over 70 people had been killed. Troops arrive, and Turner and his followers are captured or killed. Within two months, he was hanged. Nevertheless, many delegates of the Virginia State Assembly were uncertain as to what their response should be to this phenomenon. Some call for colonization in Africa for slaves; others suggest that slavery is sanctioned by God as His plan for civilizing Africans. Still others decide that future legislatures would resolve the issue. For their part, the Assembly promulgated laws limiting the movement of slaves and the gathering of free blacks and slaves.[45] (Refer to Figure 1-12.)

At this stage, it is appropriate to mention that the ownership of slaves was not exclusively practiced by whites. In the Gulf Coast region, especially in the

1-10: Thomas Jefferson's words are unfortunately prophetic in nature as he accurately describes the internal and emotional conflicts in America over slavery.

Discovery of Nat Turner.

1-11: Nat Turner shown captured, but still desiring to be free.

43   www.visitthecapital.gov
44   Ayers and Gould, *American Passages*, pp. 223–224.
45   Ibid., p. 238.

1-12: Despite the passing on any new laws governing their movements, the slaves desired one fundamental reality—freedom. Pictured here are people participating in the Underground Railroad placing themselves at great risk, as they flee toward achieving that goal.

Louisiana area, free blacks owned slaves. By 1830, approximately 1,556 free blacks in the Deep South owned a total of 7,188 slaves. While one might have thought that free blacks would be more humane toward their slaves, this was apparently not the case. "In their attitudes toward their bondsmen and treatment of their slaves, these slave owners differed little from their white neighbors."[46] Some nonwhite slaveholders were, ironically, Cherokee Indians, who had assimilated slavery from the greater white colonial society. "Records indicate that the proportion of Cherokee slave owners was slightly higher than white southerners."[47] In fact, the status of slaves was so dire that a slave revolt against the Cherokee occurred in 1842.

In the early decades of the 1800s, as alluded to earlier, an interesting legal phenomenon began to occur. State courts, especially those from free states, began adjudicating cases that culminated with the slaves being freed. On the other hand, federal judges and courts were much more likely to find for the slave owner and his rights. In its 1836 decision, the Supreme Judicial Court of Massachusetts in *Commonwealth v. Aves* began, perhaps unwittingly, to set the stage for legal battles, as well as deepening mutual antagonism between North and South about slaves and the application of law.

In the case, a slave owner visited a relative in Boston, intending to remain there for a number of months. She brought with her a six-year-old slave girl named Med. Shortly after their arrival, the Boston Female Antislavery Society sued in state court to free the girl. The chief justice, Lemuel Shaw, raises some intriguing legal concepts. The first is that according to the doctrine of comity, he might have felt bound by the fact that slavery existed in some states, and as these were their laws, they should be acknowledged universally. However, Shaw concludes that by following this line of logic, slavery would be valid in Massachusetts. Yet, he further reasons, "that comity should only apply to those commodities which are everywhere, and by all nations treated and deemed subject of property."[48] In other words, since slaves were not considered property in Massachusetts, they became free when they entered the state, based on the existing state laws. In this case, Med gained her freedom. The case allowed that a slave owner briefly passing through the state was exempt from the ruling.

To better grasp the divide that was occurring around the country about the issue of slaves and slavery, it is significant to examine the writing of South Carolina senator John C. Calhoun, an ardent states' rights advocate. In 1837, he had received a number of petitions that called for an end to slavery in the District of Columbia and the abolition of the slave trade across state lines. His response indicates the deep differences in the North and South regarding this subject and the extent that the South was prepared to take up arms to maintain their way of life.

---

46   Schweninger, Loren, Prosperous Blacks in the South, *American Historical Review* 95(February 1990): 31–56., pp. 36–37.

47   Drobak, Political Working Paper, pp. 11–14.

48   Massachusetts Supreme Court, *Commonwealth v. Aves.*

It is instructive to first read Calhoun's perspective of slaves in the South followed by his awareness, almost 25 years before the Civil War, of the vast differences between North and South. (Refer to Figure 1–14.)

I appeal to facts. Never before has the black race of Central Africa, from the dawn of history to the present day, attained a condition so civilized and improved, not only physically, but morally and intellectually. It came among us in a low, degraded, and savage condition, and in the course of a few generations it has grown up under the fostering care of our institutions, reviled as they have been to its present comparatively civilized condition. This, with the rapid increase of numbers, is conclusive proof of the general happiness of the race, in spite of the exaggerated tales to the contrary.

1-13: This rendering depicts the daily abuses, including whipping, that all slaves had to endure regardless of age.

However sound the great body of the non-slaveholding States are at present, in the course of a few years they will be succeeded by those who will have been taught to hate the people and institutions of nearly one-half of this Union, with a hatred more deadly than one hostile nation ever entertained towards another. It is easy to see the end. By the necessary course of events, if left to themselves we must become, finally, two people. It is impossible under the deadly hatred which must spring up between the two great sections, if the present causes are permitted to operate unchecked, that we should continue under the same political system. The conflicting elements would burst the Union asunder, powerful as are the links which hold it together. Abolition and the Union cannot coexist. As the friend of the Union I openly proclaim it,—and the sooner it is known the better ... [49]

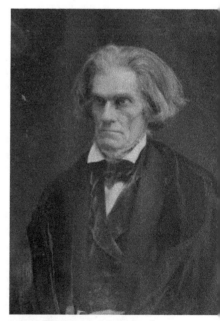

This duality of purpose and the vision of a just society are often reflected in state and federal cases regarding slaves and slavery. The *Aves* judgment in a state court might be contrasted with two other federal cases involving slaves. The first case, recently popularized by a movie, revolved around the schooner *L'Amistad*. In June of 1839, the ship, manned by a Spanish crew, left Havana, Cuba. They carried with them 49 Africans whom one of the crew claimed were his slaves. On the voyage, the Africans rebelled, killed the captain, and took possession of the ship. After this takeover, the Africans thought they were heading back to Africa; instead they were guided to the shore off of Long Island, New York. The ship and all involved were brought into

1-14: Calhoun esposed the notion that slavery had "civilized" enslaved blacks and made them happy! He also correctly anticipated the differing sectional forces that set the stage for the Civil War.

---

49 http://utk.edu, Speech of John C. Calhoun, 1837, p. 1.

port in Connecticut. Within a brief period, various individuals and the Spanish government laid claim to the ship and its cargo, including the slaves.

The response of the Africans and their counsel is clear and emphatic: "They specifically set forth and insist in this answer, that they were native born Africans; born free, and still right ought to be free and not slaves."[50] They continue to claim that every action taken against them was unlawful and fraudulent. In January 1840, a district court held "it rejected that claim made by the attorney of the United States on behalf of the Spanish minister for the restoration of the Negroes under the treaty; but it decreed that they should be delivered to the President of the United States, to be transported to Africa, pursuant to the act of March 3d, 1819."[51] This view seems to be an enlightened one. The Africans were free and would be sent back to their home of origin. The case was sent on to a circuit court, which referred it to the United States Supreme Court. The stance of the U.S. government was a tangential one at best, as noted by the Court. The United States did not pursue any legal claim on the ship or its cargo, nor did the government insist that the Africans be brought into America. The United States also did not even call for the transportation of the Africans back to Cuba. The government's position was focused on the rights of the Spanish government to reclaim property, in conjunction with a 1795 treaty between the two countries.

One of the most prominent Americans at that time, John Quincy Adams, the sixth president of the United States and the son of one of the most important founding fathers, John Adams, argued on behalf of the captured men. His focus is on the issue of personal freedom. "In a dramatic moment, Adams faces the judges, points to a copy of the Declaration of Independence hanging on the courtroom wall, and said, '[I know] no law, statute or constitution, no code, no treaty, except that law … which [is] forever before the eyes of your honors.'"[52]

The Court proceeds to analyze the case within the purview of the 1795 treaty. The ninth article of that treaty provided that all ships and merchandise rescued from the hands of pirates and robbers should be delivered to their true proprietors, as soon as due and sufficient proof was shown. The Court found, however, that this description did not fit the circumstances regarding the Africans onboard the *L'Amistad*. "If, then, these negroes are not slaves, but are kidnapped Africans, who, by the laws of Spain itself, are entitled to their freedom and were kidnapped and illegally carried to Cuba, and illegally detained and restrained on board the Amistad; there is no pretense to say, that they are pirates or robbers."[53] The Court does not allow any of the petitions claiming the Africans. Near the conclusion of this relatively short decision, the Court expresses itself on the larger issues regarding this case.

> *If the contest were about any goods on board of this ship, to which American citizens asserted a title, which was denied by the Spanish claimants, there could be no doubt of the right of such American citizens to litigate their claims before any competent American tribunal, notwithstanding the treaty with Spain. A fortiori, the doctrine must apply where human life and human liberty are in issue; and constitute the very essence of the controversy. The treaty with Spain never could have intended to take away the equal rights of foreigners, who should contest their claims before any of our courts, to equal justice; or to deprive such foreigners of the protection given them by other treaties, or by the general law*

---

50 U.S. Reports, 40–42, *United States v. Amistad*, 1841, at 589.
51 Ibid., p. 590.
52 http://history.com/Adamd, Arguments in the *Amistad* case.
53 Ibid.

of nations. Upon the merits of the case, then, there does not seem to us to be any ground
for doubt, that these Negroes ought to be deemed free; and that the Spanish treaty interposes
no obstacle to the just assertion of their rights.[54]

In its conclusion, the Court reverses the district court's ruling that had the Africans returning to Africa. The Court, continuing with its focus on freedom, declares the Africans fully free, presumably to come and go as they wished. This focus on freedom should not be mistaken as an abrupt shift for the Court. Nonetheless, it is significant to appreciate that the Court did not address the overall legality of slavery or the issue of runaway slaves in America. Indeed, other decisions reinforced the Court's view of slavery.

In the case of *Groves v. Slaughter*, also decided in 1841, the question to the Court involved a Mississippi state law concerning the sale of slaves. A group of citizens brought slaves into the state in 1836 and had been guaranteed (in a promissory note) payment on the sale of the slaves. When the payment was not forthcoming or the slaves returned, the initial buyers of the slaves sued. The defense of those who had taken the slaves was that the whole endeavor was illegal under state law. The disagreement over the legality of selling slaves revolved around the following article in the constitution of Mississippi, adopted on the 26th of October 1832.

The introduction of slaves into this State, as merchandise, or for sale, shall be prohibited,
from and after the 1st of May 1833; provided, that the actual settler, or settlers, shall not
be prohibited from purchasing slaves in any State in this Union, and bringing them into
this State for their own usage until the year 1845.[55]

The Court then proceeds to examine the major laws passed by the state regarding the sale of slaves. Sometimes, the laws seemed contradictory. In 1833, a law was passed which levied a tax on slaves that had been sold in the state. Also, an act of 1837 declares that "hereafter, the business of introducing or importing slaves into this State, as merchandise, or for sale, be and the same is hereby prohibited."[56] The Court reasons that when the sale of slaves in question was made, there was no fixed or settled policy in place, which would have voided the contract signed by the parties. The judgment of the circuit court, awarding money to the original seller, was affirmed.

What is intriguing about reading the original decisions of the Court are the other perspectives offered about varying aspects of a case. These concurring and dissenting opinions provide additional thoughts relevant to the case at hand. Occasionally, what is written as a dissenting opinion will manifest itself in a future majority or minority finding. Justice John McLean wrote one of the dissenting opinions in this (Groves v. Slaughter) case. He makes two significant points. First, he suggests that the ultimate authority to govern the issue of slaves being admitted or prohibited from the various states was a state issue, not a federal one.

If a State may admit or prohibit slaves at its discretion, this power must be in the
State, and not in congress. The constitution seems to recognize the power to be in the

---

54   Ibid., at 596.
55   U.S. Reports, *Groves v. Slaughter*, 1841, p. 497.
56   Ibid., p. 502.

States ... Each State has a right to protect itself against the avarice and intrusion of the slave-dealer; to guard its citizens against the incontinences and dangers of a slave population. The right to exercise this power, by a State, is higher and deeper than the constitution. The evil involves the prosperity, and may endanger the existence of a State. Its power to guard against, or to remedy the evil, rests upon the law of self-preservation; a law vital to every community, and especially to a sovereign State.[57]

The second point raised by Justice McLean is how he perceives the slaves themselves. "The constitution treats the slaves as persons."[58] His proof for this assertion is the second section of the first article of the Constitution, referred to above, which calls for slaves to be counted as three fifths of a vote when determining the numbers of representatives. He also references the third section of the fourth article, also mentioned above, that reads, "no person" when referring to a fugitive slave act. While he concedes that certain states refer to slaves as merchandise, McLean avers that this is a consequence of local law. "The law is respected, and all rights under it are protected by the federal authorities; but the constitution acts upon slaves as persons, not as property."[59]

Justice Henry Baldwin offers another dissenting opinion in this case. He believes very strongly that he had to take a stand against the opinion written by Justice McLean.

Other judges consider the constitution as referring to slaves only as persons, and as property in no other sense than as persons escaping from service; they do not consider them to be recognized as objects of commerce ... but I cannot acquiesce in this position ... I feel bound to consider slaves as property, by the law of the states before the adoption of the constitution, and from the first settlement of the colonies; that this right of property exists independently of the constitution, which does not create, but recognizes and protects it from violation, by any law or regulation of any state, in the cases to which the constitution applies.[60]

Baldwin continues to suggest that at the time of the adoption of the Constitution, slaves were viewed as objects of commerce with other nations and as species of merchandise that were bought and sold as chattel among the various states. After having established, in his opinion, that slaves were seen in the Constitution as goods or merchandise, he then considers the role of the states and slavery. For this justice, each state is the sole and ultimate authority regarding slavery.

It is a matter of internal police, over which the States have reserved the entire control; they, and they alone, can declare what is property capable of ownership, absolute or qualified; they may continue or abolish slavery at their pleasure, as was done before, and had been done since the constitution; which leaves this subject untouched and intangible, except by the States.[61]

---

57   Ibid., p. 507.
58   Ibid.
59   Ibid.
60   Ibid., pp. 512–513.
61   Ibid., p. 515.

Baldwin's final point is that even states that prohibited slavery had no legal grounds for interfering in any way with slaves from slaveholding states who were transiting a free state. His logic is straightforward: "Any reasoning or principle which would authorize any State to interfere with such transit of a slave, would equally apply to a bale of cotton, or cotton goods; and thus leave the whole commercial intercourse between the states liable to interruption or extinction by state laws, or constitutions."[62]

After reiterating his view that slaves were property, Justice Baldwin alludes to those who think differently from him.

1-15: The Seal of the British and American Anti-Slavery Societies clearly indicated their beliefs about that institution.

> *To consider them as persons merely, and not as property, is, in my settled opinion, the first step towards a state of things to be avoided only by a firm adherence to the fundamental principles of the state and federal governments, in relation to this species of property. If the first step taken is a mistaken one, the successive ones will be fatal to the whole system. I have taken my stand on the only position which, in my judgment, is impregnable; and feel confident in its strength; however it may be assailed in public opinion, here or elsewhere.63 (Refer to Figure 1-15.)*

One year later, in its January 1842 decisions, the Supreme Court publicized another case concerning slavery which bears examination. This case was quite indicative of the various attitudes that the states held toward the practice of slavery and the practical issues that arose as a result of these differences. In some ways, this case is a precursor to the much better known case of Dred Scott, which would be decided in 1857. The case of *Prigg v. Pennsylvania* involved a Mr. Edward Prigg, who entered Pennsylvania in search of a runaway slave, Margaret Morgan, from the state of Maryland. This case has all sorts of circumstances and quirks that add some tragic irony to it.[64] Prigg located Margaret and brought her as a fugitive from labor before

---

62   Ibid., p. 516.

63   Ibid.

64   As Finkelman notes, the status of Margaret was also in question. Her parents were slaves allowed to live in virtual freedom. She was never claimed as a slave and married a free black and then moved to Pennsylvania, a free state in 1832. In 1837, the niece and nephew of Margaret's original owner (Ashmore) hired Edward Prigg to go to Pennsylvania and claim her and her children as Ashmore's rightful property. By law, at that time, the children born in a free state (Pennsylvania) should not have been considered slaves

a Pennsylvania constable, who refused to take any legal action in the case. Prigg then took Margaret and her children back to Maryland. Subsequently, he was indicted in Pennsylvania, brought to trial, and found guilty of breaking a Pennsylvania law passed on March 26, 1826, the first section of which is summarized by the court. It provided,

> *That if any person or persons shall from and after the passing of the act, by force and violence take and carry away, or cause to be taken and carried away, and shall by fraud or false pretence, seduce, or cause to be seduced, or shall attempt to take, carry away, or seduce any negro or mulatto from any part of the commonwealth, with a design and intention of selling and disposing of, or causing to be sold, or of keeping and detaining, or of causing to be kept and detained, such negro or mulattoes a slave or servant for life, or for any term whatever; every such person or persons, his or their aiders or abettors, shall, on conviction thereof, be deemed guilty of a felony, and shall forfeit and pay a sum not less than five hundred, nor more than one thousand dollars: and more over, shall be sentenced to undergo a servitude for any term or terms of years, not less than seven years nor exceeding twenty-one years; and shall be confined and kept to hard labor, &c.*[65]

Prigg's guilty verdict was brought before the Pennsylvania Supreme Court, which affirmed it. It was then referred to the United States Supreme Court for review. The Court's finding indicates that the states involved were cooperating and wished to have this case adjudicated.

Justice Joseph Story delivered the Court's opinion. First, the Court reviews the clauses from the Constitution from the second section of the fourth article, which dealt with fugitives and runaway slaves,

> *No person charged in any State with treason, felony, or other crime who shall flee from justice, and be found in another State, shall on demand of the executive authority of the State from which he fled, be delivered up, to be removed to the State having jurisdiction of the crime.*

> *No person held to service or labor in one State under the laws thereof, escaping into another, shall in consequence of any law or regulation therein, be discharged from such service or labor; but shall be delivered up, on claim of the party to whom such service or labor may be due.*

The Court then provides a review of the purpose of these sections of the Constitution.

> *Historically, it is well known that the object of this clause was to secure to the citizens of the slaveholding States the complete right and title of ownership in their slaves, as property,*

---

at all. Nonetheless, the court ignored such facts. Finkelman, in his insightful analysis of this decision, makes two additional points. First, he notes the difficulty in understanding the justices in their opinions. "Since 1842 lawyers, judges, politicians and historians have struggled to understand what the Court actually decided in Prigg." He quotes from President John Quincy Adams, who noted that Prigg consisted of "seven judges, every one of them dissenting from the reasoning of the rest, and every one of them coming to the same conclusion—the transcendent omnipotence of slavery in these United States, riveted by a clause in the Constitution."

65   *Prigg v. Commonwealth*, 1842, p. 608.

in every State in the Union into which they might escape from the State where they were held in servitude, the full recognition of this right and title was indispensable to the security of this species of property in all the slaveholding States; and, indeed, was so vital to the preservation of their domestic interests and institutions, that it cannot be doubted that it constituted a fundamental article, without the adoption of which the Union could not have been formed. Its true design was to guard against the doctrines and principles prevalent in the non-slaveholding States, by preventing them from intermeddling with, or obstructing, or abolishing the rights of the owners of slaves.[66]

This attitude is repeated in subsequent paragraphs: "The clause manifestly contemplates the existence of a positive, unqualified right on the part of the owner of the slave, which no state law or regulation can in any way qualify, regulate, control, or restrain."[67] "We have not the slightest hesitation in holding, that, under and in virtue of the constitution, the owner of a slave is clothed with entire authority, in every State in the Union, to seize and recapture his slave, whenever he can do it without any breach of the peace or any illegal violence."[68] To bolster this finding, the Court refers to the act of February 12, 1793, which dealt with laws for handling fugitives from justice, as well as runaway slaves. This law created a sophisticated system wherein state and local authorities were required to ensure that runaway slaves were returned to their original states from which they escaped.

In fact, not only do the justices believe that the Fugitive Slave Law is quite constitutional, they further discuss the responsibility of all the states. As the decision continues, the justice quotes from Chief Justice Marshall in an earlier case establishing a principle of authority, "Wherever ... the terms in which a power is granted to congress, or the nature of the power, require that it should be exercised exclusively by congress, the subject is as completely taken from the state legislatures as if they had been forbidden to act."[69] The justices are very emphatic that the role for the states in this regard was fulfilling the constitutional mandate of returning slaves. The authority of individual states to modify the federal intention was nonexistent. "It is, therefore, in a just sense, a new and positive right, independent of comity, confined to no territorial limits, and bounded by no state institutions or policy."[70]

The finding continues to describe a chaotic situation, where every state follows its own course of action regarding runaway slaves. The justices suggest that the non-slaveholding states would not be inclined to follow through on maintaining the return of such slaves. In the end of their decision, they reiterate their main point: "But such regulations can never be permitted to interfere with or to obstruct the just rights of the owner to claim his slave, derived from the Constitution of the United States, or with the remedies prescribed by congress to aid and enforce the same."[71] Thus, the act of Pennsylvania, preventing the return of runaway slaves, was overturned and found unconstitutional. The judgment against the plaintiff, Edward Prigg, was also reversed.

Yet, as Paul Finkelman notes, part of Justice Story's finding was utilized to a large extent by abolitionists. Story has concluded that the states could not be held responsible for the enforcement of the fugitive slave constitutional clause. The justice seems clear in this point,

---

66 Ibid., p. 611.
67 Ibid.
68 Ibid., p. 613.
69 Ibid., p. 622.
70 Ibid., p. 623.
71 Ibid., p. 625.

> *The clause is found in the national constitution, and not in that of any state. It does not point out any state functionaries to whom it is intrusted ... The States cannot therefore, be compelled to enforce them; and it might well be deemed an unconstitutional exercise of power of interpretation, to insist that the states are bound to provide means to carry into effect the duties of the national government, nowhere delegated or intrusted to them by the constitution.*[72]

Thus, within a few years of this decision, Northern states passed laws which prohibited state officials from enforcing the federal act. On a practical level, using this approach, state judges declared that they had no authority to hear cases regarding runaways. While a slave-hunter's case could be heard in a federal court, often such a setting might be hundreds of miles away.[73]

This case generated a number of additional or dissenting opinions. Some of those deserve examination. The first justice to make an additional clarification was Roger Taney. While his name would be associated with the Dred Scott decisions still 15 years in the future, the language and approach he reflects in this decision will be consistent with his future ruling. It is significant to note the language he employs. Often, he uses the phrase "the right of the master" as part of his opinion. Taney believes that the judgment offered did not go far enough,

> *In other words, according to the opinion just delivered, the state authorities are prohibited from interfering for the purpose of protecting the right of the master, and aiding him in the recovery of his property. I think the states are not prohibited; and that, on the contrary, it is enjoined upon them, as a duty, to protect and support the owner when he is endeavoring to obtain possession of his property found within their prospective territories.*[74]

Taney continues in his exposition to give some pragmatic reasons why he felt that the state should actively cooperate in the returning of runaway slaves. His comments indicate a detailed knowledge of some of the contemporary issues concerning this subject, especially some of the difficulties experienced by those tracking and capturing runaway slaves.

> *Yet, during that period of time, the master was undoubtly entitled to take possession of his property wherever he might find it; and the protection of this right was left altogether to the state authorities. In attempting to exercise it, he was continually liable to be resisted by superior forces; or the fugitive might be harbored in the house of some one who would refuse to deliver him. And if a State could not authorize its officers, upon the master's application, to come to his aid, the guarantee contained in the constitution was of very little practical value. It is true he might have sued for damages. But as he would, most commonly, be a stranger in the place where the fugitive was found, he might not be able to learn even the names of the wrongdoers; and if he succeeded in discovering them, they might prove to be unable to pay damages. At all events, he would be compelled to encounter*

---

72   Ibid., p. 616.
73   Ibid., p. 625.
74   Ibid., p. 627.

the costs and expenses of a suit, prosecuted at a distance from his own home; and to sacrifice, perhaps, the value of his property in endeavoring to obtain compensation.[75]

Taney continues to address an even larger contemporary issue. He believes that every state must actively arrest and hold runaways and then contact their masters. Without the states having enforceable laws, the laws promulgated by Congress in 1793 were not adequate for the task. He notes that the state of Maryland has many laws for dealing with escaped slaves. In his opinion, Taney comments that fugitives frequently pass through Maryland from Southern states on the way to escape into Canada. It is not adequate to enable the state to arrest these refugees based on their ability to maintain law and order within the states, but rather that the states are equally bound and obligated to fulfill this constitutional mandate.

Another justice who rendered his opinion was Smith Thompson. He felt that the right of the states to add their own legislation to that of the constitutional one was valid. "I can entertain no doubt that state legislation, for the purpose of restoring the slave to his master, and faithfully to carry into execution the provision of the constitution, would be valid.[76] His opinion is that Congress has the exclusive right to legislate upon this provision of the Constitution. Thompson then proceeds to offer his synopsis of the Constitutional Convention held 60 years prior in 1787.

One of these parties, consisting of several states, required as a condition, upon which any constitution should be presented to the States for ratification, a full and perfect security for their slaves as property, when they fled into any of the States of the Union. The fact is not more plainly stated by me than it was put in the convention. The representatives from the non-slaveholding States assented to the condition ... I mention the facts as they were. They cannot be denied. I have nothing to do, judicially, with what a part of the world may think of the attitude of the different parties upon this interesting topic. I am satisfied with what was done; and revere the men and their motives for insisting, politically, upon what was done. When the three points relating to slaves had been accomplished, every impediment in the way of forming a constitution was removed ... The prohibition upon the States to discharge fugitive slaves is absolute.[77]

As part of his opinion, Justice Thompson refers to the formation of the government. In this case, prior to the Constitution,

Experience had shown that under the confederacy [Articles of Confederation], the reclamation of fugitive slaves was embarrassed and uncertain ... There was no doubt that it would become more so. It was foreseen, unless the delivery of fugitive slaves were made part of the constitution, and that the right of the States to discharge them from service, was taken away, that some of the States would become the refuge of runaways; and, of course, that in proportion to the facility and certainty of the State being a refuge, so

---

75 Ibid., p., 629–630.
76 Ibid., p. 635.
77 Ibid., pp. 638–639.

1-16: While state and federal courts argued about legal issues, in the Southern states, slave auctions, such as the one depicted here, were commonplace occurrences.

would the rights of individuals, and the institutions of the slaveholding States, be impaired.[78]

In another instance of reflecting the subtleties of the contemporary problems, Thompson writes about another aspect of this issue.

The claim for the States to legislate is mainly advocated upon the ground, that they are bound to protect free blacks and persons of color residing in them, from being carried into slavery by any summary process. The answer to this is that legislation may be confined to that end, and be made effectual, without making such a remedy applicable to fugitive slaves.[79]

Near the end of this finding is another dissenting opinion by Justice Peter Daniel. This justice disagrees with his judicial colleagues in that he believes that the states have authority in this matter: "it seems unquestionable that the States retain concurrent authority with congress, not only under the eleventh amendment of the constitution, but upon the soundest principles of general reasoning."[80] Daniel's concern is that without the non-slaveholding states having an incentive or legal authority to capture fugitives, many would escape. "By the removal of every incentive of interest in state officers, or individuals, and by the inculcation of a belief that any cooperation with the master becomes a violation of the law, the most active and efficient auxiliary which he could possibly call to his aid is neutralized."[81] In effect, this justice is suggesting that the government and the state work together to enforce the capture and return of runaways. (See Figure 1-16.)

A final dissenting outlook is offered by Justice John McLean. He initially turns to history as an explanation for the varying views on slavery.

In some of the States, it was considered an evil, and a strong opposition to it, in all its forms, was felt and expressed. In others it was viewed as a cherished right, incorporated into the social compact, and sacredly guarded by law. Opinions so conflicting, and which so deeply pervaded the elements of society, could be brought to a reconciled action only by an exercise of exalted patriotism. ... A law is better understood by a knowledge of the evils which led to its adoption. And this applies most strongly to a fundamental law.[82]

---

78 Ibid., p. 645.
79 Ibid., p. 650.
80 Ibid., p. 654.
81 Ibid., p. 657.
82 Ibid., p. 660.

His focus on history also unearths a much earlier incident which paralleled the case of Prigg. According to Justice McLean, around the time of the adoption of the Constitution, a man of color was seized by several people and forcibly removed from the state of Pennsylvania with the intention of enslaving him. Apparently Virginia citizens, some of these men who evicted the black man were indicted by the state of Pennsylvania. In 1791, the governor of Pennsylvania demanded that the governor of Virginia turn them over to Pennsylvania as fugitives from justice. The attorney general of Virginia ruled that the offense charged in the indictment was not a crime, and thus the governor of Virginia refused to arrest the suspects and deliver them to the authorities of Pennsylvania. The correspondence about this case was transmitted to the president of the United States and to Congress. Justice McLean believes that it was that incident that led to the 1793 act, which mandated the return of the runaway slave to the state from which he came.

1-17: The photograph shows an Atlanta storefront, prior to the Civil War that reads, "Auction & Negro Sales." A frightening aspect of such sales was the fact that they had become mundane and routine, a regular aspect of Southern society.

Near the end of his comments, Justice McLean attempts to show that federal laws and state laws, even of those of the state of Pennsylvania, were not really irreconcilable: "Now, here is no conflict between the law of the State and the law of Congress. The execution of neither law can, by any just interpretation, in my opinion, interfere with the execution of the other. The laws in this respect stand in harmony with each other."[83]

Incidents raised by Justice McLean in the *Prigg* case help remind the reader of a few facts. First, some of these issues have a long and tortured history. From the early decades of this country's development, the issues of slavery and its many manifestations were debated. As reflected in the Constitution, it was clear that the disagreements about the whole institution were deeply embedded in the hearts and souls of the American people. What is also apparent is that even in these early decades of the new country, this entire institution was causing a schism in the country. Another fact, often obscured and obliterated by the legal theories of Supreme Court deliberations, was the reality and inhumanity of slavery. (Refer to Figure 1-17.)

Narrative of the Life of Frederick Douglass, written by Douglass about his own experiences, and other such works helped illustrate the day-to-day reality of slaves. It is relevant to quote from Douglass's work to imagine his life and its risks at the same time the Court reached some of its decisions, such as in the *Prigg* case. In January of 1833, Douglass, then a young man, is sent by his master to work for a year with a Mr. Edward Covey. "Mr. Covey was a poor man, a farm-renter … Mr. Covey had acquired a very high reputation for breaking young slaves, and this reputation was of immense value to him."[84] Douglass writes that he lived with Covey for a year. During the first six months, he was whipped almost weekly. These whippings began to take their toll.

> *If at any one time of my life more than another, I was made to drink the bitterest dregs of slavery that time was during the first six months of my stay with Mr. Covey. We were worked in all weathers. It was never too hot or too cold; it could never rain, blow, hail, or snow, too hard for us to work in the field. Work, work, work, was scarcely more the order*

83 Ibid., p. 669.
84 Andrews and Gates, *Slave Narratives*, p. 320.

for the day than the night ... Mr. Covey succeeded in breaking me. I was broken in body, soul, and spirit.[85]

On Sunday, his one day off, Douglass dreams and prays about one thing: freedom. Looking at the ships moored in the nearby Chesapeake Bay, he yearns for liberty.

You are loosed from your moorings, and are free; I am fast in my chains, and am a slave! You move merrily before the gentle gale, and I sadly before the bloody whip! You are freedom's swift-winged angels that fly round the world; I am confined in bands of iron! O that I were free![86]

After yet another beating from Covey, Douglass escapes and returns to his original master and pleads that he not be returned to his abuser. His owner says that he and Covey have an agreement that he would work there a year. After his return, Covey attempts to tie him up to whip him, when something unexpected happens.

Mr. Covey seemed now to think that he had me, and could do as he pleased; but at this moment—from whence came the spirit I don't know—I resolved to fight; and, suiting my action to the resolution, I seized Covey hard by the throat; and as I did so, I rose. He held on to me, and I to him. My resistance was so entirely unexpected, that Covey seemed taken all aback. He trembled like a leaf. ... we were at it for nearly two hours. Covey at length let me go, puffing and blowing at a great rate, saying that if I had not resisted, he would not have whipped me half so much. The truth was that he had not whipped me at all. I considered him as getting the entirely the worst end of the bargain; for he had not drawn blood from me, but I had from him. The whole six months afterwards, that I spent with Mr. Covey, he never laid the weight of his finger upon me in anger.[87]

Douglass's story is illuminating and at the same time depressing. He writes about teaching other slaves how to read and conducting secret Bible classes. This secret education is all done under the constant fear of punishment by their respective masters for pursuing intellectual and religious studies. "Every moment that they spent in that school, they were liable to be taken up, and given thirty-nine lashes. They came because they wished to learn. Their minds had been starved by their cruel masters. They have been shut up in mental darkness. I taught them, because it was the delight of my soul to be doing something that looked like bettering the condition of my race."[88]

---

85 Ibid., p. 324.
86 Ibid., p. 325.
87 Ibid., p. 331.
88 Ibid., pp. 337–338.

Douglass's perils continue as he organizes a group of runaways to flee their confinement, only to be discovered in the final hours before leaving. Ultimately, in September of 1838, he escapes to New York and then into the New England area, where he found his advocacy and became one of his generation's most prominent spokesmen for abolition. In the appendix to his story, Douglass raises a challenge which is profoundly prophetic.

1-18: Frederick Douglass ca. 1855

> *What I have said respecting and against religion, I mean strictly to apply to the slaveholding religion of this land, and with no possible reference to Christianity proper ... I love the pure, peaceable, and impartial Christianity of Christ: I therefore hate the corrupt, slaveholding, women whipping, cradle-plundering, partial and hypocritical Christianity of this land ... I am filled with unutterable loathing when I contemplate the religious pomp and show, together with the horrible inconsistencies, which every where surround me. The man who wields the blood-clotted cow skin during the week fills the pulpit on Sunday, and claims to be a minister of the meek and lowly Jesus. The man who robs me of my earnings at the end of each week meets me as a class-leader on Sunday morning, to show me the way of life, and the path to salvation. He who sells my sister, for purposes of prostitution, stands forth as the open advocate of purity. He who proclaims it a religious duty to read the bible denies me the right of learning to read the name of God who made me ... the warm defender of the sacredness of the family relation is the same that scatters whole families—sundering husbands and wives, parents and children, sisters and brothers—leaving the hut vacant, and the hearth desolate.*[89] *(See Figure 1-18.)*

The heartfelt emotions expressed by Douglass capture the stark realities associated with this institution. Brought to the colonies in the 1600s, supported by increasingly discriminatory laws, and vigorously debated at the 1787 Constitutional Convention, slavery was very much present at America's founding. Unfortunately, even the greatest of our forefathers was unable to end its existence. At best, the year 1808, which banned the importation of slaves, was settled upon as an incomplete resolution of this issue. One of the unintended consequences of the 1808 ban on the importation of slaves was a new market for domestic chattel-slaves that were in increasing demand.

It was also around the turn of the century, 1794, when Eli Whitney patented the cotton gin, a machine that revolutionized the production of cotton by greatly speeding up the process

---

89   Ibid., p. 363.

of removing seeds from cotton fiber.[90] This invention greatly expanded the production and demand for cotton, creating a new demand for slaves to harvest the crop.

As demonstrated above, the distinctions between Northern states, whose state courts were deciding cases favoring the end of slavery, were in stark contrast with the federal Supreme Court, which strongly backed the moral correctness of the Constitution's acceptance of slavery. As the mid-1800s approached, these differences would only intensify.

---

90   http://history.com

Discussion Questions

1. What must it have felt like for an African to be captured, taken captive, and ultimately transported for months to a destination thousands of miles away? Did they experience post-traumatic stress disorder?

2. Why would civil authorities in New Jersey and New York in the 1700s choose to burn slaves at the stake?

3. Do you agree with the three-fifths compromise worked out in the Constitutional Convention in 1787?

4. Why didn't the authors of the Convention use the words slaves or slavery in that document?

5. What is the role of the Supreme Court in our governmental system? Can their findings be changed?

6. If slavery was legal in the 1800s, what should be the legal status of someone taking their slaves with them on a trip that transited a free state for a short time? Should they be arrested? The slave freed? Or no action should be taken, as they are waiting on a ship to take them home?

7. What do you think about the statements of John C. Calhoun? Should his words been paid more heed? Could the Civil War have been averted?

8. Which governmental entity should have ultimate control over the issue of slavery, the states or the federal government? Why?

9. If you lived in a free state during this time and a runaway slave came to you for assistance, what would your legal, moral, and personal responses be?

10. How do you relate to the writings of Frederick Douglass?

THE DARK CLOUDS OF WAR GATHER

chapter 2

The heart-wrenching emotions expressed by Douglass capture in a symbolic way the powerful feelings associated with the institution of slavery. As the decade of the 1840s ended and the 1850s began, the country's heightened sensitivity and reactions to slavery became even more volatile. California had drafted a state constitution, which contained a provision that neither slavery nor involuntary solitude would be tolerated in the state. Southerners, ever vigilant about maintaining power in Congress, reacted vigorously to this development. Some Southerners called for a convention of Southern states, and Southern congressmen talked of commercial boycotts and secession. In January 1850, three prominent American statesmen, John C. Calhoun, Henry Clay, and Daniel Webster, worked on creating legislation that defused the immediate crisis and addressed the many diverse issues of the period. They proposed legislation whose features reflected their process of balancing competing ideologies. For example, slavery would be left in the District of Columbia, but the District's slave trade would be abolished. This bill provided a stronger law to capture fugitive slaves in the North, but declared that Congress had no power to regulate the slave trade among the states, despite the reality

2-1: This picture shows white men in the a field shooting at black men who presumably were slaves, now free. Ca. 1850.

that Congress depended on the Commerce Clause to establish these acts. California was admitted as a free state, but the role of slavery in territories won from Mexico would be undetermined.[1]

Initially, it appeared that this compromise legislation would not pass, but over time, with the aid of less prominent, yet conciliatory congressmen, the bill became law in September 1850. The details of this new, harsher Fugitive Slave Act were especially unsetting to many Northerners who opposed slavery. Rewards were paid for all runaway slaves returned, and bystanders were by law required to aid in the capture of the runaways. The runaway was not allowed to testify in his or her own defense or call any witnesses. Most disturbing was the provision that the number of years that a former slave had lived in freedom building a new life was irrelevant under this act. Soon, armed resistance against the fulfillment of this act occurred. Mobs broke into jails to free ex-slaves, and slave owners heading north to recapture an escaped slave were often threatened.[2] (See Figure 2-1.)

Additional accounts, such as those of Harriet Jacobs, describe in vivid, realistic details the perils that existed for runaways. The following story details the selling of Benjamin, a 20-year-old man who had run away from captivity. After sitting in jail for six months, covered by vermin, he was being sold to a slave trader. His mother, who had tried to help him all along, had this reaction to his being sold: "Could you have seen that mother clinging to her child, when they fastened the irons upon his wrists; could you have heard her heart-rending groans, and seen her bloodshot eyes wander wildly from face to face, vainly pleading for mercy; could you have witnessed that scene as I saw it, you would exclaim, Slavery is damnable."[3]

Other works such as *Uncle Tom's Cabin*, written by Harriet Beecher Stowe, sharpened and heightened even more people's feelings about the topic of slavery. In 1852 alone, the novel sold over 300,000 copies and became the subject of the most popular play in American history.[4]

Into this maelstrom of countrywide emotions, a new bill proposed in Congress created more fissures across America. Senator Stephen Douglas put forward a bill called the Kansas-Nebraska Act, which contained a few explosive elements. In a nod to Southern congressmen, the bill—which organized the territories of the West—invalidated the Missouri Compromise, which had previously prohibited slavery in all territories north of the northern boundary of the Missouri Compromise land. Douglas proposed that the new territories decide for themselves whether or not their state would permit slaves and slaveholders.

This plan unleashed enormous resentment and increased opposition to slavery and the Southern states. Northern ministers and newspapers attacked the proposal. Nevertheless,

---

1   Ayers, Gould, et al., *American Passages*, p. 287.
2   Ibid., p. 288.
3   Jacobs, *Incidents in the Life of a Slave Girl*, p. 48.
4   Ayers, Gould, et al., *American Passages*, p. 289.

the bill passed through the Congress and became law. Northerners felt they no longer had to honor the 1850 Fugitive Slave Act. Tempers grew raw. In Boston, 1500 militia men had to be called out when a runaway slave was to be returned to slavery in Virginia. Nevertheless, even in Boston, racial topics were contentious issues. In its 1849 term, the supreme court of the state of Massachusetts ruled that the General School Committee of Boston was able to maintain separate primary schools for white and black children. The findings of the state supreme court seem eerily similar to the findings of later federal courts, which advocated that it is not the role of courts to cause people of different races to be in proximity with each other.

> *The committee, apparently upon great deliberation, have come to the conclusion, that the good of both classes of schools will be best promoted, by maintaining the separate primary schools for colored and white children ... It is urged, that this maintenance of separate schools tends to deepen and perpetuate the odious distinction of caste, founded in a deep-rooted prejudice of public opinion. This prejudice, if it exists, is not created by law, and probably cannot be changed by law.[5] (Refer to Figure 2-2.)*

This type of ruling reflects the contemporary reality of varying rulings by state and federal courts about slavery and its many aspects. Similarly, sometimes the state courts changed their own interpretations, given ever changing, contemporary social thinking. This tension is best illustrated by a series of cases decided in the state of Missouri regarding runaway slaves, and how and when they became free.

In 1807, a Missouri statute held that a person kept in wrongful servitude could sue for freedom. Most of the people using this law were enslaved Africans. The legal process involved fulfilling numerous requirements each slave had to take to gain their freedom. They had to prove they were free and had been physically abused while being held as slaves. These proceedings were called freedom suits. The provisions of this law were added into a Missouri state law written in 1824. In fact, the years between 1824 and 1844 were considered the "golden age" of such suits, since many slaves won their freedom through this legal process. In an 1824 decision, the Missouri Supreme Court created a legal precedent referred to as "once free, always free." The court held that if a slave were taken to live in a territory or state where slavery was not allowed, at that point the slave became a free person, even if he or she later returned to a slave state such as Missouri.[6]

This legal principle set the stage for many gaining their freedom, as exemplified

2-2: This picture from the twentieth century indicates the sad legacy of children being separated for educational purposes in America.

---

5   *Roberts v. Boston*, 1849.
6   http://sos.mo.gov/archives/education/aahi/beforedredscotthistory

in subsequent cases. For example, in 1833, Ralph, a man of color, sued Coleman Duncan for his freedom in St. Louis, Missouri. Ralph claimed that he had been enslaved by Duncan and taken to work for him in the free state of Illinois, thereby making him a free man. Initially, the St. Louis District Court denied his petition for freedom. However, on appeal to the Missouri Supreme Court in 1833, the court ruled that the established doctrine—"once free, always free"—applied, and Ralph was freed.[7]

In an 1836 case, Rachel, a female slave to an officer in the U.S. Army, sued for her freedom in the St. Louis Circuit Court. Rachel alleged that she had been taken to an area known as the Michigan Territory. Slavery had been outlawed in this expansive geographical area by Congress in the 1787 Northwest Ordinance. As in the prior case, the decision was appealed to the Missouri Supreme Court, where the court held that once the officer had taken his slave to a free territory, he lost his ownership rights. They freed Rachel.[8]

What is especially striking about these cases is that the very issues raised in them, i.e., living in a free state and in a territory in which Congress had outlawed slavery, served as conduits for freedom on the 1830s and 1840s. The doctrine of "once free, always free," which had been so openly and often applied by the Missouri Supreme Court, was transformed as the political and social attitudes toward slavery and runaway slaves became more strident in the 1850s. Federal decisions, as well as local ones, came into play, with two major cases decided in the 1850s.

In *Strader v. Graham*, an 1850 case, the reality of slaves moving back and forth from slave to free states is brought once again into question. In this case, Christopher Graham was the owner of three slaves who had a history of performing music in free states and then returning to Kentucky, their home state, which was a slave state. The permit that he gave them to travel amid the various states is illuminating.

> *This is to give liberty to my boys, Henry and Reuben, to go to Louisville, with Williams and to play with him till I may wish to call them home ... My object is to have them well trained in music. They are young, one 17 and the other 19 years of age. They are both of good disposition and strictly honest, and such is my confidence in them that I have no fear that they will ever (act) knowingly wrong, or put me to trouble. They are slaves for life, and I paid for them an unusual sum; they have been faithful, hard-working slaves, and I have no fear but that they will always be true to their duty, no matter in what situation they may be placed.*[9] *(See Figure 2-3.)*

What Henry and Rueben had done was take the steamboat *Pike* from Louisville, Kentucky, to Cincinnati, Ohio, where they escaped to Canada. Graham sued the owners and captain of the boat for having taken the slaves to their freedom. The owners and captain countered that Henry and Rueben were actually already free individuals, as they had spent time in Ohio, a free state, on previous visits.

The laws in Kentucky seemed clear. A statute approved in January of 1824 in some ways describe this case.

---

7   Ibid.

8   Ibid., Rachel-petitions.asp.

9   http://supremejustia.com/US/51/82/case., p. 3.

Any master or commander of a steamboat or other vessel who shall hire or employ, or take as passengers on board of such steamboat or other vessel or suffer it to be done or otherwise take out of the limits of the commonwealth any slave or slaves without permission of the master of such slaves shall be liable to damages to the party aggrieved by such removal, and the steamboat or other vessel on board of which such offense was committed shall be liable, and may be proceeded against in chancery, and may be condemned and sold to pay such damages and costs of suit.[10]

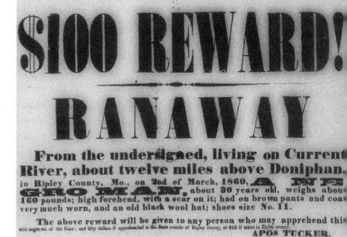

$100 REWARD!

RANAWAY

From the undersigned, living on Current River, about twelve miles above Doniphan, in Ripley County, Mo., on 2nd of March, 1860, **A NEGRO MAN**, about 30 years old, weighs about 160 pounds; high forehead, with a scar on it; had on brown pants and coat very much worn, and an old black wool hat; shoes size No. 11.

The above reward will be given to any person who may apprehend this said negro out of the State; and fifty dollars if apprehended in this State outside of Ripley county, or $25 if taken in Ripley county.

APOS TUCKER.

2-3: This poster indicates the reality for slaves attempting to be free. A reward for $100 was offered as an incentive to capture a runaway slave. Ca. 1860.

Graham won a judgment in a Louisville chancery court for three thousand dollars in damages against the owners and the ship's captain. If the money was not paid, the boat could be seized and sold to recover the money. The case was sent to the Kentucky Court of Appeals, which affirmed the original finding against the owners and captain. The case was then referred to the federal Supreme Court. The Court made two explicit determinations that are significant on their own, but also very important, as they are active principles that would be applied in the deciding of the well-known Dred Scott case. The first decision applies to the powers of the state regarding the status of slaves.

Every state has an undoubted right to determine the status, or domestic and social condition of the persons domiciled within its territory except insofar as the powers of the states in this respect are restrained, or duties and obligations imposed upon them, by the Constitution of the United States. There is nothing in the Constitution that can in any degree control the law of Kentucky upon this subject. And the condition of the Negroes, therefore, as to freedom or slavery after their return depended altogether upon the laws of that state, and could not be influenced by the laws of Ohio. It was exclusively in the power of Kentucky to determine for itself whether their employment in another state should or should not make them free on their return. The Court of Appeals has determined that by the laws of the state, they continued to be slaves. And their judgment upon this point is, upon this writ of error, conclusive upon this Court, and we have no jurisdiction over it.[11]

A second legal argument that had been advanced from the side of the owners and captain was that the slaves were also free due to their time spent in Ohio, based on the articles of the Ordinance of 1787 dealing with the Northwest Territories of the United States. One of the articles provided, "There shall be neither slavery nor involuntary servitude in the said territory

---

10 Ibid.
11 Ibid., p. 4

otherwise that in punishment for crimes whereof the party shall have been duly convicted, provided always that any person escaping into the same from whom labor is lawfully claimed in anyone of the original states, such fugitive may be lawfully reclaimed and conveyed to the person claiming his or her labor or service as foresaid."[12]

The Court, in 1850, foreshadowing the 1857 *Dred Scott* case, quickly determined that the ordinance and its provisions were no longer legally binding, despite the fact this ordinance had been reaffirmed by Congress in 1789. "The six articles, said to be perpetual as a compact, are not made a part of the new Constitution. They certainly are not superior and paramount to the Constitution, and cannot confer power and jurisdiction upon this Court ... As we have already said; it ceased to be in force upon the adoption of the Constitution, and cannot now be the source of jurisdiction of any description in this Court."[13] The Court dismissed the claim of the owners and captain and backed the judgment of the state of Kentucky for Mr. Graham and the damages he suffered upon his slaves being free.

Clearly, the country was rapidly moving away from cooperation and compromise and toward a period of increased tension and confrontation. One legal action that originated in the state of Missouri was slowly making its way to the Supreme Court. This case, decided over the course of a few years, was announced to the country in March 1857. The *Dred Scott* case (*Scott v. Sandford*) was perhaps one of the best known of the Court's decisions. Nevertheless, the findings of the court in the majority and minority opinions deserve close analysis and examination. The basic facts of the case are summarized by Justice Stephen Breyer in his book entitled, *Making Our Democracy Work*.

> *Dred Scott was born a slave on a Virginia plantation around 1800. His first owner, Peter Blow, took him to St. Louis, Missouri, where he sold him to an army doctor, John Emerson. Emerson took Scott with him from base to base, including Fort Armstrong in the free state of Illinois and Fort Snelling in the free territory of Wisconsin (now in the state of Minnesota). During his two-year stay at Fort Snelling, Scott married Harriet, a slave who also lived there. Emerson then returned to St. Louis with Scott, Harriet, and their newly born child, Eliza. After Emerson died, Scott, and his family became the property of Emerson's wife and, eventually, of his wife's brother, John Sanford. Scott, or perhaps Harriet, was not satisfied with this arrangement, so the couple brought a lawsuit, first in state court, then in federal court. They argued that their lengthy stay in free territory made Scott legally a free man.[14] (Refer to Figure 2-4.)*

This case had the potential to answer many of the pressing questions of the day regarding slavery, the status of slaves as they passed from slaveholding to free states, and other legal issues connected with this major fact of contemporary American life. In an extensive and comprehensive decision, the Court chose not only to respond to this specific case, but to address other issues as well. The Court's judgment was delivered by Chief Justice Roger Taney. He first acknowledges that the case's final adjudication was held for over a year to give the Court and the justices ample time to consider the many ramifications of the case. The first major question addressed by Taney is amazingly fundamental, as it affects the rest of his response.

---

12   Ibid.
13   Ibid., p. 6.
14   Breyer, Stephen, *Making Our Democracy Work: New York*, Vintage Books, 2010, pp. 32–33. Scott and his wife had a second daughter born upon their return to Missouri.

The question is simply this: can a negro, whose ancestors were imported into this country, and sold as slaves, become a member of the political community formed and brought into existence by the Constitution of the United States, and as such become entitled to all the rights, and privileges, and immunities, guaranteed by that instrument to the citizen? One of which rights is the privilege of suing in a court of the United States in the cases specified in the Constitution.

It will be observed, that the plea applies to that class of persons only whose ancestors were Negroes of the African race, and imported into this country, and sold and held as slaves. The only matter in issue before the court, therefore, is, whether the descendants of such slaves, when they shall be emancipated, or who are born of parents who had become free before their birth, are citizens of a State, in the sense which the word citizen is used in the Constitution of the United States. … that is, of those persons who are descendants of Africans who were imported into this country, and sold as slaves.[15] *(See Figure 2-5.)*

2-4: *An excellent family portrait of Dred Scott, his wife Harriet, and daughters Eliza and Lizzie. He and his family were pioneers in the field of race relations for our country.*

Before answering the question posed, the chief justice makes a few comments about Native Americans and their legal status.

It is true that the course of events has brought the Indian tribes within the limits of the United States under subjection to the white race; and it has been found necessary, for their sake as well as our own, to regard them as in a state of pulpilage, and to legislate to a certain extent over them and the territory they occupy. But they may, without doubt, like the subjects of any other foreign Government, be naturalized by the authority of Congress, and become citizens of a State and the United States; and if an individual should leave his nation or tribe, and take up his abode among the white population, he would be entitled

---

15   *Dred Scott v. Sandford*, U.S. Reports, December 1856, p. 403.

CHIEF JUSTICE ROGER B. TANEY

2-5: Chief Justice Roger Taney generally negatively associated with the Dred Scott decision.

to all the rights and privileges which would belong to an emigrant from any other foreign people.[16]

Taney then answers the question of the rights that slaves and their children may have.

The question before us is, whether the class of persons described in the plea of abatement compose a portion of this people, and are constituent members of this sovereignty? We think they are not, and that they are not included, and were not intended to be included, under the word "citizens" in the Constitution, and can therefore claim none of the rights and privileges which that instrument provides for and secures to citizens of the United States. On the contrary, they were at that time considered as a subordinate and inferior class of beings, who had been subjugated by the dominant race, and, whether emancipated or not, yet remained subject to their authority, and had no rights or privileges but such as those who held the power and the Government might choose to grant them.[17]

Taney qualifies his answer somewhat with the following paragraph.

It is not the province of the court to decide upon the justice or injustice, the policy or impolicy, of these laws. The decision of that question belonged to the political or law making power; to those who framed the sovereignty and framed the Constitution. The duty of the court is, to interpret the instrument they have framed, with the best lights we can obtain on the subject, and to administer it as we find it, according to its true intent and meaning when it was adopted.[18]

As his analysis continues, Taney makes an important distinction that will be employed by future courts. He predicates that there are two types of citizenship which exist in America, United States citizenship and citizenship of an individual state. His strong contention is that being a member of a state does not mean one is also a member of the United States.

---

16 Ibid., p. 404.
17 Ibid.
18 Ibid., p. 405.

It is very clear, therefore, that no State can, by an act or law of its own, passed since the adoption of the Constitution, introduce a new member into the political community created by the Constitution of the United States. It cannot make him a member of this community by making him a member of its own. And for the same reason it cannot introduce any person, or description of persons, who were not intended to be embraced in this new political family, which the Constitution brought into existence, but were intended to be excluded from it.[19]

Thus, in one of his first major findings, Taney—along with the majority of the Court—concludes, "The plaintiff in error could not be a citizen of the State of Missouri, within the meaning of the Constitution of the United States, and, consequently was not entitled to sue in its courts."[20] Despite this finding, the Court addresses other issues associated with slaves and slavery.

Taney continues with a historical overview describing the time of the Declaration of Independence as he attempts to justify his opinions.

In the opinion of the court, the legislation and histories of the times, and the language used in the Declaration of Independence, show, that neither the class of persons who had been imported as slaves, nor their descendants, whether they had become free or not, were then acknowledged as a part of the people, nor intended to be included in the general words used in that memorable instrument.

It is difficult at this day to realize the state of public opinion in relation to that unfortunate race, which prevailed in the civilized and enlightened portions of the world at the time of the Declaration of Independence, and when the Constitution of the United States was framed and adopted. But the public history of every European nation displays it in a manner too plain to be mistaken.

slaves → *They had for more than a century before been regarded as beings of an inferior order, and altogether unfit to associate with the white race, either in social or political relations; and so far inferior, that they had no rights, which the white man was bound to respect; and that the negro might justly and lawfully be reduced to slavery for his benefit. He was bought and sold, and treated as an ordinary article of merchandise and traffic, whenever a profit could be made by it. This opinion was at that time fixed and universal in the civilized portion of the white race.*[21] *(Refer to Figure 2-6.)*

As his opinion develops, Taney first refers to the attitude of the British regarding slaves: "They not only seized them on the coast of Africa, and sold them or held them in slavery for their own use; but they took them as ordinary articles of merchandise to every country where they could make a profit on them, and were far more extensively engaged in this commerce than any other nation in the world."[22]

The justice then references some of the colonial laws specifically directed against slaves. First, he quotes a Maryland law of 1717, which spoke to the status of the children of interracial

---

19 Ibid., p. 406.
20 Ibid.
21 Ibid., p. 407.
22 Ibid., p. 408.

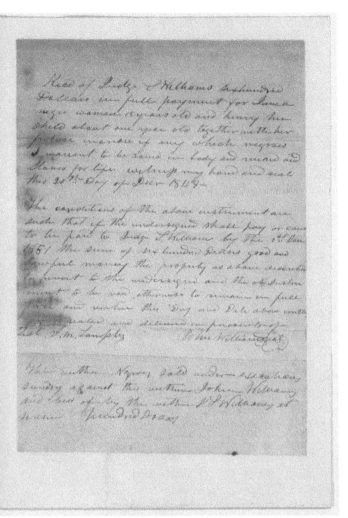

2-6: While the courts addressed the issue of slavery, the reality for millions of people of color was harsh and unforgiving. This receipt showed that a judge in Alabama purchased Jane, an 18-year-old black woman, her one-year-old son Henry, and any future children for the price of $600.00.

marriages. "If any free negro or mulatto intermarry with any white woman, or if any white man shall intermarry with any negro or mulatto woman, such negro or mulatto shall become a slave for life, excepting mulattoes born of white woman, who, for such intermarriage shall only become servants for seven years."[23] The second colonial law was from the province of Massachusetts. This 1705 law was clear in its intent: "If any Negro or mulatto shall presume to smite or strike any person of the English or other Christian nation, such Negro or mulatto shall be severely whipped, at the discretion of the justices before whom the offender shall be convicted."[24]

From both of these laws, Justice Taney reaches a conclusion about race relations at the time of the Declaration of Independence.

They show that a perpetual and impassable barrier was intended to be erected between the white race and the one which they had reduced to slavery, and governed as subjects with absolute and despotic power, and which they then looked upon as so far below them in the scale of created beings, that intermarriages between white persons and negroes or mulattoes were regarded as unnatural and immoral, and punished as crimes, not only in the parties, but in the person who joined them in marriage. And no distinction in this respect was made between the free Negro or mulatto, and the slave, but this stigma, of the deepest degradation, was fixed upon the whole race.[25] *(Reference Figure 2-7.)*

The justice then addresses a question that has been asked by generations of Americans. How can we reconcile the poetic and stirring verses of the Declaration of Independence with the harsh reality of slavery and racial prejudice? First, Taney quotes the verses we are

---

23 Ibid.
24 Ibid.
25 Ibid., p. 409.

all familiar with. "We hold these truths to be self-evident; that all men are created equal; that they are endowed by their Creator with certain unalienable rights; that among them is life, liberty, and the pursuit of happiness; that to secure these rights, Governments are instituted, deriving their just powers from the consent of the governed."[26]

Taney's answer to why these verses don't apply to all Americans is breathtakingly significant in its ramifications and meaning.

2-7: Despite the words above which discuss "scale of created beings," "unnatural," and "degradation," perhaps the most important word is "freedom." The rendering in this 1863 picture represents that ongoing endeavor. The title of this drawing is quite appropriate: In Search of Freedom.

The general words above quoted would seem to embrace the whole human family, and if they were used in a similar instrument at this day would be so understood. But it is too clear for dispute, that the enslaved African race were not intended to be included, and formed no part of the people who framed and adopted this declaration; for if the language, as understood in that day, would embrace them, the conduct of the distinguished men who framed the Declaration of Independence would have been utterly and flagrantly inconsistent with the principles they asserted; and instead of the sympathy of mankind, to which they so confidently appealed, they would have deserved and received universal rebuke and reprobation ... they knew that it would not in any part of the civilized world be supposed to embrace the negro race, which, by common consent, had been excluded from civilized Governments and the family of nations, and doomed to slavery.[27]

Justice Taney then reviews earlier references to the Constitution (mentioned above), which were the clauses that allowed the importation of slaves until the year 1808 and spoke about runaway slaves having to be returned to their masters. He then proceeds to offer more legal justification for his conclusions. He argues that states that were slaveholding ones, as well as those that didn't have slaves, equally did not recognize the rights of African Americans as being on a par with white citizens. To make this point, Taney refers to a number of state laws concerning slaves.

Thus, Massachusetts, in 1786, passed a law similar to the colonial one which we have spoken. The law of 1786, like the law of 1705, forbids the marriage of any white person with any negro, Indian, or mulatto, and inflicts a penalty of fifty pounds upon any one who shall join them in marriage; and declares all such marriages absolutely null and void, and degrades thus the unhappy issue of the marriage by fixing upon it the stain of bastardy. And this mark of degradation was renewed, and again impressed upon the

---

26 Ibid., p. 410.
27 Ibid.

race, in the careful and deliberate preparation of their revised code published in 1836. This code forbids any person from joining in marriage any white person with any Indian, negro, or mulatto, and subject the party who shall offend in this respect, to imprisonment, not exceeding six months, in the common jail, or to hard labor, and to a fine of not less than fifty nor more than two hundred dollars; and, like the law of 1786, it declares the marriage to be absolutely null and void [28]

The next state he examines is Connecticut. In this instance, the state very early on outlawed slavery. Yet, Taney finds laws which he believes reflects the view of blacks in that state. "And again, in 1833, Connecticut passed another law, which made it penal to set up or establish any school in that State for the instruction of persons of the African race not inhabitants of the State, or to instruct or teach in any such school or institution, or board or harbor for that purpose, any such person, without the previous consent in writing of the civil authority of the town in which such school or institution might be." [29] In fact, Taney uses Connecticut as an example of a state which should have had the most lenient and favorable laws regarding former slaves in the nation. "And if we find that at the time of the Constitution was adopted, they were not even raised to the rank of citizens, but were still held and treated as property, and the laws relating to them passed with reference altogether to the interest and convenience of the white race, we shall hardly find them elevated to a higher rank anywhere else." [30]

One other example from a Northern state will suffice to illustrate his thinking. He quotes from the laws of New Hampshire passed in 1815 and revised in 1855 regarding the state militia, that only "free white citizens" were permitted to enroll in the militia. Taney's conclusion is obvious at this stage,

Nothing could more strongly mark the entire repudiation of the African race. The alien is excluded, because, being born in a foreign country, he cannot be a member of the community until he is naturalized. But why is the African race, born in the State, not permitted to share in one of the highest duties of the citizen? The answer is obvious; he is not, by the institutions and laws of the State, numbered among its people. He forms no part of the sovereignty of the State, and is not therefore called on to uphold and defend it. [31].

The only state which in Taney's opinion treated blacks equally in both civil and political rights was the state of Maine. His next point is that the process of naturalization, which granted citizenship for new immigrants to America, is a federal power alone and would not be permissible for the children of slaves: "And this power granted to Congress to establish an uniform rule of naturalization is, by the well understood meaning of the word, confined to persons born in a foreign country, under a foreign Government. It is not a power to raise to the rank of a citizen any one born in the United States, who, from birth and parentage, by the laws of the country, belongs to an inferior and subordinate class." [32]

---

28 Ibid., p. 413.
29 Ibid., pp. 414–415.
30 Ibid.
31 Ibid.
32 Ibid., p. 417.

Taney's use of historical precedents continues with references to a document long forgotten by most—the Articles of Confederation, America's first governing document, which preceded the Constitution. The Articles made two references to race that Taney quotes. The first is the term "free inhabitants" when referring to the rights of citizenship. For Taney, this meant, "And, notwithstanding the generality of the words "free inhabitants," it is very clear that, according to their accepted meaning in that day, they did not include the African race, whether free or not."[33] A second more explicit reference to "white inhabitants" is found in the fifth section of the ninth constitutional article which speaks of the power of Congress, "to agree upon the number of land forces to be raised, and to make requisitions from each State for its quota in proportion to the number of white inhabitants in such State, which requisition should be binding."[34] For Taney, such terms indicate the chasm between the free and the slave races.

After reviewing these points, the chief justice uses more recent legal decisions made by different attorneys-general of the government regarding the definition of the term "citizen of the United States,"

> *The question was brought officially before the late William Wirt, when he was the Attorney General of the United States in 1821, and he decided that the words "citizens of the United States" were used in the acts of Congress in the same sense as in the Constitution; and that free persons of color were not citizens, within the meaning of the Constitution and laws; and this opinion has been confirmed by that of the late Attorney General Caleb Cushing, in a recent case, and acted upon by the Secretary of State, who refused to grant passports to them as "citizens of the United States."*[35]

As this lengthy finding continues, Justice Taney seems to anticipate criticism of this finding, as he states, "No one, we presume, supposes that any change in public opinion or feeling, in relation to this unfortunate race, in the civilized nations of Europe or in this country, should induce the court to give to the words of the Constitution a more liberal construction in their favor than they were intended to hear when the instrument was framed and adopted. Such an argument would be altogether inadmissible in any tribunal called on to interpret it."[36] Taney was not about to be persuaded by any contemporary abolitionist philosophy concerning slavery. In this section of the decision, he reiterates the Court's finding about Dred Scott's legal standing. "Dred Scott was not a citizen of Missouri within the meaning of the Constitution of the United States, and not entitled as such to sue in its courts; and consequently, that the Circuit Court had no jurisdiction of the case, and that the judgment on the plea in abatement is erroneous."[37]

After some discussion about whether the circuit court should have taken jurisdiction in this matter, the finding turned to another key legal point raised in Dred Scott's defense. Did the geographic locations of Dred Scott and his family in their travels grant him his freedom, as he and they resided in areas that were created by Congress or the state of Illinois to be free of slavery? Taney and his Court address both questions and make some significant decisions about them.

---

33 Ibid., p. 418.
34 Ibid.
35 Ibid., p. 421.
36 Ibid., p. 426.
37 Ibid., p. 427.

The issue of land purchased from France is addressed. The act of Congress, upon which the plaintiff relies, declares that slavery and involuntary servitude, except as a punishment for crime, shall be forever prohibited in all that part of the territory ceded by France, under the name of Louisiana, which lies north of thirty six degrees thirty minutes north latitude, and not included within the limits of Missouri. And the difficulty is, whether Congress was authorized to pass this law under any of the powers granted to it by the Constitution; for if the authority is not given by that instrument, it is the duty of this court to declare it void and inoperative, and incapable of conferring freedom upon any one who is held as a slave under the laws of any one of the States.[38] *(Refer to Figure 2-8.)*

The logic and reasoning of the Court is illustrative and educational. In the Constitution, the power of Congress vis à vis new territory seems clear as found in Article Four, Section 3, second paragraph,

2-8: The vast area of the country deemed to be free of slavery by Congress, voided by the Dred Scott decision.

"The Congress shall have the power to dispose of and make all needful Rules and Regulations respecting the Territory or other Property belonging to the United States; and nothing in this Constitution shall be so construed as to Prejudice any Claims of the United States, or of any particular State." Yet, in this instance, the court finds that, in the judgment of the court, that provision has no bearing on the present controversy, and the power there given, whatever it may be, is confined, and was intended to be confined, to the territory which at that time belonged to, or was claimed by, the United States, and was within their boundaries as settled by the treaty with Great Britain and can have no influence upon a territory afterwards acquired from a foreign Government. It was a special provision for a known and particular territory, and to meet a present emergency, and nothing more.[39]

---

38 Ibid., p. 432.
39 Ibid.

Next, the justice discusses the formation of the Ordinance of 1787 as an agreement between the various states to prohibit slavery in that territory. Nonetheless, according to Justice Taney, "As this league of States would, upon the adoption of the new Government, [C]ease to have any power over the territory, and the ordinance they had agreed upon be incapable of execution and a mere nullity.[40]

The interpretation continues with a detailed analysis of the wording used in the Constitution, especially the words, "to dispose of and make all needful rules and regulations respecting the territory or other property belonging to the United States." In this finding, the words are parsed for meaning: "It does not speak of any territory, or of Territories, but uses language which, according to its legitimate meaning points to a particular thing. The power is given in relation only to 'the' territory of the United States—that is, a territory then in existence, and then known or claimed as to the territory of the United States."[41] At the end of this rather forced and labored explanation, the conclusion is clear, "Consequently, the power which Congress may have lawfully exercised in this Territory, which it remained under a Territorial Government, and which may have been sanctioned by judicial decision, can furnish no justification and no argument to support a similar exercise of power over territory afterwards acquired by the Federal Government. We put aside, therefore, any argument, drawn from precedents, showing the extent of the power which the General Government exercised over slavery in the Territory, as altogether inapplicable to the case before us."[42]

The next line of reasoning of the justices concerns itself with the nature of law in the territories. The rights and privileges that any citizens enjoy in these territories must conform to parameters of the Constitution. For example, the justices asserted that Congress cannot pass any laws which would deprive citizens in the territories their rights to freedom of religion, speech, or the right to assemble peacefully. Included in these rights, which no one can abridge, are the rights of property. "Thus, the rights of property are united with the rights of person, and placed on the same ground by the Fifth Amendment to the Constitution, which provides that no person shall be deprived of life, liberty, and property without due process of law. And an act of Congress which deprives a citizen of the United States of his liberty or property, merely because he came himself or brought his property into a particular Territory of the United States, and who had committed no offense against the laws, could hardly be dignified with the name of due process of law."[43]

In short, what Taney is postulating is that the slaves were the property of those people living in the territories, and that as such, the Congress, when it did not allow slavery in the territory, acted inappropriately. "And if the Constitution recognizes the right of property of the master in a slave, and makes no distinction between that description of property and other property owned by a citizen, no tribunal, acting under the authority of the United States, whether it be legislative, executive, or judicial, has a right to draw such a distinction, or deny to it the benefit of the provisions and guarantees which have been provided for the protection of private property against the encroachments of the Government."[44]

The conclusion of the Court seems easy to discern regarding this aspect of the case. "Upon these considerations, it is the opinion of the court that the act of Congress which prohibited a citizen from holding and owning property of this kind in the territory of the United States north

---

40 Ibid., p. 435.
41 Ibid., p. 436.
42 Ibid., p. 442
43 Ibid., p. 450.
44 Ibid., p. 451.

of the line therein mentioned, is not warranted by the Constitution, and is therefore void; and that neither Dred Scott himself, nor any of his family were made free by being carried into this territory; even if they had been carried there by the owner, with the intention of becoming a permanent resident."[45]

The final issue for the Court to decide was accomplished in short order. Concerning the question of whether Scott's time in Illinois—a free state—granted him the status of freedom, the Court, which had judged in a prior case about this issue, makes a few brief points. They reason that the case had been already heard in the supreme court of the state of Missouri, which had reversed the findings of a lower state court and found that Scott was a slave. They further decide, as mentioned previously, that the federal circuit court had no jurisdiction in the case. The state of your birth determined your status regarding slavery or freedom. Dred Scott's birth in a slaveholding state legally bound him to a life of slavery, regardless of his travels to free territories or states.

After this lengthy opinion, there were a few justices who wished to add their own opinions to the record. Some of them argue that the circuit court should have had jurisdiction of the case. Justice Nelson makes a strong argument for the right of each state to make its own laws regarding slavery. "Our conclusion, therefore, is, upon this branch of the case, that the question involved is one depending solely upon the law of Missouri and that the Federal court sitting in the State, and trying the case before us, was bound to follow it."[46]

At this stage, it is appropriate to offer a brief synopsis of this monumental decision. First, the *Dred Scott* decision overturned nearly 70 years of established precedent, wherein Congress had power over territories. Second, it took over a case that had already been decided on a state level and used it as the basis for such historical findings. Third, it addressed the entire question of citizenship for slaves and free blacks that had not been part of the initial case in the first place. Fourth, it overturned the Missouri Compromise, which had been in effect for approximately 30 years. Fifth, it defined slaves as property that was beyond the legal protection of the states.

It is not difficult to imagine the impact that the *Dred Scott* decision had on the proponents of slavery and their opponents. For those opposed to slavery, some may have concluded that a more militant approach would be required to end its existence. For those who desired its continued practice, this finding reinforced their ideas and allowed little room for moderation or compromise.

At this stage, it is appropriate to delve into the backgrounds and political affiliations of the justices sitting at that time. It is plausible to suggest that their state of birth or allegiances may have influenced their votes regarding slaves and slavery. An analysis of this kind may also serve as a template for future justices and their decisions. Beginning with the chief justice and those who voted as he did in the *Dred Scott* case, followed by those who dissented, a brief overview of their lives and beliefs is presented for consideration.

Chief Justice Roger Taney of Dred Scott notoriety was born in Calvert County, Maryland, in 1777. After graduation from college, he studied law and was admitted to the Maryland bar. He spent the early years of his career in Frederick, Maryland, building a successful law practice and being elected to the state senate in 1816. While Taney did free slaves he had inherited, it was his belief that each state had complete control over slaves held in its borders, and whatever problems this created must also be solved by the states, not the federal government.[47]

---

45   Ibid., p. 452.
46   Ibid., p. 465.
47   Friedman and Israel, Eds., *The Justices of the Supreme Court*, vol. I., p. 340.

As his career continued, he was chosen in 1826 as the state attorney general. In this position, Taney aligned with many who thought that both federal and state governments had shared powers. Taney believed it was the Supreme Court's role to decide which of those powers should be shared and which were to be reserved to one or the other locus of sovereignty.[48] Slavery in this regard was a state issue, yet some questions such as the problem of fugitive slaves that crossed state borders became a federal concern as well.

During these years, Taney developed close ties with President Andrew Jackson and was a strong advocate for his economic and national policies. When the United States Supreme Court's chief justice John Marshall died in July of 1835, Taney was nominated by Jackson for his position. He was confirmed by the Senate in 1836. His basic philosophy of governance remained that the states held a wide range of powers that were exclusively theirs. At the same time, there were concurrent powers, which linked the states and federal government together.

Taney's Court, as can be imagined, offered decisions that ran the gamut of economic, regulatory, and political issues. It is the arena of topics regarding slaves and slavery that requires further examination. As mentioned above, there were a number of cases such as *Groves v. Slaughter*, *Prigg v. Pennsylvania*, and *Strader v. Graham* where Taney's thoughts were consistent. For example, in the *Prigg* case, he agrees that a Pennsylvania law of 1826 severely limiting the ability to track down and return runaway slaves is indeed unconstitutional. He also affirms that it was the obligation of the states to protect the property of slaveholders—i.e., slaves who had come into their boundaries.

In many ways, the *Dred Scott* case was a continuation in the line of such cases. There was a confluence of events which brought about its notoriety. First were the passions regarding slavery that were boiling in 1856 America. Second, due to Justice McLean's insistence on offering an antislavery opinion, Taney, whose original notion was to give a limited decision based on *Strader v. Graham*, now felt compelled to present a comprehensive opinion, with the hope that this would give judicial finality to the contentious issues surrounding slaves and slavery in America.[49] The response to the decision given on March 7, 1857, three days after the inauguration of James Buchanan, was immediate and emotional. Taney and Buchanan were pictured in the North as having conspired in advance for the benefit of Southern slaveholders.[50]

Ironically, Taney's personal actions did not reflect what one might assume. In the same year as the *Scott* decision, he explains his thoughts on this subject: "I am not a slaveholder. More than thirty years ago I manumitted every slave I owned except two who were too old when they became my property to provide for themselves. These two I supported in comfort as long as they lived."[51] Like other Southerners, he believed that abolition had impeded the tendency to improve the slave's lot. He felt that the abolitionists' focus caused the masters to be more sensitive to criticism and more fearful of the loyalty of his slaves. Taney died in the midst of the Civil War on October 12, 1864. (See Figure 2-9.)

One of the pre–Civil War Supreme Court justices who best illustrates the difficulties of trying to reconcile a belief in effective, delegated national powers with the concept of state sovereignty was Justice James Moore Wayne.[52] He was born in Savannah, Georgia, in 1790. After graduating from Princeton University, then the College of New Jersey, he studied law. In 1819, Wayne was elected to a judgeship in the Savannah Court of Common Pleas, followed a year later by an appointment

---

48   Ibid., p. 341.
49   Ibid., p. 354.
50   Ibid., p. 355.
51   Ibid.
52   Ibid., p. 326.

2-9: Justice James M. Wayne

to the state's superior court. He also pursued a career in politics and was elected to Congress in 1829. During that time, he often took moderate political stands. When the state of South Carolina introduced the concept of states having the prerogative to nullify federal laws, Wayne—as did the rest of Georgia—disagreed with that extreme stand. "As a Unionist, Wayne took a careful middle position between the extremes of nullification and consolidation."[53] In January of 1835, he was nominated and confirmed for a position on the United States Supreme Court. Over his years on the Court, he became known as an expert on admiralty law.

It is, however, his stance on slavery that was especially telling. "As both a constitutionalist and a southerner, Wayne, of course, believed that the institution of slavery enjoyed full constitutional protection."[54] His attitude was rather straightforward. He never entertained the notion that blacks could or should be allowed citizenship. "The black's inferior status, whether slave or free, was in the nature of things and the law should be firm in maintaining that status."[55] In the decisions regarding the *Dred Scott* case, he aligned himself completely with the findings of Justice Taney.

Wayne's concerns for the union of American states were exemplified during the Civil War. His son, an Army major, resigned his commission and returned to Georgia to serve in the Confederacy as the adjutant general for the state of Georgia. Nonetheless, Wayne kept his position on the Court and did not resign, as Justice Campbell of Alabama had done. Wayne was denounced in his native state of Georgia and branded as an enemy alien. A Confederate court confiscated his property in Georgia. During the Civil War, he supported the president's actions in the blockade of Southern ports. Despite these many difficulties, after the war, he returned to Georgia to reestablish his presence there. He died in July 1867 and was buried in Savannah.

Justice John Catron's date of birth and place of birth are not fully known. He was most likely born in 1786 in Pennsylvania. After military service during the war of 1812, he was admitted to the Tennessee bar in 1815. After years of practicing law, he was appointed by the legislature to the Tennessee Supreme Court in 1824. In 1831, Catron received the honor of being the state's first chief justice. He was also active with his family in the ironworks industry. Throughout his

---

53   Ibid., p. 328.
54   Ibid., p. 332.
55   Ibid., p. 333.

legal career in Tennessee, many aspects of racism and slavery were addressed. The issues of the emancipation of slaves and the legal status of free blacks were considered in an 1834 case. His attitude toward slaves who had been freed by manumission is emphatically expressed: "Degraded by their color and condition in life, the free negroes are a very dangerous and most objectionable population where slaves are numerous."[56] Catron felt that socially, the status of these free blacks was intolerable. "The free black man lives amongst us without motive and without hope."[57] (Refer to Figure 2-10.)

Dealing with the free black population, Catron proposed that manumissions be valid only if the freed individuals were sent to Liberia. He did not recommend sending these folks to other states in the Union, even when they accepted free slaves as citizens. "Nothing can be more untrue than that the free Negro is more respectable as a member of society in the non-slaveholding, than in the slaveholding States. In each, he is a degraded outcast and his fancied freedom a delusion ... Generally, and almost universally, society suffers, and the Negro suffers by manumission."[58]

2-10: Justice John Catron

It is also around this time, the mid-1830s, that Catron renders a decision regarding Native Americans. His attitude toward them and their status is clear: "Civilized men should not be misled by misapplied pity for 'mere wandering tribes of savages.' They deserve to be exterminated as savage and pernicious beasts."[59] His thinking about the control of Cherokee lands in the Southeast is straightforward: "Catron defended the state's authority over lands within its boundaries. The states had full jurisdiction over Indians when they entered the Union." [60] He also referred to them in a disparaging manner. "The Cherokees are overrun by whites, their government is broken up and suppressed by Georgia, their few people within our limits are so scattered and feeble, as not only to be incapable of self-government, but they are wholly incapable of protecting themselves, or the whites among them ... Theirs is, emphatically, a land without law, if our laws do not reach it, and so to all appearance it must remain."[61] This view sharply

56   Ibid., p. 374.
57   Ibid.
58   Ibid.
59   Ibid., p. 376.
60   Ibid., p. 377.
61   Ibid.

2-11: Justice Samuel Nelson

contrasted his own views about the Cherokee civilization given in an 1826 case. At that time, he spoke in appreciative terms about the Indians. "The Cherokees did have rights, which rights I am proud to say, have for the past thirty years, been respected with that good faith on our part, that became us as honest men and Christians."[62]

On President Andrew Jackson's last day in office, March 3, 1837, he nominated John Catron to the U.S. Supreme Court. Catron served on the High Court for almost three decades. In this time, he addressed the many issues brought to the Court about slavery. In the *Prigg* case, he agreed with Justice Story that federal powers and laws regarding fugitive slaves were exclusive and had to be followed by the states. His role in the *Dred Scott* case was a significant one. He had been in communication with a longtime friend, James Buchanan, the president elect. Catron and Buchanan corresponded about the various issues, including the property rights of citizens living in areas known as the Louisiana Purchase, and whether the Congress had made appropriate law in outlawing slavery in the Purchase area.

As the justices began their deliberations about which issues they would address in this case, Catron recommended that Buchanan write to Justice Grier of Pennsylvania to remind him about the importance of resolving many of the national questions regarding slavery presented by this case. "Buchanan complied, and in his inaugural address on March fourth he promised to abide by the Court's decision," adding disingenuously, "Whatever this may be."[63] In this case, Catron agreed with the majority that Scott's status was determined by the laws of the state of Missouri, where he was considered a slave for life.

It is important to note that Catron's principles about the supremacy of federal law put his life at risk. Ten days after President Abraham Lincoln's inauguration, Catron rushed from Washington to the states of Kentucky, Tennessee, and Missouri to perform his circuit court responsibilities. He believed that the maintenance of federal power in those possibly Confederate states was every important, regardless of the risk. In Nashville, he was warned by the federal marshal that his life was at risk and that the marshal could not offer any assistance. "In St. Louis he did meet his court, and there denounced the secessionists as rebels while denying writs of

---

62   Ibid.
63   Ibid., p. 381.

habeas corpus to several men then being held as traitors by federal officials. Catron's Unionism was unshakable."[64] This public and principal stance literally cost him a fortune. In a letter to the president, he detailed that, due to forfeiture of property in Nashville and elsewhere, he had lost over $100,000. But, as he concluded, "I have to punish Treason & will."[65] Catron died in May of 1865, shortly after the preservation of the Union had been assured by the defeat of the Confederacy. (Refer to Figure 2-11.)

Born in Washington County, New York, in 1792, Justice Samuel Nelson studied law and became involved in local and state politics. By 1823, he began his judicial career as a state circuit judge. After eight years, he was appointed to the New York Supreme Court, becoming its chief justice in 1837. After service in this position, he was nominated by President John Tyler for a seat on the U.S. Supreme Court in 1845.

Nelson's judicial approach in the *Dred Scott* case was that of restraint and discretion. He urged his fellow justices to delay a decision until the end of the next year, 1857. His task in the sculpting of the Court's decision had been to prepare a limited opinion on those questions of law included in the lower court's decision. When Justice Taney decided to write an opinion which he hoped would speak for the majority, Justice Nelson did not discard his own draft opinions. His judgment is emphatic: "In other words, except in cases where the power is restrained by the constitution of the United States, the law of the State is supreme over the subject of slavery within its jurisdiction."[66]

For his part in this decision, he received public criticism. "He hesitated to go with the Southern

2-12: Justice Robert C. Grier

Judges in their revolutionary opinions, yet he had not sufficient virtue to boldly stand up against their heresies."[67] Nelson's reaction to the Civil War is one of profound sorrow. In mid-1862, he laments the twin evils brought on by the war: "the plunge of Emancipation," and the "military despotism imposed in the loyal states."[68]. He died in December of 1873. (See Figure 2-12.)

---

64   Ibid., pp. 382–383.
65   Ibid.
66   Friedman and Israel, Eds., *The Justices of the Supreme Court*, vol. II, p. 415.
67   Ibid., p. 417.
68   Ibid., p. 437.

Justice Robert Grier was born in Cumberland County, Pennsylvania, on March 5, 1794. Grier's father operated a grammar school, so he was raised with knowledge of Greek and Latin. After graduation from college, he took over the operation of this school. In his spare time, he studied the law with a local attorney and was accepted to the bar in 1817.

After marriage and years of practice as an attorney, Grier accepted a judgeship in 1833 and moved to Pittsburgh. This experience and his political contacts led to his appointment by President James Polk to the U.S. Supreme Court in 1846. Within a brief period, he had established a place of some influence on the Court. Chief Justice Taney assigned to him a fair number of opinions in constitutional cases.[69]

His views regarding slaves and slavery were presented in various cases. In an 1852 decision regarding runaway slaves, he writes, "State laws were permissible, if they did indeed aid in the capture of fugitives, and did not interfere with federal powers in any way."[70] Concerning the *Dred Scott* case, president-elect James Buchanan corresponded with Justice Grier, who responded that, "He would work closely with Taney and Wayne to produce an acceptable and authoritative majority opinion."[71] In this case, his decision was a half-page, agreeing with the conclusions of Justices Nelson and Taney.

While Grier was a defender of Southern constitutional rights and opposed abolition, he, like many, was not supportive of the notion of seceding from the Union. His thoughts of the war were in some ways prophetic. "We must conquer this rebellion or declare our republican government a failure, if it should cost 100,000 men and millions of money."[72] His view about the Confederacy is also expressed in an 1861 case: "Consequently, this court ... can view those in rebellion ... in no other light as traitors to their country."[73] Near the end of his judicial career, with his health failing, he resigned from the Court and died six months later in 1870.

Justice Peter V. Daniel was born in Stafford County, Virginia, on April 24, 1784. Daniel was educated by a series of private tutors. He studied law in Richmond and gained admission to the bar in 1808. Through his family connections, he was able to become part of Virginia's social hierarchy. In 1809, he was elected to the state legislature. In 1818, he became lieutenant governor of Virginia. By virtue of his political work and connections, Daniel developed a strong friendship with future president Martin Van Buren. In 1836, he was appointed to the federal bench as judge of the United States District Court of Eastern Virginia by President Andres Jackson.

Daniel's legal philosophy centered on the concept of constitutional fundamentalism. "Stripped of verbiage this meant that judges should expound the Constitution and laws narrowly, especially when it came to national powers."[74] Federal encroachment and the threat of consolidated government were his greatest concerns. In 1841, his friend and political supporter, Martin Van Buren, nominated him to the U.S. Supreme Court. While his position changed, his basic philosophy did not. "These principles, never abandoned and hardly modified, made Daniel the Court's extreme agrarian, the sworn enemy of consolidation, corporations and banks; the extreme defender of states rights, and finally the extreme sectionalist and radical partisan in the slavery question."[75]

---

69   Ibid., p. 440.
70   Ibid.
71   Ibid., p. 442.
72   Ibid.
73   Ibid., p. 459.
74   Ibid., p. 399.
75   Ibid., p. 401.

His thoughts regarding the abolition movement were consistent with his overall philosophy: "For him the maintenance of the South's socio-economic system was bound up with the very foundations of constitutional government."[76] In the 1842 *Prigg* case, much of Daniel's opinion would be consistent with his findings 15 years later in the *Dred Scott* case. "The Missouri Compromise was thus wholly unconstitutional and void. The question of the existence of slavery was a matter to be determined solely by the people of each territory without any interference by the federal government.[77]

Daniel's thoughts in that later case left little doubt of his beliefs. "The African Negro race never had been acknowledged as belonging to the family of nations ... that this race has been by all the nations of Europe regarded as subjects of capture or purchase; as subjects of commerce or traffic; and that the introduction of that race into every section of this country was not as members of civil or political society, but as slaves."[78] He further held that slaves were the property of their owner. In that category of property, a slave could not be a citizen. "A slave owner could by his own act of emancipation make a free

2-13: Justice John A. Campbell

man, but he could not create a citizen."[79] After the Court's adjournment for its 1859 term, Daniel returned to Richmond, where he passed away on May 31, 1860. (See Figure 2-13.)

Justice John A. Campbell was born in Georgia on June 24, 1811. He graduated the University of Georgia with honors in 1826 and then spent a few years at the West Point Military Academy, resigning after the death of his father. He was admitted to the Georgia bar in 1829 at the young age of 18. He became involved in the legal and political arenas of his day. In 1853, Chief Justice Roger Taney sent Supreme Court justices John Catron and Benjamin Curtis to President Franklin Pierce to advise him that John Campbell should be nominated to the High Court. This occurred on March 21, 1853. Campbell's work on the Taney Court included areas such as corporate charities, determining corporate liability, drawing boundary lines between states, and deciding jurisdiction of rivers.[80] As a circuit rider in the Fifth Circuit, he judged cases in

76   Ibid., p. 403.
77   Ibid., p. 404.
78   Ibid.
79   Ibid.
80   Ibid., p. 468.

Alabama and Louisiana. Some of the cases involved smuggling slaves into the South. In this regard, as Justice Curtis enforced fugitive slave regulations in antislavery New England, Justice Campbell upheld the laws against slave smuggling in the proslavery South.

His thoughts in the *Dred Scott* case parallel those of Chief Justice Taney, agreeing that the laws of Missouri governed the legal status of Dred Scott. "He concluded that the opinion of the federal circuit court was correct; Scott remained a slave and therefore could not sue in court."[81] Campbell's views had changed over the years. In 1847, he proposed that slave families be maintained and not broken up for sale. In 1848, he wrote that Congress could determine how territories should be governed, including their property. He freed his own slaves around 1853.[82] It is impossible to fully explain the gap between his personal and fairly moderate views and those expressed in the *Dred Scott* case. It might be due to the general hardening of positions in the North and South regarding slavery, states' rights, and the continuity of the Union.

In the months leading up to the Civil War, Campbell acted as an intermediary between Confederate commissioners and Secretary of State William Seward. The hope of these talks was to somehow avoid war through compromise and negotiations. This effort failed when the war began in April of 1861.

Within weeks, he tendered his resignation from the Supreme Court. There is much speculation on the reasons motivating his resignation, particularly in light of the fact that Justice Wayne of Georgia did not resign. Nevertheless, Campbell did and returned to Alabama. "In short, he had always been a loyal southerner within the Union; he now sadly followed Alabama when it marched into war."[83] Ironically, his return to Alabama was scorned by many who misrepresented his various political stands. In May of 1861, Campbell returned to Mobile, Alabama, where he was threatened with lynching. Eventually, after moving to New Orleans, he became the Confederate Assistant Secretary of War on October 21, 1862. After the war, he was jailed for four months and then released upon the order of President Andrew Johnson. "As he left prison, Campbell in middle age was bankrupt in every sense. His property and home were destroyed, his reputation was suspect, he was about to be excluded from public office, federal practice and the polls. ... but like the fabled phoenix, he was to rise from the ashes."[84]

He returned to New Orleans where he set up a law practice. In this role, he was intimately involved in the 1873 Slaughterhouse Cases, which became well known for its analysis by the Supreme Court of the parameters and potency of the newly passed Fourteenth Amendment. Campbell died on March 12, 1889.

Justice Benjamin R. Curtis was born in Watertown, Massachusetts, just outside of Boston on November 4, 1809. An early affinity for books and reading created the stage for him to enter Harvard College in 1825. After graduation from college, he immediately was accepted into Harvard Law School. Under the tutelage of legal giants such as Joseph Story, an associate justice of the U.S. Supreme Court, Curtis excelled. He was admitted to the bar in 1832, establishing a practice in Northfield, Massachusetts. In October 1834 he returned to the Boston area to join a prominent law firm. He remained with this firm for 17 years, where he primarily represented large private corporations engaged in trade concerned about governmental interference.[85]

---

81   Ibid., p. 469.
82   Ibid., p. 470.
83   Ibid., p. 472.
84   Ibid., p. 474.
85   Ibid., p. 449.

Curtis's beliefs about the contemporary issues of the 1850s were typical of many at that time. "When the sectional dispute over slavery broke out, he stood at Daniel Webster's side as a staunch nationalist and conservative—both being prepared to defend the constitution and the Union in fair weather or foul."[86] He publicly supported sectional accommodation as the price for the maintenance of the Union. In this regard, he endorsed enforcement of the 1850 Fugitive Slave Act.

Curtis was nominated to the U.S. Supreme Court by President Millard Fillmore. His confirmation occurred in December 1851. Interestingly, he served six years on the High Court. One of the responsibilities that the justices had at this time was "circuit riding" throughout their judicial area, judging cases. In this regard, Curtis's First Circuit area included the four New England states of Maine, New Hampshire, Massachusetts, and Rhode Island. As such, he judged a number of cases involving runaway slaves who had been tracked down with the purpose of returning them to slavery. As mentioned previously, much of the populace of the North was especially determined not to comply with the Fugitive Slave Act and return escaped slaves to a life of slavery. Curtis, however, in his judicial role stood firm in upholding and enforcing this unpopular law. His reasoning is important to consider. "He maintained that flouting the law by incitement to violence would undermine order, which is indispensable to liberty, and would reduce government to a shambles, to a mere tool of the violent and the strong operating at the expenses of the peaceful and the weak."[87] For these stances, the New England press dubbed him "the slave-catcher judge."[88]

Justice Curtis was one of two dissenters on the *Dred Scott* decision. His conclusions about the case are the opposite of Justice Taney's and the majority of the justices. Simply put, he felt that blacks were citizens of America and voters as well. He argued that citizens of a state were also citizens of the Unites States, and with the appropriate rights and privileges, could sue in federal courts. He reasoned that residence in a free state gave freedom to any slaves and that Congress had the legal right to prohibit slavery in the Missouri Compromise territory. The aftermath of the *Scott* decision occurred on many levels. Curtis gave a copy of his dissent to a Boston newspaperman for publication, which angered Justice Taney. Due to a combination of personal, financial, and political factors, Justice Curtis resigned from the Court on September 1, 1857, at the age of 47.

He returned to Boston and resumed his law practice, which eventually included arguing many cases in front of the U.S. Supreme Court, as well as the Massachusetts Supreme Judicial Court. He served as counsel to President Andrew Johnson in his impeachment trial. His words reflect his skills as an eminent attorney: "I am here to speak to the Senate sitting in its judicial capacity as a court of impeachment, presided over by the Chief Justice for the trial of the President of the United States ... here party spirit, political schemes, foregone conclusions, outrageous biases can have no fit operation."[89] After this trial, Curtis's health gradually failed, and he died on September 15, 1874. (Refer to Figure 2-14.)

Born in New Jersey in 1785, Justice John McLean had an interesting career. In his early adult years, he moved his family to Ohio and became involved in the newspaper business. At this time of his life, he converted from a Presbyterian to a Methodist, becoming, according to some, the leading Methodist layman in the country. McLean's legal career progressed with an appointment to the Ohio Supreme Court in 1816. In his second year in that position, he decided a case

---

86   Ibid., p. 451.
87   Ibid., p. 454.
88   Ibid.
89   Ibid., p. 459.

2-14: Justice John McLean

involving a slave who traveled between Kentucky, a slaveholding state, and Ohio, a free one. In this decision, he communicated some of his thoughts about slavery: "he would incline toward granting freedom to all slaves, according to the immutable principles of natural justice."[90] He also contended that if a master uses slave labor in a free state, by such an act he forfeits the right of property in slaves.[91]

His work on a national scale continued with an appointment as U.S. postmaster general in 1823. This was followed by his confirmation to the United States Supreme Court in 1829. McLean served as a justice for 31 years. While he had presidential aspirations, these never came to fruition.

During McLean's many years on the Court, his position about slavery revolved around the tension between upholding the Constitution and the natural opinions and affinities he held against the institution of slavery. In the 1842 *Prigg* case, he argues that states might prevent the seizure of alleged fugitive slaves. "In a State where slavery is allowed, every colored person is presumed to be a slave; and on the same principle, in a non-slaveholding State, every person is presumed to be free, without regard to color." [92] In an 1847 case, *Jones v. Van Zandt*, he agrees with the majority in upholding the conviction of Van Zandt, who had broken a federal law against harboring a fugitive slave. McLean believed that the laws as written in the Constitution needed to be enforced and followed.

Most interestingly, his dissent in the *Dred Scott* case is seen as pivotal to the historical significance of the case. The case was argued in February 1856. One year later, the justices met and decided to dispose of the case on the narrow grounds that Scott's case must be determined by Missouri law. If that state had concluded that he was a slave, then he had no legal right to sue in federal courts. McLean and Justice Curtis decided to go beyond this minor point. They felt that a free black was a citizen on the basis of interstate comity. McLean argued that the Missouri court which had ruled against Scott should have given more weight to the constitution and laws of Illinois. He concluded that the lower court's order should be reversed.[93]

---

90   Friedman and Israel, Eds., *The Justices of the Supreme Court*, vol. I, p. 303.
91   Ibid., p. 304.
92   Ibid., p. 310.
93   Ibid., p. 311.

Based on McLean and Curtis taking more aggressive positions, the proslavery justices decided to address larger issues in the case. As mentioned above, they decided that Scott was not a citizen, and they declared the unconstitutionality of the early prohibitions about slavery in U.S. territories. Justice McLean died within a few days of the commencement of the Civil War on April 4, 1861.

This summary of the beliefs and life experiences of the justices involved in the Scott case was given to help readers appreciate that the justices were somewhat influenced in their decisions based on their places of origin and early upbringing, but it is impossible to know how much of an effect this had. In some cases, their opinions changed over time; in other instances, their initial beliefs were retained over a lifetime. Some had to make gut-wrenching decisions such as supporting the Union or the new Confederacy, often dealing with the splitting up of their families and financial well-being as a consequence of such decisions.

What might be most significant is to use these beliefs and life experiences as a standard by which future decisions can be judged. Once the Civil War was concluded and the Thirteenth, Fourteenth, and Fifteenth Amendments were ratified, America changed. The reality of slavery and its existence could no longer be used in a historical or legal context when deciding future cases. Nonetheless, did the notion of the freed slaves being separate but equal become the defining philosophical attitude of the Court in the late 19th and mid-20th centuries? These questions will be addressed in the analysis of future Court cases.

After the *Dred Scott* case, the mood in the country seemed to become increasingly polarized by the inability to find a peaceful resolution to slavery. This decision did little to calm the emotions of the nation. In fact, one could surmise that it had an antagonizing effect on America. A case decided in the Court's next term accurately reflected the increased tension and even danger to the framework of the country, as states began actively ignoring some of the statutes regarding slavery and especially runaway slaves. Public outrage in the North had been slowly increasing with the enforcement of the newly strengthened Fugitive Act of 1850. The sight of black men and women, many long-time residents of the North, being dragged off to jail in chains and taken South to bondage by federal authorities converted hundreds of indifferent Northerners to antislavery sentiments overnight. (See Figure 2-15.)

Emotions were so strong that nine Northern states enacted new personal liberty laws, allowing state attorneys to defend fugitives, appropriated funds to pay defense costs, and denied the use of public buildings to detain accused escapees. These state laws were challenged by the federal government in the little-known cases of *Ableman v. Booth* and *United States v. Booth*. In this instance, the state of Wisconsin, on two occasions, did not comply with the legal requirements of the act of 1850. The actions that the state took are summarized in the High Court's decision,

> *It will be seen from the foregoing statement of facts, that a judge of the Supreme Court of the State of Wisconsin in the first of these cases, claimed and exercised the right to supervise and annul the proceedings of a commissioner of the United States, and to discharge a prisoner, who had been committed by the commissioner of an offence against the laws of this Government, and that this exercise of power by the judge was afterwards sanctioned and affirmed by the Supreme Court of the State.*
>
> *In the second case, the state court has gone a step further, and claimed and exercised jurisdiction over the proceedings and judgment of a District Court of the United states, and upon a summary and collateral proceeding, by habeas corpus, has set aside and annulled its judgment, and discharged a prisoner who had been tried and found guilty of an offence against the laws of the United States, and sentenced to imprisonment by the District court.*

CAUTION!!
COLORED PEOPLE
OF BOSTON, ONE & ALL,
You are hereby respectfully CAUTIONED and
advised, to avoid conversing with the
Watchmen and Police Officers
of Boston,
For since the recent ORDER OF THE MAYOR &
ALDERMEN, they are empowered to act as
KIDNAPPERS
AND
Slave Catchers,
And they have already been actually employed in
KIDNAPPING, CATCHING, AND KEEPING
SLAVES. Therefore, if you value your LIBERTY,
and the *Welfare of the Fugitives* among you, *Shun*
them in every possible manner, as so many *HOUNDS*
on the track of the most unfortunate of your race.

Keep a Sharp Look Out for
KIDNAPPERS, and have
TOP EYE open.
APRIL 24, 1851.

2-15: This April 1854 poster warns "The Colored People" of Boston to stay away from police officers as they might act as slave catchers and return them to slavery.

And it further appears that the State court have not only claimed and exercised this jurisdiction, but have also determined that their decision is final and conclusive upon all the courts of the United States, and ordered their clerk to disregard and refuse obedience to the writ of error issued by this court, pursuant to the act of Congress of 1789, to bring here for examination and revisions the judgment of the State court.[94]

The Court responds with a number of powerful statements reinforcing their role as the ultimate legal arbiter for the country. Nevertheless, the fact that the state courts acted so defiantly regarding the handing over of runaway slaves offers a glimpse into the level of emotions involved with this issue. First, the Court takes the state to task for assuming legal powers without authority.

The judges of the Supreme Court of Wisconsin do not distinctly state from what source they suppose they have derived this judicial power. There can be no such thing as judicial authority, unless it is conferred by a Government or sovereignty ... It certainly has not been conferred on them by the United States; and it is equally clear it was not in the power of the State to confer it, ... And although the state of Wisconsin is sovereign within its territorial limits to a certain extent, yet that sovereignty is limited and restricted by the Constitution of the United States. ... And the sphere of action appropriated to the United States is as far beyond the reach of the judicial process issued by a State judge or a State court, as if the line of division was traced by landmarks and monuments visible to the eye.[95]

94   *Ableman v. Booth* and *United States v. Booth*, 1858, pp. 513–514.
95   Ibid., pp. 515–516.

The justices' remarks continue with a strong defense of the Constitution itself. The ruling reiterates the fact that the Constitution allows that it "shall be the supreme law of the land, and the judges in every State shall be bound thereby, anything in the Constitution or laws of any State to the contrary notwithstanding." [96] The next argument is a recapitulation of the role that the Supreme Court justices have in regard to the Constitution.

> *It was essential, therefore, to its very existence as a Government, that it should have the power of establishing courts of justice, altogether independent of state power, to carry into effect its own laws; and that a tribunal should be established in which all cases which might arise under the Constitution and laws and treaties of the United States, whether in a State court or a court of the United States, should be finally and conclusively decided.*
>
> *This judicial power was justly regarded as indispensable, not merely to maintain the supremacy of the laws of the United States, but also to guard the States from any encroachment upon their reserved rights by the General government ... And as the final appellate power in all such questions is given to this court ... and no one can fail to see, that if such an arbiter had not been provided, in our complicated system of government, internal tranquility could not have been preserved; and if such controversies were left to arbitrament of physical force, our Government, State, and national, would soon cease to be Governments of laws, and revolutions by force of arms would take the place of courts of justice and judicial decisions.* [97]

After establishing their ultimate legal authority, the High Court explicitly reiterated its support for the process of capturing runaway slaves. "The act of Congress commonly called the fugitive slave act is, in all its provisions, fully authorized by the Constitution of the United States."[98] They reversed the findings of the Wisconsin Supreme Court in both of these cases, which had offered state laws that differed from the federal ones regarding fugitive slaves.

The almost palpable animosity between the states was exemplified by the case of *Lemmon v. the People*, decided by New York's supreme court in 1860. In this case, slaveholders traveling to Texas onboard a ship with their eight slaves awaiting a steamboat to their destination transited in New York City. Despite a warning not to disembark, they did. Within a day, the slave owners were served with a writ of habeas corpus to free the slaves. Early in the 19th century, New York State had passed a law that freed all slaves who remained there for nine months.[99] The judge in the habeas corpus hearing freed the slaves immediately, as he noted that in 1841 the nine-month waiting period had been repealed.

While the actual slave owners in this case did not appeal the ruling, they were compensated for the value of their slaves by the state of Virginia. Virginia appropriated state funds to appeal this decision through the state legal system. *Lemmon v. the People* ultimately was decided by the New York Supreme Court in April 1860. "In a five to three decision to free the slaves, the court affirmed that the 1841 statute freed all slaves upon their entry to New York."[100]

As one can easily understand, such decisions only heightened and exacerbated the difficult relations that existed between the Northern states wishing to abolish the practice of slavery and

---

96   Ibid., p. 517.
97   Ibid., pp. 518–521.
98   Ibid., p. 526.
99   Drobak, Political Working Paper, p. 14.
100   Ibid., p. 16.

the Southern states, which increasingly felt that their way of life was being threatened. Slave owners felt that such decisions created incentives for slaves to escape and even revolt.[101]

It seems clear from these cases that the country was moving inexorably on a course of frustration and tension that would ultimately end in a deadly conflict.

---

101   Ibid., p. 17.

Discussion Questions

1. Can you imagine how it felt for enslaved parents to see their children sold and taken away, perhaps forever?

2. Why did the General School Committee of Boston decide in the 1840s to maintain separate schools for black and white students?

3. Do you agree with the justifications of Justice Taney that blacks were never considered "citizens" when the Constitution was written?

4. Should Dred Scott have received his freedom after residing in a free state and territory?

5. If you were a justice on the *Dred Scott* case, how would you have voted, and why?

6. What must it have felt like for a runaway slave to cross a natural boundary such as a river and transition from a slave state to a free state?

7. During the Civil War, what were some of the very personal and economic challenges faced by some of the justices?

8. After reading the biographical synopses of the justices in the *Dred Scott* case, have you reached any conclusions about their beliefs and decisions?

9. If the case had been decided differently, could the Civil War have been averted?

10. If you were alive in the 1800s and could own slaves, would you have done so?

THE BATTLEFIELD SHIFTS TO THE SUPREME COURT

With the country becoming increasingly agitated and divided regarding slavery and states' rights, war seemed sadly inevitable. The Civil War began in April 1861 at Fort Sumter, South Carolina, and lasted for four long years. While estimates vary, the number of fatalities exceeded 700,000 people. In the midst of the war, new laws were promulgated by the North regarding slaves and slavery. Initially, the Civil War did not focus solely on slavery, but rather on maintaining the Union. In fact, in the months prior to the war's beginning, a possible Thirteenth Amendment was proposed, which would have prohibited future amendments from interfering with slavery where it already existed.[1] The onset of the war removed any possibility of this proposed amendment's passage. (See Figure 3-1.)

As always, with this issue, there was no shortage of opinions, all very strongly held. Some opponents of freeing the slaves were afraid. "They feared that emancipation would propel two or three million semi-savages northward, where they would crowd into white neighborhoods, compete for white jobs,

---

1   http://13thamendment.harpweek.com

and mix with white 'sons and daughters.'"[2] Abolitionists strongly argued "That by seceding, Southerners had forfeited their right to the protection of the Constitution. Lincoln could now—as the price of treason—legally confiscate their property in slaves."[3]

3-1: This picture symbolizes the battle wounds, bravery, and sacrifices of war.

The Republican-dominated Congress quickly formulated laws affecting slaves. In August of 1861, Congress passed the Confiscation Act, which allowed the seizure of any slave employed by the Confederate military. As the war commenced and battles were fought, tens of thousands of slaves escaped and headed toward the North or Union-controlled areas. By August 1861, Congress established a national policy when it forbade the practice of returning fugitive slaves to their owners. Lincoln utilized a variety of approaches to this issue that evolved as the war proceeded. An initial attitude of noninterference was altered to a new one: colonization. To placate the fears of those Northerners who did not favor the emancipation of slaves, Lincoln suggested that African Americans be deported to Haiti, Panama, or other sites. In the summer of 1862, he spoke to a delegation of black visitors to the White House,   .

> *He told them that deep seated racial prejudice made it impossible for them to achieve equality in this country. For blacks to be truly free, he said, they had to immigrate to countries where opportunities existed. An African-American from Philadelphia spoke for the group when he told the president, "This is our country as much as it is yours, and we will not leave it.*[4]

At the same time, military commanders in the field of battle were making ad hoc decisions about freeing slaves in areas under their control. Congress responded with a second Confiscation Act. This law declared all slaves of rebel masters "forever free of their servitude."[5] In effect, this law outlawed slavery in much of the Confederacy. In the same month, Lincoln drafted a version of an emancipation proclamation. Upon the advice of his cabinet, he waited until after a Union victory—the battle at Antietam in Maryland in September of 1862—to offer his proclamation. Lincoln presented the emancipation as a military necessity. In it, he called for the rebel states to lay down their arms; if they did not, their slaves would be forever free. It is valuable to read sections of this proclamation to understand what was written and intended, as well as some qualifiers that were also found in the document. On January 1, 1863, Lincoln issued the final version of the Emancipation Proclamation. (Refer to Figure 3-2.)

---

2   Roark, Johnson, et al., *American Promise*, p. 507.

3   Ibid.

4   Ibid., p. 509.

5   Ibid.

Simultaneously, events on the ground were rapidly changing. The Militia Act of 1862 encouraged blacks to enroll in the Union's armed forces. By the time of the Emancipation Proclamation, blacks were joining in large numbers and taking active roles in the fighting. Even though they were not treated as fairly as white soldiers, blacks made an enormous contribution to the Union cause. By the end of the war, approximately 180,000 African American men had served in the Union military, representing 10 percent of the total force. Of these, 130,000 black soldiers came from the slave states, perhaps 100,000 of them ex-slaves. More than 38,000 black soldiers died in the Civil War, a mortality rate higher than that of white troops. Blacks played a crucial role in the triumph of the Union and the destruction of slavery.[6] (Refer to Figure 3-3.)

3-2: Imagine what it must have felt like to learn that freedom, so long denied, was close at hand.

With the conclusion of the war in 1865, the country entered a new relationship between the North and South: the Reconstruction period. This 12-year cycle deserves much attention and examination, as the dynamics involved at that time created paradigms of racial relations which lasted for decades. While the South had been defeated on the battlefields, another cultural war front was rapidly developing. A myriad of questions arose concerning the conquered South: What would be the economic, educational, cultural, and racial future of the South? Who would have responsibility for this transformation? Would the freed slaves be integrated in the remnants of the defeated South?

Initially, President Lincoln led the movement to spearhead this massive Reconstruction effort. On April 11th, 1865, with the war finally over, he shared his attitude toward the South and its reintegration into the Union.

> *Speaking from the White House balcony, he dismissed the theoretical question of whether the Confederate states had technically remained in the Union as "good for nothing at all— a mere pernicious abstraction." … Lincoln wanted "no persecution, no bloody work," no dramatic restructuring of southern social and economic life.[7]*

Sadly, within days of this speech, Abraham Lincoln was assassinated. His vice president—Andrew Johnson, now elevated to the presidency—had his own philosophy about Reconstruction. He went further than Lincoln in his willingness to forgive the South and welcome them back into the Union. He offered this attitude about the secession from the North: "There is no such thing as Reconstruction. Those states have not gone out of the

---

6   Ibid., p. 510.
7   Tindall and Shi, *The Essential America*, p. 292.

3-3: This mid-1860s photograph indicates the bravery and military bearing of black soldiers. The saying on the top of the picture is self-explanatory, "Rather die freemen, than live to be slaves."

Union. Therefore Reconstruction is unnecessary."[8] At the same time, many in Congress who eventually formed a coalition of members called Radical Republicans pressed for an immediate sweeping transformation of Southern society. For the moment, the views of the executive branch in the person of the president prevailed. In the eight months between Lincoln's assassination and the convening of a new postwar Congress, the South reflected its attitudes about reconciliation with two significant gestures. In December of 1865, the South sent the following individuals to represent its interests in Congress: "Among the new members presenting themselves to Congress were Georgia's Alexander H. Stephens, late vice-president of the Confederacy, four Confederate generals, eight colonels, six cabinet members, and a host of lesser Rebel officials."[9]

Of even greater importance was that the Southern governments began passing restrictive laws directed against the former slaves. These laws became known as the "Black Codes." These new laws set up a disparate system of justice in the Southern states,

Furthermore, the new southern legislatures, in passing repressive "Black Codes" restricting the freedom of blacks, baldly revealed that they intended to preserve the trappings of slavery as nearly as possible. As one southerner stressed, the "ex-slave was not a free man; he was a free Negro."[10] (See Figure 3-4.)

These laws were pernicious in their effects on the newly freed slaves. The details varied from state to state, but some provisions were common. Black marriages were recognized, but interracial marriage was prohibited. In some Southern states, blacks could not own farmland or city lots. Vagrant blacks were punished with severe fines, and, if unable to pay, were forced to work in the fields for whites, who paid the courts for this cheap labor.[11]. In Mississippi, for example, the "Black Code" law read, "Every civil officer shall, and every person may, arrest and carry back to his or her legal employer any freedman, free Negro, or mulatto who shall have quit the service of his or her employer before the expiration of his or her term of service without good

8   Ibid.
9   Ibid., p. 293.
10   Ibid.
11   Ibid.

cause."[12] These laws also placed the former slaves into legal circumstances that created situations akin to slavery. "If any freedman, free Negro or mulatto, convicted of any of the misdemeanors provided against in this act, shall fail or refuse for the space of five days after conviction, to pay the fine and costs imposed, such person shall be hired out by the sheriff or other officer, at the public outcry, to any white person who will pay said fine and all costs, and take the convict for the shortest time."[13]

3-4: One of the first priorities for the freed slave community was education for their children.

Other provisions found in the Black Codes barred blacks from many businesses without obtaining a special license and forbade them from renting or leasing land, except in towns and cities. These codes were laws which helped maintain the legal supremacy of whites over those of blacks. In several states, blacks could not own guns. Blacks were barred from jury duty. Central to the codes was a sense of economic inequality.

Faced with the death of slavery and the disintegration of plantations, legislators sought to hustle freedmen back into traditional tasks. South Carolina attempted to limit blacks to either farm work or domestic service by requiring them to pay annual taxes of $10 to $100 to work in any other occupation. Mississippi declared that blacks who did not possess written evidence of employment could be declared vagrants and be subject to fines or involuntary plantation labor. Most states allowed judges to bind black children—orphans and others whose parents they deemed unable to support them—to white employers. Under these so called apprenticeship laws, courts bound out thousands of black children to planter "guardians."[14]

At this juncture, Congress, led by Radical Republicans believing that President Johnson's approach of a gracious and nonthreatening attitude toward Reconstruction was unsuccessful, began to assert its power. Laws and constitutional amendments were passed in direct response to the Black Codes and the South's intransigence in general and over Johnson's veto. The first of these amendments was the Thirteenth Amendment, ratified in December of 1865.

This short amendment contains two brief sections.

Section 1. Neither slavery nor involuntary servitude, except as a punishment for crime, whereof the party shall have been duly convicted, shall exist within the United States, or any place subject to their jurisdiction."

Section 2. Congress shall have power to enforce this article by appropriate legislation.

This amendment gave additional legal authority to the wartime Emancipation Proclamation. One of the functions of this amendment, as well as the Fourteenth and Fifteenth amendments, was that their acceptance by the former Confederate states was mandated in order for the

12   Barrett and Cohen, *Constitutional Law*, p. 22.
13   Ibid.
14   Roark, Johnson, et al., *The American Promise*, p. 547.

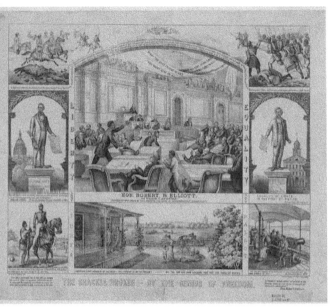

3-5: This picture shows Congressman Robert B. Elliot of South Carolina giving an empassioned speech on January 6th, 1874, about freedom. A famous quote from that occasion is, "What you give to one class you must give to all. What you deny to one class, you deny to all."

Southern states to reenter the Union, as part of the reconstruction process unfolding in the country in the months and years after the Civil War.

One significant dynamic to be expressed at this juncture is one of tension or stress between the defeated Confederacy and the Radical Republicans in Congress. As the South produced Black Codes and gave other indications that the prejudice toward people of color was still very much alive and well, Congress responded with various acts and amendments, whose purpose was to dampen and ultimately diminish through the use of law, any tendencies that the South might have had for perpetuating various discriminatory practices and laws. (Refer to Figure 3-5.)

The Civil Rights Act of 1866 was designed to directly counter such unequal laws and also to provide for a legal remedy for any infractions against former slaves. This 1866 act would be followed by subsequent civil rights acts in 1870, 1871, and 1875. It is instructive to view the law of 1866 and note its specificity. Clearly, its authors wanted to enumerate the rights which the freed slaves should enjoy. The first section of the 1866 act addresses the issue of citizenship for the former slaves. It enacted that:

> *All persons born in the United States and not subject to any foreign power, excluding Indians not taxed, are hereby declared to be citizens of the United States; and such citizens, of every race and color, without regard to any previous condition of slavery or involuntary servitude, except as a punishment for crime whereof the party shall have been duly convicted, shall have the same right in every State and Territory in the United States to make and enforce contracts, to sue, be parties, and give evidence, to inherit, purchase, lease, sell, hold, and convey real and personal property, and to full and equal benefit of all laws and proceedings for the security of person and property as is enjoyed by white citizens, and shall be subject to like punishment, pains, and penalties, and to none other, any law, statute, ordinance, regulation, or custom to the contrary notwithstanding.[15]*

The intent of this act could not be more explicit: whites and blacks should have equal benefit of the law, and thus be entitled to full legal participation in a new Southern society.

The words of one of the bill's original Senate cosponsors, Lyman Trumbull, indicated his thinking on January 5, 1866, about the significance and meaning of this civil rights act, created months after the Civil War.

---

15   Barrett and Cohen, *Constitutional Law*, pp. 22–23.

Mr. President, I regard the bill to which the attention of the Senate is now called as the most important measure that has been under its consideration since the adoption of the constitutional amendment abolishing slavery. That amendment declared that all persons in the United States should be free. This measure is intended to give effect to that declaration and secure to all persons within the United States practical freedom. There is very little importance in the general declaration of abstract truths and principles unless they can be carried into effect, unless the persons who are to be affected by them have some means of availing themselves of their benefits ... the Senator said, the bill would "break down all discrimination between black men and white men."[16] *(See Figure 3-6.)*

It is unfortunate that the goals of Senator Trumbull were not realized for a least a century or longer. The penalties of not following this act are clearly delineated in the next section of the bill.

That any person who, under color of any law, statute, ordinance, regulation, or custom, shall subject, or cause to be subjected, any inhabitant of any state or Territory to the deprivation of any right, secured or protected by this act, or to different punishment, pains, or penalties, on account of such person having at any time been held in a condition of slavery, or involuntary servitude, except as a punishment for crime, whereof the party shall have been duly convicted or by reason of his color, or race, than is prescribed for the punishment of white persons, [exactly what the "Black Codes" were doing] shall be deemed guilty of a misdemeanor, and shall, on conviction thereof, be punished by fine not exceeding one thousand dollars, or imprisonment not exceeding one year, or both, in the discretion of the court.[17]

FREE!

3-6: Clearly, the goal of these amendments and the 1866 Civil Rights Act is crystalized in this art work: Freedom.

This portion of the law is immediately followed by others that list the legal offices and officers whose job it was to pursue legal actions regarding this act.

That the District Courts of the United States, within their respective districts, shall have, exclusively of the courts of the several States, cognizance of all crimes and offences committed against the provisions of this act, and also concurrently with the Circuit Courts of the United States, of all causes, civil and criminal, affecting persons who are denied, or cannot enforce in the courts or judicial tribunals of the State, or locality, where they may be, any of the rights secured to them by the first section of the act.

---

16 http://scholar.google.com, *Jones v. Alfred H. Mayer Co.*
17 http://wikisource.org, *Civil Rights Act of 1866*, p. 2.

And it be further enacted, That the district attorneys, marshals, and deputy marshals of the United States, the commissioners appointed by the circuit and territorial courts of the United States, with powers of arresting, imprisoning, or bailing offenders against the laws of the United States, the officers and agents of the Freedmen's Bureau, and every officer who may be specially empowered by the President of the United States, shall be, and they are hereby, specially authorized and required, at the expense of the United States, to institute proceedings against all and every person who shall violate the provisions of this act and cause him or them to be arrested and imprisoned, or bailed, as the case may be, for trial before such court of the United States or territorial court as by this act has cognizance of the offence.[18]

This act is unique in that the above provisions anticipate that if justice is not found on a local level, then citizens who believed that their rights had been abused would have a remedy in a federal circuit or district court. The clear intention is explicitly spelled out in the paragraphs above: the former slaves were to have equal benefit of all laws and proceedings for the security of person and property as is enjoyed by white citizens. It seems apparent as well that the act was passed into law with the belief that its provisions would be vigorously enforced.

Interestingly, President Johnson, who had taken over after Lincoln's assassination, had chosen to veto this bill. His reasoning in this decision makes for fascinating reading.

In all our history, in all our experience as people living under Federal and State law, no such system as that contemplated by the details of this bill has ever before been proposed or adopted. They establish for the security of the colored race safeguards which go infinitely beyond any that the General Government has ever provided for the white race. In fact, the distinction of race and color is by the bill made to operate in favor of the colored and against the white race.[19]

The Senate and the House overrode the president's veto, and the bill became law. Other forceful laws and amendments were also passed to help ensure the kind of equality-based society the Radical Republicans envisioned.

Despite the specificity and force of the 1866 Civil Rights Act, the South continued in its extreme recalcitrance to give the freed slaves full rights. Congress responded to this situation by creating and having the country ratify in 1868 the Fourteenth Amendment to the Constitution. The amendment's first section would be part of many subsequent legal cases.

All persons born or naturalized in the United States, and subject to the jurisdiction thereof, are citizens of the United States and of the State wherein they reside. No State shall make or enforce any law which shall abridge the privileges or immunities of citizens of the United States; nor shall any State deprive any person of life, liberty, or property, without due process of law; nor deny to any person within its jurisdiction the equal protection of the laws.

This amendment is a direct refutation of the Dred Scott decision, which predicated that blacks could not be citizens. The second section concerns itself with the right of the black

---

18   Ibid., pp. 2–3.
19   Ibid., p. 9.

community to vote, and warns that the number of representatives in Congress would be reduced based on those males who are denied their right to vote. The third and fourth sections deal with issues related to membership in the Confederacy and debts owed to the Confederacy. (Refer to Figure 3-7.)

Again, the goal of passing the Fourteenth Amendment was multileveled. First, to reinforce the aims promulgated by the Civil Rights Act of 1866: Anyone born in the country was a citizen, and as such was entitled to the full protection of the laws which no state shall abridge, deprive, or deny. A second purpose of the amendment was that its acceptance became part of the legislative process put in place, by which the states within the former Confederacy were allowed to reenter the Union. Its ac-

3-7: President Grant signs the Ku-Klux Force Bill, 1871. The goal, as its name implied, was to reduce Klan violence.

ceptance, along with that of the Thirteenth Amendment, would hopefully help create a more equal society.

Nonetheless, to further make this point of equal rights, especially in the area of voting rights, Congress proposed and the states ratified the Fifteenth Amendment in 1870. This amendment specifically addresses the ability of the former slaves to vote and thus achieve real political power in the postwar South. It is a succinct, yet powerful amendment.

Section 1. The right of citizens of the United States to vote shall not be denied or abridged by the United States or by any State on account of race, color, or previous condition of servitude.

Section 2. The Congress shall have the power to enforce this article by appropriate legislation.

Unfortunately, despite the Civil Rights Act of 1866 and the Thirteenth, Fourteenth, and Fifteenth amendments, which seemingly guaranteed basic legal rights to all former slaves, groups and individuals arose to challenge this basic social premise. In the year after the war, bloody race riots in Memphis and New Orleans presaged future violence. The attitude of most southern whites was to accept the former slaves as just that, and nothing more. Formed in Pulaski, Tennessee, by former Confederate general Nathan Bedford Forrest, the Ku Klux Klan became the embodiment of the South's resistance to the notion of equality for the former slaves and the goals of Reconstruction. By 1868, wearing robes and hoods, members of the Klan became a highly organized organization, whose goals were the humiliation, subjugation, and intimidation of the black and sympathetic white communities. Newly formed black schools went up in flames throughout the South. The aim of this violence was spelled out in an Alabama newspaper in 1869 reporting on the burning of a black school, "It should be a warning for them to stick hereafter to 'de shovel and de hoe' and let their dirty-backed primers go."[20] The violence seemed to escalate annually. Between 1868 and 1871, political violence reached astounding levels. Arkansas experienced nearly 300 political killings, both of blacks and whites, in the three months before the fall elections of 1868. Louisiana, in a period of a few months in the spring and summer of 1868, was the locale for over a thousand such murders.[21]

The reach of the Klan was pervasive. It intervened in almost every arena of a person's personal and professional life, with the sole purpose of maintaining the subjugation of the black community. The scope of the Klan on a communal level was significant as well. Its influence cut across all strata of Southern society: "Although most Klansmen were poor farmers and tradesman, middle class whites—planters, merchants, bankers, lawyers, doctors, even ministers—also joined the group and participated in its brutalities."[22]

Congress did not take the growth of the Klan as an accomplished fact. Their response was to pass three enforcement laws that they hoped would blunt and counter the potency of the Klan's actions. In fact, the first of these laws was known as the Ku Klux Klan Act. The language of the act and the significant fines prescribed in it are indications of how serious the Klan's attacks were viewed by Congress.

If two or more persons conspire to injure, oppress, threaten, or intimidate any citizen in the free exercise or enjoyment of any right or privilege secured to him by the Constitution or laws of the United states, or because of his having so exercised the same; or

> *If two or more persons go in disguise on the highway, or on the premises of another, with intent to prevent or hinder his free exercise or enjoyment of any right or privilege so secured—They shall be fined not more than $10,000 or imprisoned not more than ten years, or both; and if death results, they shall be subject to imprisonment for any term of years or for life.*[23]

The second of these enforcement laws provided that federal elections be monitored by federal election supervisors and marshals. The third law imposed criminal penalties upon anyone who interfered with any citizen's right to vote. It might seem that with the passing of these laws that not only the Klan, but the rest of those opposed to an integrated society, would acquiesce and accept equal rights for all, especially the former slaves. This would not be the case for a number of reasons.

At this juncture, it is important to paint a broad picture of events. In brief, there was an immensely significant struggle occurring for the direction of the rebuilt South. There were those in the Congress who felt that by passing new laws and amendments that the South would feel compelled to obey these laws, thus creating a more socially balanced society. On the other hand, as noted by the detailed research of Robert J. Kaczorowski, the practical, on-the-ground enforcement of these laws and amendments was an especially difficult challenge. One of his major points—often misunderstood by many—is that laws are only as good as their enforcement. There were a number of political, logistical, and legal issues making the enforcement of these laws difficult, if not impossible. (Refer to Figure 3-8.)

---

20   Roark, Johnson, et al., *The American Promise*, p. 558.
21   Ibid., p. 559.
22   Tindall and Shi, *The Essential America*, vol. II, p. 301.
23   Barrett and Cohen, *Constitutional Law*, p. 1049.

The ineffectiveness of the Freedmen's Bureau and the military in protecting civil rights was not the result of inadequate civil legal authority to enforce civil rights. Rather, it was the result of a number of factors including: the confusion over military authority and policy caused by conflicting orders issued by the President and the Commissioner of the Freedmen's Bureau; political pressures to restore local authority as soon as possible; the insufficient numbers of federal legal officers, troops and courts; the immense distances that had to be covered; the enormous number of crimes that had to be prosecuted; the inefficiency of the case method of dispensing justice; the personal opposition of many of the Bureau agents to protecting civil rights; the ubiquitous resistance of Southern whites to federal law; and, the deeply felt Southern defiance of, and hatred for, federal authority.[24]

3-8: This picture symbolizes the attitudes of many in the Reconstruction South. The headline from this 1875 Birmingham, Alabama, newspaper partially reads, "We intend to beat the Negro in the battle of life and defeat means one thing—extermination."

Based on all of the above, it might be fair to suggest that winning a battle in the war was easier than prosecuting a major violation of a civil rights case. Imagine a small town in the South, where a form of violence of any sort has been perpetrated on a person or persons who had been slaves. Perhaps a small group of former slaves had approached an elections building with the idea of enjoying their newly won freedom of voting. Prior to reaching the polling place, they are accosted by a group of armed whites, who inform them that they shouldn't be thinking about voting. When the black citizens persist in their walk toward the polling place, they are brutally attacked. This attack prevents them from voting and is also a stark warning to the rest of the black community of what might happen to them if they attempt a similar act. Now the question posed is, how do these folks, clearly deprived of their Fifteenth Amendment rights and more, get justice? Who will hold these thugs responsible? Will the local sheriff prosecute and arrest them? Hardly. If arrested, will a judge bind them over for trial? Hardly. If bound over for trial, will a jury of their peers find them guilty of a crime? Hardly. Would federal troops, fully occupied with more heinous crimes throughout the South, give this case a high priority? Hardly. If there are troops and federal lawyers sent to this town, will they stay over the many months needed to persuade town members that they should testify in federal court against their neighbors? Once again, hardly. (See Figure 3-9.)

In this contest of wills between those who wanted to change and reconstruct the South to a society more integrated, as opposed to those who didn't want to see blacks as their equals,

---

24   Kaczorowski, *Politics of Judicial Interpretation*, p. 43.

3-9: This artwork vividly and eeriely captures the reality of the
Blyew case with masked men invading the sanctity of
the Foster homestead.

those opposed to equality persisted longer. Historians have long noted that the interest from the North in affairs of the South rapidly waned as time moved forward. Westward expansion, Indian wars, economic development, a business panic in 1873, all reflected a weariness and diminished interest in the outrages of the South.[25] This lack of will and interest can be documented by the number of federal prosecutions over the years of the Reconstruction period. "In the peak year of 1873 there were 1271 prosecutions under their criminal provisions in Southern federal courts. Even before the decisions in the Civil Rights Cases, the end of Reconstruction and the withdrawal of federal troops marked a dramatic change in enforcement. In 1878 there were 25 criminal cases."[26]

In the midst of the maelstrom of causes, changing political currents, and the myriad of new laws, stood the United States Supreme Court. As the sole and ultimate arbiter of legality in our country, the Court's decisions in many of these cases had enormously significant implications for decades to come. It is my contention that the Court was racially motivated and oriented in their thinking. Despite the apparent change in the country as a result of the Civil War as manifested in the Thirteenth, Fourteenth, and Fifteenth amendments, as well as the various civil rights acts, the Court's attitude for decades continued to follow the tradition of earlier courts, which had espoused the notion of inequality between black and white Americans. I do not take this position lightly; other scholars such as Michael J. Klarman are much more delicate and deliberate in their assessment of the justices voting. He argues "that judicial decision making involves a combination of legal and political factors. A legal axis, which consists of sources such as text, original understanding, and precedent, exists along a continuum that ranges from determinacy to indeterminacy … A political axis … exists along a continuum that ranges from very strong preferences to relatively weak ones."[27] In my view, however, there is less wiggle room. Once the Court gave their interpretations in favor of limiting efforts to eradicate discrimination and impede true equal rights, those who followed this approach were emboldened in their cause. I will attempt to prove that the large majority of the Court's findings had the practical effect of delaying the full implementation of civil rights in our country for decades—even generations.

One particularly brutal case which reflected the Court's reluctance to fully support the rights of the newly freed slaves or the various laws written for their defense is found in the little- known case of *Blyew et al v. United States*, decided in December 1871. The thrust of the case was the efficacy of the Civil Rights Act of 1866 mentioned above, which "gave jurisdiction to the Circuit Court of all causes, civil and criminal, affecting persons who are denied or cannot

25   Tindall and Shi, *The Essential America*, p. 302.
26   Barrett and Cohen, *Constitutional Law*, p. 1050.
27   Klarman, *From Jim Crow to Civil Rights*, p. 5.

enforce in the courts of the State or locality where they may be, any of the rights given by the act among which is the right to give evidence, and to have full and equal benefit of all laws and proceedings for the security of person and property as is enjoyed by white citizens."[28]

This case, as described in the Court's summary, is especially heinous.

3-10: *This drawing accurately illustrates the general knowledge of the on-the-ground circumstances of Southern life for the newly freed slaves.*

> *A number of witnesses testified that on a summer evening of 1868 (August 29th), towards eleven o'clock, at the cabin of a colored man named Jack Foster, there were found the dead bodies of the said Jack, of Sallie Foster, his wife, and of Lucy Armstrong, for the murder of whom Blyew and Kennard stood convicted; this person, a blind woman, over ninety years old, and the mother of Mrs. Foster; all persons of color; their bodies yet warm. Lucy Armstrong was wounded in the head; her head cut open as with a broad-axe. Jack Foster and Sallie, his wife, were cut in several places, almost to pieces. Richard Foster, a son of Jack, who was in his seventeenth year, was found about two hundred yards from the house of his father, at the house of a Mr. Nichols, whither he had crawled from the house of his father, mortally wounded by an instrument corresponding to one used in the killing of Lucy Armstrong, Jack and Sallie Foster. He died two days afterwards from the effects of his wounds aforesaid, having made a dying declaration tending to fix the crime on Blyew and Kennard. Two young children, girls, one aged ten years and the other thirteen (this last, the Laura Foster above mentioned), asleep in a trundle-bed, escaped, and the latter was a witness on the trial.*
>
> *Evidence was produced on the part of the United States, that a short time previous to the murder, Kennard was heard to declare, in presence of Blyew, "that he (Kennard) thought there would soon be another war about the niggers; that when it did come he intended to go to killing niggers, and he was not sure that he would not begin his work of killing them before the war should actually commence.[29] (Refer to Figure 3-10.)*

The witnesses and the victims in this case were all black citizens of the state of Kentucky. As such, and the reason that the case was tried in the federal circuit court rather than the state court was the following Kentucky statute of 1860, "That a slave, negro, or Indian, shall be a competent witness in the case of the common wealth for or against a slave, negro, or Indian, or in a civil case to which negroes or Indians are parties, but in no other case."[30]

On October 7, 1868, both men were indicted by the Circuit Court for the District of Kentucky on three counts of murder. The indictments contained the statements that the surviving witnesses were unable to testify against Blyew and Kennard due to their race and color. The men initially claimed that the state should have been the authority to rule on their guilt or innocence. The circuit court took on the case and ultimately found them guilty under the provisions of the statute known as the Civil Rights Act of April 9, 1866. Once the case was removed

---

28   *Bylew v. United States*, p. 581.
29   Ibid., pp. 584–585.
30   Ibid., p. 581.

from the state level and moved to the federal level and the men found guilty, the General Assembly of Kentucky directed the governor to ensure that the state would be represented, as the case was taken to the U.S. Supreme Court for review. The legal view espoused by Kentucky was that the circuit court did not have jurisdiction in such cases. In this regard, lawyers for the state appeared before the Supreme Court and argued,

> *That it was an insult to her dignity and an outrage on the peace of a community which, by the organic law of the land, was placed under her protection; that her law was offended by it, and that none but she had a right to enter into judgment with the perpetrators of it … that the United States had never pretended that a murder within the limits of a State was an offense against them, and that it was no more an offense against the United States than it was against the republic of France or the empire of Germany.*[31]

The Kentucky lawyers contended that the Constitution, in the second section of Article Three, limited the judicial power of the federal government. That section says that the judicial power shall extend to cases affecting ambassadors, controversies between two or more states, between citizens of different states, and between a state, or the citizens thereof, and foreign states, citizens, or subjects. The lawyers strongly argued,

> *Yet this act (the 1866 Civil Rights Act) gave exclusive jurisdiction to the Federal courts and a total denial of all rights on the part of the State to interfere in any case that affects a Negro; which a case no doubt does where a Negro is a party. Such a condition of things could not be tolerated by any State, even if it extended to great cases. But the act extended the jurisdiction of the Federal courts exclusively of that of the State to all cases affecting Negroes; i.e., to all cases where Negroes are parties.*[32]

The attorneys continue this line of reasoning by suggesting that the consequences of this act eliminated the state from its proper legal responsibilities: "If a negro robbed a hen-roost, the suffering party was now obliged to let him go unpunished or to take him for justice to wherever the Federal court sat, often hundreds of miles off … The Act of Congress had, in cases where it did apply, dislocated all of the machinery of the State courts and rendered them powerless to perform their duty."[33]

Another line of reasoning advanced by the state lawyers is based on an earlier Supreme Court ruling, which concluded that a criminal case affects nobody but the party accused and the public. In this case, they argue that the blacks in the case were not "affected" by the events which occurred, and would only be so if they had witnessed a crime themselves.

Solicitor General of the United States B. H. Bristow answers these arguments with statements of his own. He first spoke about the Thirteenth Amendment passed in 1865. "The Thirteenth Amendment to the Constitution worked a radical change to the existence of the United States. But it did not execute and was not meant to execute itself. Appropriate Congressional legislation was provided for. The amendment as a remedial one must be construed. The obvious intention

---

31 Ibid., p. 586.
32 Ibid., pp. 586–587.
33 Ibid., p. 587.

was to remove an existing evil, which was recognized as the cause of the civil strife in which the country was engaged, and to confer freedom upon the slave as a reward for his military service in the preservation of the government."[34]

The next argument Bristow makes is that the newly freed slaves and other members of the black community needed protection from abuses before they truly achieved their freedom. "So long as he is denied the right to testify against those who violate his person or property he has no protection, and is denied the power to defend his own freedom."[35] As previously mentioned, this point was an extremely crucial one throughout the history of Reconstruction. While there were laws on the books concerning equal rights, the difficulty in enforcing these laws and amendments often made a mockery of them, and at the very least, impotent.

The solicitor expresses the consequences of the State law, "The condition of things in Kentucky under its law excluding the evidence of blacks where white persons have committed crime is disgraceful to a Christian community. A band of whites shall set upon and murder half a congregation of blacks, their minister included, and though a hundred blacks who saw the massacre survive, and can identify their murderers, conviction is impossible."[36]

The next argument once again concerns the language of the act and also responds to the previous position that the former slaves were not "affected" in this case. "The murder did affect persons who were denied in the State courts rights which the act of Congress secured. It affected the murdered Negro, the Negro witnesses in the case, and the whole Negro population of Kentucky."[37]

Justice William Strong delivers the opinion of the Court. He focuses on the issue of whether the Circuit Court had the legal authority to pursue this case based on the third section of the Civil Rights Act of 1866 mentioned above. He poses the question in this manner, "Was, then, the prosecution, or indictment, against these defendants a cause affecting such persons or persons? If it was, then by the provisions of the act it was within the jurisdiction of the court, and if it was not, that court had no jurisdiction."[38]

After some brief propositions regarding the 1866 act and its scope, the Court seems about to reach a logical conclusion.

> *On the contrary, it concedes to it a far-reaching purpose. That purpose was to guard all the declared rights of colored persons, in all civil actions to which they may be parties in interest, by giving to the District and Circuit Courts of the United States jurisdiction of such actions whenever in the state courts any right enjoyed by white citizens is denied them. And in criminal prosecutions against them, it extends a like protection. We cannot be expected to be ignorant of the condition of things which existed when the statute was enacted, or of the evils which it was intended to remedy. It is well known in many of the States, laws existed which subjected colored men convicted of criminal offences to punishments different from and often severer than those which were inflicted upon white persons convicted of similar offences ... It is well known that in many quarters prejudices existed against the colored race, which naturally affected the administration of justice in the state courts, and operated harshly when one of that race was a party accused. These were evils doubtless which the act of Congress had in view, and which it intended to*

---

34 Ibid., p. 588.
35 Ibid., p. 589.
36 Ibid.
37 Ibid.
38 Ibid., p. 591.

remove. And so far as it reaches, it extends to both races the same rights, and the same means of vindicating them.[39]

They then reach their conclusion, which seemingly contradicts the points just made.

In view of these considerations we are of the opinion that the case before us is not within the provisions of the act of April 9th, 1866 and that the Circuit Court had not jurisdiction of the crime of murder committed in the district of Kentucky, merely because two persons who witnessed the murder were citizens of the African race, and for that reason incompetent by the law of Kentucky to testify in the courts of that State. They are not persons affected by the cause.[40]

The Court continues with the following surreal assertion,

We need hardly add that the jurisdiction of the Circuit Court is not sustained by the fact averred in the indictment that Lucy Armstrong, the person murdered, was a citizen of the African race, and for that reason denied the right to testify in the Kentucky courts. In no sense can she be said to be affected by the cause. Manifestly the act refers to persons in existence. She was the victim of the frightful outrage which gave rise to the cause, but she is beyond being affected by the cause itself.[41]

It is worthwhile to reread the last quote. The murdered victims of this atrocity were not "affected" by it, because they had been killed!

The Court goes on to justify its interpretation based on an understanding of the word "affecting" from an earlier case, *The United States v. Ortega*. It is important to briefly explore that case and determine its applicability to the Blyew one. In the mid-1820s, Juan Ortega was indicted in the United States Circuit Court for an assault on Rivas y Salmon, the Spanish chargé d'affaires. The jury found Ortega guilty. He contested the findings by alleging that the circuit court did not have jurisdiction over the case, as it was a diplomatic one that should have been adjudged, according to the Constitution, by the U.S. Supreme Court. In 1826, the Court found that this was not a case "affecting a public minister" within the plain meaning of the Constitution. It was a public prosecution brought about by a private citizen. The minister was not affected as a diplomat, but as an individual. The judgment was that the punishment set by the circuit court was valid and binding.[42]

What the reader can focus on is the question of how similar these cases are, and does the Ortega decision fit here? In the Ortega case, justice was achieved, in that Ortega was punished for his assault on the ambassador, and the question revolved around jurisdiction, with the Court deciding that the circuit court was the proper legal venue for this episode. Ironically, in this case—which had proceeded far beyond a simple assault—the justices concluded that there will not be an acceptable venue for justice. If the state courts will not allow the testimony of those

---

39 Ibid., p. 593.
40 Ibid.
41 Ibid., pp. 593–594.
42 http://press-pups/uchicago/edu/founders/documents

terrorized and the federal courts have no standing as the judgment suggests, then where indeed were the victims supposed to receive any modicum of justice? In my view, the *Blyew* case is very dissimilar to the *Ortega* one.

Ultimately, despite the fact that there was overwhelming physical evidence in this case, including death-bed declarations and eye-witness accounts, the perpetrators of this brutal attack by ax-wielding assassins, who had been found guilty, had their sentences reversed.

There were two strong dissents to this decision, written by Justice Joseph P. Bradley with the concurrence of Justice Noah H. Swayne. The first point made by Justice Bradley was to review the history and reason behind the 1866 Civil Rights Act. He reiterates the point that the goal of the act was "to place persons of African descent on an equality of rights and privileges with other citizens of the United States. To do this effectually ... to counteract those unjust and discriminating laws of some of the States by which persons of African descent were subjected to punishments of peculiar harshness and ignominy, and deprived of rights and privileges enjoyed by white citizens."[43] After reviewing the first section of the act mentioned above, Justice Bradley offers an assessment of contemporary practices which infringe on the rights of former slaves, as well as free blacks. This section is a treasure trove of historical data that can help contemporary readers appreciate the reality of life for people of color in the immediate years after the Civil War. These state laws reflect the actuality of the "Black Codes" and other mores and social patterns that developed in the South, helping to preserve the inequality in society between whites and blacks.

> *This section (of the Civil Rights Act) is in direct conflict with those State laws which forbade a free colored person to remove or pass through the State, from having firearms, from exercising the functions of a minister of the gospel, and from keeping a house of entertainment; laws which prohibited all colored persons from being taught to read and write, from holding or conveying property, and from being witnesses in any case where a white person was concerned; and laws which subjected them to cruel and ignominious punishments not imposed upon white persons, such as to be sold as vagrants, to be tied to the whipping post, &c., &c. All these, and all other discriminations, were intended to be abolished and done away with.*[44]

The certainty of the two justices' beliefs about the need for the Civil Rights Act is explained in the following paragraph.

> *To deprive a whole class of the community of this right, to refuse their evidence and their sworn complaints, is to brand them with a badge of slavery; is to expose them to wanton insults and fiendish assaults; is to leave their lives, their families, and their property unprotected by law. It gives unrestricted license and impunity to vindictive outlaws and felons to rush upon these helpless people and kill and slay them at will, as was done in this case. To say that actions or prosecutions intended for the redress of such outrages are not "causes affecting the persons who are the victims of them, is to take, it seems to me, a view of the law too narrow, too technical, and too forgetful of the liberal objects it had in view. If, in such a raid as I have supposed, a colored person is merely wounded or maimed, but is*

---

43   Ibid., pp. 596–597.
44   Ibid.

still capable of making complaint, and on appearing to do so, has the doors of justice shut in his face, on the ground that he is a colored person, and cannot testify against a white citizen, it seems to me almost a stultification of the law to say that the case is not within its scope ... If the case above supposed is within the act (as it assuredly must be), does it cease to be so when the violence offered is so great as to deprive the victim of life? Such a construction would be a premium on murder.[45]

Justice Bradley continues his impassioned dissent. The words and tenor of the emotions expressed speak volumes.

The object of prosecution and punishment is to prevent crime, as well as to vindicate public justice. The fear of it, the anticipation of it, stands between the assassin and his victim like a vindictive shade. It arrests his arm, and loosens the dagger from his grasp. Should not the colored man have the aegis of this protection to guard his life, as well as to guard his limbs, or his property? Should he not enjoy it in equal degree with the white citizen? In a large and just sense, can a prosecution for his murder affect him any less than a prosecution for an assault upon him? He is interested in both alike. They are his protection against violence and wrong.[46]

In a final, almost prophetic comment, the justice writes, "Merely striking off the fetters of the slave, without removing the incidents and consequences of slavery, would hardly have been a boon to the colored race."[47] This single insight succinctly and clearly reflects the grim reality of the former slaves and free blacks. Without full legal acceptance, as well as full social acceptance, people of color would never be afforded the opportunity to transition into full and participatory members of American society. (Refer to Figure 3-11.)

It crucially important to note the 1868 date of this case. The daily violence against the former slaves was quite real, brutal, and in many cases such as this, quite gruesome. Those who committed crimes were not brought to justice. As mentioned above, these were the years that the Klan was beginning its activities in the South. In many cases, the absence of law enforcement and punishment for those initiating acts of brutality created an atmosphere of "open season of violence" on former slaves. This brief—and largely unknown—Supreme Court case was part of a movement that ultimately negated much of the moral force and legal potency of the Civil Rights Act of 1866, as well as the Fourteenth and Fifteenth amendments to the Constitution.

Impossible to gauge, but nevertheless significant to contemplate, is what the perception was of the people at the time who were prone to violence. It is reasonable to surmise that the news of the Supreme Court reaching this decision in this and other cases caused people to conclude—quite correctly—that violence against black citizens was acceptable, or at the very least, something the highest court of the land would not hold them responsible for.

Even in other cases decided that initially did not focus on racism or prejudice, the topic was not far from the surface. In the 1872 case known as the *Slaughterhouse Cases*, the meaning of the three post–Civil War amendments—the Thirteenth, Fourteenth, and Fifteenth—is addressed. In March of 1869, the Louisiana legislature created a corporation which received exclusive

---

45   Ibid., p. 599.
46   Ibid., p. 600.
47   Ibid., p. 601

rights for the whole process of slaughtering animals in the parishes of Orleans, Jefferson, and St. Bernard. All other people were forbidden to build or maintain any slaughterhouses in those parishes. If others chose to slaughter their animals in this area, they had to use the facilities of the corporation and pay a set fee for that service. This privilege was given for a 25-year period. The butchers, most of whom were white, and others opposed to this corporation and its apparent monopoly sued in state court. The Supreme Court of Louisiana decided in favor of the corporation, and the cases made their way up to the United States Supreme Court in December of 1870. The judgment was given in December 1872.

THE 'RAIL SPLITTER' AT WORK REPAIRING THE UNION.

3-11: Despite the leadership of Presidents Lincoln and Johnson to "sew" together the North and South, the task was almost impossible given the reality of Southern resistance to ideas of social integration and full equality for the former slaves.

Those arguing against the corporation went back into medieval European law sources about monopolies. They next argue that this process violated the Thirteenth Amendment, which prohibits slavery and involuntary servitude. The point is that the formation of this type of exclusive entity forced the other butchers into a kind of involuntary servitude outlawed by the amendment. Also, the lawyers arguing for those opposed to the corporation suggest that the Fourteenth Amendment had also been breached. Their very passionate argument was that the amendment, which reads, "No state shall make or enforce any law which shall abridge the privileges or immunities of citizens of the United States, nor shall any state deprive any person of life, liberty, or property, without due process of law, nor deny to any person within its jurisdiction the equal protection of the laws," was violated. The lawyers further argue the plaintiffs did not have the equal protection of the laws, as called for in the amendment: "It is equally in violation of it, since it deprives them of their property without due process of law."[48]

Justice Samuel Miller delivers the Court's findings to these arguments. First, the Court found that the creation of the corporation by the legislature was done for the good of the city. They then go on to verify the authority of the state,

> *It may, therefore, be considered as established, that the authority of the legislature to pass the present statute is ample, unless some restraint in the exercise of that power be found in the constitution of that State or in the amendments to the Constitution of the United States, adopted since the date of the decisions already cited.*[49]

In this instance, the notion of the "police power" of the local municipality to make such public health decisions was part of the justices' considerations. The Court then addresses the arguments raised against the corporation based on the Thirteenth and Fourteenth amendments. It acknowledges that this is the first time that the justices had an opportunity to explain their views of these amendments.

---

48 *Slaughterhouse Cases*, p. 56.
49 Ibid., p. 66.

> *We do not conceal from ourselves the great responsibility which this duty devolves upon us. No questions so far-reaching and pervading in their consequences, so profoundly interesting to the people of this country, and so important in their bearing upon the relations of the United States, and of several States to each other and to the citizens of the States and the United States, have been before this court during the official life time of any of its present members.*[50]

They continue this finding, which they themselves have labeled as historic, with an overview of the then recent Civil War and its causes.

> *The institution of African slavery, as it existed in about half the States of the Union, and the contests pervading the public mind for many years, between those who desired its curtailment and ultimate extinction and those who desired additional safeguards for its security and perpetuation, culminated in the effort, on the part of most of the States in which slavery existed, to separate from the Federal government, and to resist its authority. This constituted the war of the rebellion, and whatever auxiliary causes may have contributed to bring about the war, undoubtedly the over shadowing and efficient cause was African slavery.*[51]

This review is followed by a synopsis of the amendments' purposes.

> *But the war being over, those who had succeeded in re-establishing the authority of the Federal government were not content to permit this great act of emancipation to rest on the actual results of the contest or the proclamation of the Executive, both of which might have been questioned in after times, and they determined to place this main and most valuable result in the Constitution of the restored Union as one of its fundamental articles. Hence the thirteenth article of amendment of that instrument. [They then quote from the amendment.] To withdraw the mind from the contemplation of this grand yet simple declaration of the personal freedom of all the human race within the jurisdiction of this government—a declaration designed to establish the freedom of four millions of slaves ... The word servitude is of larger meaning than slavery, as the latter is popularly understood in this country, and the obvious purpose was to forbid all shades and conditions of African slavery.*[52]

The Court, as it did for previous cases, goes on to detail the reality of the Black Codes, which were prevalent in the postwar South,

> *Among the first acts of legislation adopted by several of the States in the legislative bodies which claimed to be in their normal relations with the Federal government, were laws which imposed upon the colored race onerous disabilities and burdens, and curtailed their rights in the pursuit of life, liberty, and property to such an extent that their freedom was*

---

50 Ibid., p. 67.
51 Ibid., p. 68.
52 Ibid.

of little value, while they had lost the protection which they had received from their former owners from motives both of interest and humanity.

They were in some States forbidden to appear in the towns in any other character than menial servants. They were required to reside on and cultivate the soil without the right to purchase or own it. They were excluded from many occupations of gain, and were not permitted to give testimony in the courts in any case where a white man was a party. It was said that their lives were at the mercy of bad men, either because the laws for their protection were insufficient or were not enforced.[53]

As the justices' historical review continues, they discuss the need for the Fourteenth and Fifteenth amendments.

And on the most casual examination of the language of these amendments, no one can fail to be impressed with the one pervading purpose found in them all, lying at the foundation of each, and without which none of them would have been suggested; we mean the freedom of the slave race, the security and firm establishment of that freedom, and the protection of the newly-made freeman and citizen from the oppressions of those who had formerly exercised unlimited dominion over them.[54]

The Court then reviews the *Dred Scott* case in light of these amendments. When referring to the first section of the Fourteenth Amendment, the justices correctly observe, "That its main purpose was to establish the citizenship of the Negro can admit of no doubt."[55] The Court then makes a distinction that had enormous significance for their understanding of the Fourteenth Amendment. The justices maintain there existed two types of citizenship, one for the United States and the other for the States. This distinction of dual sovereignties was one made in the framing of the Constitution. The two are different, and not one and the same. "It is quite clear, then, that there is a citizenship of the United States, and a citizenship of a State, which are distinct from each other, and which depend upon different characteristics or circumstances in the individual."[56] This type of dual citizenship is a significant element in the *Dred Scott* case decided in 1857.

The Court continues to incorporate additional details to their historical interpretation, which had dramatic consequences.

The language is, "No State shall make or enforce any law which shall abridge the privileges or immunities of citizens of the United States. It is a little remarkable, if this clause was intended as a protection to the citizen of a State against the legislative power of his own State, that the word citizen of the State should be left out when it is so carefully used and used in contradistinction to citizens of the United States, in the very sentence which precedes it ... It is too clear for argument that the change in phraseology was adopted understandingly and with a purpose.[57]

53 Ibid., p. 70.
54 Ibid., p. 71.
55 Ibid., p. 73.
56 Ibid., p. 74.
57 Ibid.

This distinction between the rights of citizens of the United States, as opposed to the rights that people have as citizens of the various states, has enormous ramifications. "But we wish to state here that it is only the former which are placed by this clause under the protection of the Federal Constitution, and that the latter, whatever they may be, are not intended to have any additional protection by this paragraph of the amendment.[58]

This conclusion, that there are substantial legal differences between the rights of the citizens of the United States compared to the rights of citizens of states, was developed further by the justices. They surmise that the real power regarding rights is a function of the individual states, as opposed to the federal government: "The entire domain of the privileges and immunities of citizens of the States, as above defined, lay within the constitutional and legislative power of the states, and without that of the Federal government."[59] They ask and answer the following question,

> Was it the purpose of the fourteenth amendment, by the simple declaration that no State should make or enforce any law which shall abridge the privileges and immunities of citizens of the United States, to transfer the security and protection of all the civil rights which we have mentioned, from the States to the Federal government? And where it is declared that Congress shall have the power to enforce that article, was it intended to bring within the power of Congress the entire domain of civil rights heretofore belonging exclusively to the States?[60]

The justices go on with this line of reasoning as they speak about the amendments and their effect on the relations between the state and federal governments: "When in fact it radically changes the whole theory of the relations of the State and Federal governments to each other and of both these governments to the people; the argument has a force that is irresistible, in the absence of language which expresses such a purpose too clearly to admit of doubt ... We are convinced that no such results were intended by the Congress which proposed these amendments, nor by the legislatures of the States which ratified them."[61]

The Court then continues to more fully express its views on the privileges and immunities guaranteed to all United States citizens. "He has the right of free access to its seaports. ...

Another privilege of a citizen of the United States is to demand the care and protection of the Federal government over his life, liberty, and property when on the high seas or within the jurisdiction of a foreign government ... The right to peaceably assemble and petition for redress of grievances, the privilege of the writ of habeas corpus, are the rights of the citizen guaranteed by the Federal Constitution."[62] But after listing some rights enjoyed by all citizens, the court reiterates its main interpretation: "But it is useless to pursue this branch of inquiry, since we are of opinion that the rights claimed by these plaintiffs in error, if they have any existence, are not privileges and immunities of citizens of the United States within the meaning of the clause of the Fourteenth Amendment under consideration."[63]

---

58 Ibid.
59 Ibid., p. 77.
60 Ibid.
61 Ibid., p. 78.
62 Ibid., p. 79.
63 Ibid., p. 80.

Next, and most significantly for our topic, the justices directly address the amendment and its potency in the area of civil rights.

> *The existence of laws in the States where the newly emancipated Negroes resided, which discriminated with gross injustice and hardship against them as a class, was the evil to be remedied by this clause, and by it such laws are forbidden.*
>
> *If, however, the States did not conform their laws to its requirements, then by the fifth section of the article of amendment Congress was authorized to enforce it by suitable legislation. We doubt very much whether any action of a State not directed by way of discrimination against the Negroes as a class, or on account of their race, will ever be held to come within the purview of this provision. It is so clearly a provision for that race and that emergency, that a strong case would be necessary for its application to any other. But as it is a State that is to be dealt with, and not alone the validity of its laws, we may safely leave that matter until Congress shall have exercised its power, or some case of State oppression, by denial of equal justice in its courts, shall have claimed a decision at our hands.*[64] *(Refer to Figure 3-12.)*

In a final analysis, the justices touch on recent history, "Under the pressure of all the excited feeling growing out of the war, our statesmen have still believed that the existence of the States with powers of domestic and local government, including the regulation of civil rights—rights of person and property—was essential to the perfect working of our complex form of government, though they have thought proper to impose additional limitations on the states, and to confer additional power on that of the Nation."[65] The justices affirm the judgment of the Louisiana high court, which allowed the monopoly of the butchers in New Orleans.

Justice Stephen Field offers a lengthy dissent to the majority finding. His opinion was that the recent amendments to the Constitution did, indeed, protect citizens of the United States against the deprivation of their common rights by state legislation. His reading of the Thirteenth Amendment is an expansive one. "Still it is evident that the language of the amendment is not used in a restrictive sense. It is not confined to African slavery alone. It is general and universal in its application. Slavery of white men as well as of black men is prohibited, and not merely slavery in the strict sense of the term, but involuntary servitude in every form."[66] Regarding the Fourteenth Amendment, Justice Field's interpretation is clear: "Notwithstanding all the pomp and display of eloquence on the occasion, every citizen is a citizen of some State or Territory, and as such, under an express

3-12: The ratification of the Fifteenth Amendment was the occasion for celebration across the country.

---

64   Ibid., p. 81.
65   Ibid., p. 82.
66   Ibid., p. 90.

provision of the Constitution, is entitled to all privileges and immunities of citizens in the several States; and it is in this and no other sense that we are citizens of the United States."[67] For this justice, the rights shared by all are fundamental and broad in their application. "The privileges and immunities designated are those which of right belong to the citizens of all free governments."[68] Chief Justice Noah Swayne and Justice Joseph Bradley also concurred with this dissent.

Justice Bradley felt compelled to offer additional comments of dissent. His comments center on his interpretation of the force of the Fourteenth Amendment.

> *That question is now settled by the fourteenth amendment itself, that citizenship of the United States is the primary citizenship in this country; and that State citizenship is secondary and derivative, depending upon citizenship of the United States and the citizen's place of residence ... A citizen of the United States has a perfect constitutional right to go to and reside in any State he chooses, and to claim citizenship therein, and an equality of rights with every other citizen; and the whole power of the nation is pledged to sustain him in that right. He is not bound to cringe to any superior, or to pray for any act of grace, as a means of enjoying all the rights and privileges enjoyed by other citizens.*
>
> *And when the spirit of lawlessness, mob violence, and sectional hate can be so completely repressed as to give full practical effect to this right, we shall be a happier nation, and a more prosperous one than we are now ... If a man is denied full equality before the law, he is denied one of the essential rights of citizenship as a citizen of the United States.*[69]

In his impassioned dissent, the justice harkens back to the Magna Carta to establish the liberties that should be experienced equally by all citizens. He then quotes the well-known sentiments referred to earlier about all men enjoying certain unalienable rights. "Here again we have the great threefold division of the rights of freemen, asserted as the rights of man. Rights to life, liberty, and the pursuit of happiness ... These are the fundamental rights which can only be taken away by due process of law, and which can only be interfered with, ... by lawful regulations necessary or proper for the mutual good of all; and these rights, I contend, belong to the citizens of every free government."[70] Justice Bradley reinforces the notion that there are fundamental privileges and immunities that should be enjoyed by all citizens: "Their very citizenship conferred these privileges, if they did not possess them before. And these privileges they would enjoy whether they were citizens of any state or not."[71] The justice makes a final point about the relationship of the state and national governments. He suggests that there would not be any inconveniences to the states if federal courts became involved in ensuring that the principles of the amendment were legally met. "But even if the business of the national courts should be increased, Congress could easily supply the remedy by increasing their number and efficiency."[72]

---

67 Ibid., p. 94.
68 Ibid., p. 97
69 Ibid., pp. 112–113.
70 Ibid., p. 116.
71 Ibid., p. 119.
72 Ibid., p. 124.

Finally, Justice Swayne adds in his own dissent to the decision of the Court. First, he reviews the Thirteenth, Fourteenth, and Fifteenth amendments and their purposes. His explanation of the role of the federal government in the reinforcement was clear and compelling.

> *By the language "citizens of the United States" was meant all such citizens; and by "any person" was meant all persons within the jurisdiction of the State. No distinction is intimated on account of race or color. This court has no authority to interpolate a limitation that is neither expressed nor implied. Our duty is to execute the law, not to make it. The protection provided was not intended to be confined to those of any particular race or class, but to embrace equally all races, classes, and conditions of men.*[73]

Swayne concludes his remarks with words that seem eerily prophetic to those of us who are aware of what the future held for civil rights and race relations in the decades following the Civil War.

> *By the Constitution, as it stood before the war, ample protection was given against oppression by the Union, but little was given against wrong and oppression by the States. That want was intended to be supplied by this amendment. Against the former this court has been called upon more than once to interpose. Authority of the same amplitude was intended to be conferred as to the latter. But this arm of our jurisdiction is, in these cases, stricken down by the judgment just given. Nowhere, than in this court, ought the will of the nation, as thus expressed, to be more liberally construed or more cordially executed. This determination of the majority seems to me to lie far in the other direction. I earnestly hope that the consequences to follow may prove less serious and far-reaching then the minority fear they will be.*[74]

Around the same time as this case was being decided, the post–Civil War legal and social battles for equality were being fought in the South. By October of 1871, the federal government had begun prosecuting hundreds of Klansmen in North Carolina and Mississippi. President Grant sent federal troops to occupy nine South Carolina counties, rounding up thousands of Klan members.[75] Sadly, these actions on behalf of the former slaves and the many laws and constitutional amendments that had been passed were the exception rather than the rule in post–Civil War America.

In a pair of 1875 decisions, the Court offered two findings which continued the process of diluting and neutering the various post–Civil War amendments and civil rights acts. In the first of two rulings in *United States v. Reese et al.*, the Court places a significantly restrictive interpretation on the newly ratified Fifteenth Amendment. The essence of the case is succinctly summarized by Chief Justice Morrison R. Waite: "It presents an indictment containing four counts, under sects. 3 and 4 of the act of May 31, 1870 (16 Stat. 140), against two of the inspectors of a municipal election in the State of Kentucky, for refusing to receive and count at such election

---

73 Ibid., pp. 128–129.
74 Ibid., p. 129.
75 Unger, *The United States*, p. 405. In fact, violence would continue against blacks and sympathetic whites throughout the South almost continuously in some form for a century.

the vote of William Garner, a citizen of the United States of African descent."[76] The act of May 1870 was written with the purpose of enforcing the Fifteenth Amendment that had been ratified in February of that same year.

This act had four sections, all concerned with ensuring that the notion of providing the vote guaranteed in the Fifteenth Amendment would be a reality. All the sections are explicit in their intent. It is worthwhile to list the sections.

> *Its first section provides that all citizens of the United States, who are or shall be otherwise qualified by law to vote at any election, &c., shall be entitled and allowed to vote thereat, without distinction of race, color, or previous condition of servitude, any constitution, &c., of the State to the contrary notwithstanding.*

> *The Second section provides for the punishment of any officer charged with the duty of furnishing to citizens an opportunity to perform any act, which by the constitution or laws of any State, is made a prerequisite or qualification of voting, who shall omit to give all citizens of the United States the same and equal opportunity to perform such prerequisite, and become qualified on account of race, color, or previous condition of servitude of the applicant.*

> *The third section is to the effect, that, whenever by or under the constitution or laws of any State, &c., any act is or shall be required to be done by any citizen as a prerequisite to qualify or entitle him to vote, the offer of such citizen to perform the act required to be done "as aforesaid" shall, if it fail to be carried into execution by reason of the wrongful act or omission "aforesaid" of the person or officer charged with the duty of receiving or permitting such performance, or offer to perform, or acting thereon, be deemed as held as a performance in law of such act; and the person so offering and failing as aforesaid, and being otherwise qualified, shall be entitled to vote in the same manner, and to the same extent, as if he had, in fact, performed such act; and any judge, inspector, or other officer of election, whose duty it is to receive, count, &c., or give effect to, the vote of any such citizen, who shall wrongfully refuse or omit to receive, count, &c., the vote of such citizen, upon the presentation by him of his affidavit stating such offer, and the time and place thereof, and the name of the person or officer whose duty it was to act thereof, and that he was wrongfully prevented by such person or officer from performing such act, shall, for every offence, forfeit, and pay, &c.*

> *The fourth section provides for the punishment of any person who shall, by force, bribery, threats, intimidation, or other unlawful means, hinder, delay, &c., or shall combine with others to hinder, delay, prevent, or obstruct, any citizen from doing any act required to be done to qualify him to vote, or from voting, at any election.*[77]

What is fascinating about this law is that it offers a clear and contemporary perspective of the very valid concerns that legislators had in the immediate years following the Civil War

---

76 *United States v. Reese et al.*, p. 215.

77 Ibid., pp. 216–217.

regarding the right to vote. With the ratification of the brief Fifteenth Amendment, "Section 1, The right of citizens of the United States to vote shall not be denied or abridged by the United States on account of race, color, or previous condition of servitude. Section 2, The Congress shall have power to enforce this article by appropriate legislation." The real fear was that people in the South were actively working to prohibit and prevent that vote.

Eerily, the second section of the Enforcement Act directly addresses circumstances when state election officials prevented people from voting. This is similar to what the state of Mississippi would devise in the 1890s as part of a successful movement to disenfranchise black voters. The third section, in its specificity, is anticipating the reality of election officials not taking the word of a possible voter that they had fulfilled all preelection qualifications. These laws were written with a very clear notion of stopping abuses already occurring. The fourth section provides punishment for an array of offenses, all focused on those Klan like-minded people who were indeed intimidating, hindering, delaying, and unlawfully preventing blacks from voting. Although the black community did develop and have representatives in subsequent congresses, it is valid to suggest that this right to vote was certainly not considered as an absolute right among many in the South.

Unfortunately, the Supreme Court in its findings with this case (Reese) bolstered that philosophy greatly. The chief justice effects a major definition of the Fifteenth Amendment that in many ways reduced its potency. "The Fifteenth Amendment does not confer the right of suffrage upon any one. It prevents the States, or the United States, however, from giving preference, in this particular, to one citizen of the United States over another on account of race, color, or previous condition of servitude."[78] (See Figure 3-13.)

The chief justice continues to explain this finding by suggesting that before the adoption of the amendment, states could exclude citizens from voting due to factors such as race, property, or education. After the Fifteenth Amendment, they could not do so. He also notes that Congress may enforce the amendment by "appropriate legislation."

However, he quickly offers an important qualifier to that notion as well.

> *This leads us to inquire whether the act now under consideration is "appropriate legislation" for that purpose. The power of Congress to legislate at all upon the subject of voting at State elections rests upon this amendment. The effect of art.1, sect.4, of the Constitution, in respect to elections for senators and representatives, is not now under consideration. It has not been contended, nor can it be, that the amendment confers authority to impose penalties for every wrongful refusal to receive the vote of a qualified elector at State elections. It is only when the wrongful refusal at such an election is because of race, color, or previous condition of servitude that Congress can interfere, and provide for its punishment. If, therefore, the third and fourth sections of the act are beyond that limit, they are unauthorized.*[79]

It is clear in which direction Chief Justice Waite is going. In short order, he finds various objectionable components with the Enforcement Act. "This act interferes with this practice, and prescribes rules not provided by the laws of the states."[80] Even though the language of the enforcement sections noted above seems quite explicit in its focus, the justice decides that it is not: "Penal statutes ought not to be expressed in language so uncertain. If the legislature un-

---

78   Ibid.
79   Ibid., p. 218.
80   Ibid., p. 219.

3-13; This wonder ing depicts the aftermath of the violence experienced in the Colfax, Louisiana Massacre, 1873.

dertakes to define by statute a new offence, and provide for its punishment, it should express its will in language that need not deceive the common mind. Every man should be able to know with certainty when he is committing a crime."[81] Their reaction to the act is fairly obvious. "In view of all these facts, we feel compelled to say, that, in our opinion, the language of the third and fourth sections does not confine their operation to unlawful discriminations on account of race, &c."[82]

What the decision concludes is that the language of the Enforcement Act was partially constitutional and partially not. The justices took the Congress directly to task: "Within its legitimate sphere, Congress is supreme, and beyond the control of the courts; but if it steps outside of its constitutional limitations, and attempts that which is beyond its reach, the courts are authorized to … annul its encroachments upon the reserved power of the States and the people."[83] Based on this reasoning, they reached a significant conclusion. "We must, therefore, decide that Congress has not yet provided by 'appropriate legislation' for the punishment charged in the indictment; and that the Circuit Court properly sustained the demurrers, and gave judgment for the defendants."[84]

To be clear, in this one relatively obscure and unstudied case, decided ten years after the end of the Civil War and five years after the ratification of the Fifteenth Amendment, supposedly guaranteeing the right to vote for all citizens, clarity was mudded. First, the Court doesn't guarantee the vote, but suggests that the amendment is in place to help avoid discrimination, and the elaborate legislation to enforce the amendment, quite explicit in its words, is voided by the justices. The lone dissenter in the case, Justice Ward Hunt, offers these observations.

> *That the intention of Congress on this subject is too plain to be discussed. The Fifteenth Amendment had just been adopted, the object of which was to secure to a lately enslaved population protection against violations of their right to vote on account of their color or previous condition … The second section [of the Enforcement Act] requires that equal opportunity shall be given to the races in providing every prerequisite for voting, and that any officer who violates this provision shall be subject to civil damages to the extent of $500, and to fine and imprisonment. To suppose that Congress, in making these provisions, intended to impose no duty upon, and subject to no penalty, the very officers who were to perfect the exercise of the right to vote,—to wit, the inspectors who receive or reject the votes,—would be absurd.[85]*

Hunt further continues his spirited dissent by almost mocking the Court's focus on the word "aforesaid" and the minute dissection of the various components of the indictment: "The particularity required in an indictment or in the statutory description of offences has at times been extreme, the distinctions almost ridiculous. I cannot but think that in some cases good sense is

---

81   Ibid., p. 220.
82   Ibid.
83   Ibid., p. 221.
84   Ibid., pp. 221–222.
85   Ibid., p. 241.

sacrificed to technical nicety, and a sound principle carried to an extravagant extent."[86] He goes on to note the obvious elements of the case. "The refusal to receive an affidavit as evidence that the tax had been paid by Garner, and the rejection of his vote, are the essential acts of the defendants which constitute their guilt."[87]

Justice Hunt proceeds with an excellent overview of the reasoning behind the devising of the Fifteenth Amendment. After reviewing the purpose of the Thirteenth and Fourteenth amendments, he reminds the reader that in the second section of the Fourteenth Amendment, the number of representatives in the Congress might be reduced if the former slaveholding states choose to exclude any of its black population from voting. This created an unacceptable situation.

> *The existence of a large colored population in the Southern States, lately slaves and necessarily ignorant, was a disturbing element in our affairs. It could not be overlooked. It confronted us always and everywhere. Congress determined to meet the emergency by creating a political equality, by conferring upon the freemen all the political rights possessed by the white inhabitants of the State. It was believed that the newly enfranchised people could be most effectually secured in the protection of their rights of life, liberty, and the pursuit of happiness, by giving to them that greatest of rights among freemen,—the ballot. Hence the Fifteenth Amendment was passed by Congress, and adopted by the States. The power of any State to deprive a citizen of the right to vote on account of race, color or previous condition of servitude, or to impede or to obstruct such right that account, was expressly negatived.*[88]

For this justice, it was apparent that when the election officials in the state of Kentucky did not allow the votes of a black citizen that they violated the law. "I am of the opinion, therefore, that the refusal of the defendants, inspectors of elections, to receive the vote of Garner, was a refusal by the state of Kentucky, and was a denial by that State, within the meaning of the Fifteenth Amendment, of the right to vote."[89]

At this point, Hunt's dissent might have concluded, but the justice ends with a historical overview which turned the tables completely on those who decried the role of the federal government vis à vis the rights of the states.

> *The statute-books of all countries abound with laws for the punishment of those who violate the rights of others, either as to property or person and this not so much that the trespassers may be punished as that the peaceable citizen may be protected. Punishment is the means; protection is the end. The arrest, conviction, and sentence to imprisonment, of one inspector, who refused the vote of a person of African descent on account of his race, would more effectually secure the right of the voter than would any number of civil suits in the State courts, prosecuted by timid, ignorant, and penniless parties against those possessing the wealth, the influence, the sentiment of the community. It is certain that in fact*

---

86 Ibid., p. 243.
87 Ibid.
88 Ibid., pp. 247–248.
89 Ibid., p. 252.

the legislation taken by Congress, which we are considering, was not only the appropriate, but the most effectual, means of enforcing the amendment.[90]

In a final biting comment, the justice reminds his colleagues and the country that since the inception of the Constitution, there have been laws that the Congress has enforced in favor of slaveholders. He notes that a 1793 law allowed, in line with the Constitution, fugitive slaves to be captured and returned to their "masters." Anyone who sheltered a runaway or hindered their return was also subject to a fine and imprisonment. He further established that in the cases previously mentioned above, in *Prigg v. Pennsylvania* and *Ableman v. Booth*, the Court upheld these slave fugitive laws without the federal government being inappropriately involved in the business of the state. "The clause protecting the freedmen, like that sustaining the rights of slaveholders, is found in the Federal Constitution only. Like the former, it provides the means of enforcing its authority, through fines and imprisonments, in the Federal courts; and here, as there, the national government is bound, through its own departments, to carry into effect all the rights and duties imposed upon it by the Constitution."[91]

Despite this sharp dissent, the *Reese* case greatly diluted the potency of the Fifteenth Amendment. It is important to view this case in the context of other Supreme Court decisions made at this time to accurately gauge their social effects. Thus, within a decade of the conclusion of the Civil War, slavery had ended as an American normative practice; however, former slaves were still not accepted on a social level as being coequal citizens and neighbors. It is fair to assert that this thinking—apparently enthusiastically approved by the justices of the Supreme Court—became the standard in the entire country. The next case reinforces this notion.

In the same year, 1875, the *Cruikshank* case was decided as well. This decision was also about the right to vote; however, in this matter, the intentions of those opposed to the former slaves voting employed an approach that was direct, savage, and deadly. This situation began in 1873, with a brutal confrontation in Colfax, Louisiana. An election dispute pitted white Democrats against black Republicans. In March 1873, black voters, who feared that whites planned to seize the county government, gathered at the courthouse, dug trenches, and drilled with shotguns. They had been deputized by the local sheriff to protect the county office.[92] On Easter Sunday after three weeks of sporadic gunfire, a band of whites armed with rifles and cannons blasted the courthouse, set it ablaze, and massacred the blacks who poured out, waving a white flag of surrender.[93] The estimate of the number of victims varies from 50 to over 280. Despite the brutality and gruesome details of this slaughter, local officials did not prosecute the attackers. Federal investigators identified 96 men who had violated provisions of the Enforcement Act of 1870 mentioned in the *Reese* case, also known as the Ku Klux Klan Act.

Of the 96 men accused, only nine stood trial. Of the nine, six were acquitted by jurors who heard conflicting testimony about their participation at the massacre. Three men, William Cruikshank, John Hadnot, and William Irwin, were indicted and subsequently convicted on 32 counts for conspiracy under the sixth section of the Enforcement Act by a federal circuit court jury in the District of Louisiana. The first eight counts of the 32 give an example of what these men were accused of. (Refer to Figure 3-14.)

---

90   Ibid., p. 254.
91   Ibid., p. 256.
92   Irons, *A People's History*, p. 202.
93   Ibid.

The first count was for banding together, with intent "unlawfully and feloniously to injure, oppress, threaten, and intimidate" two citizens of the United States (Levi Nelson and Alexander Tillman) "of African descent and persons of color," "with the unlawful and felonious intent thereby" them "to hinder and prevent in their respective free exercise and enjoyment of their lawful right and privilege to peaceably assemble together with each other and with other citizens of the United States for a peaceable and lawful purpose."

The second avers an intent to hinder and prevent the exercise by the same persons of the "right to keep and bear arms for a lawful purpose."

The third avers an intent to deprive the same persons "of their respective several lives and liberty of person, without due process of law."

The fourth avers an intent to deprive the same persons of the "free exercise and enjoyment of the right and privilege to the full and equal benefit of all laws and proceedings for the security of persons and property" enjoyed by white citizens.

3-14: The faded words of this 1876 picture read: Is this a republican form of government? Is this protecting life, liberty or property? Is this the equal protection of the laws? **All are very valid and relevant questions.**

The fifth avers an intent to hinder and prevent the same persons "in the exercise and enjoyment of the rights, privileges, immunities, and protection granted and secured to them respectively as citizens of the said United States, and as citizens of the said State of Louisiana, by reason of and for and on account of the race and color" of the said persons.

The sixth avers an intent to hinder and prevent the same persons in "the free exercise and enjoyment of the several and respective rights and privileges to vote at any election to be thereafter by law and held by the people in and of the said State of Louisiana."

The seventh avers an intent "to put in great fear of bodily harm, injure, and oppress" the same persons, "because and for the reason" that, having the right to vote, they had voted.

The eighth avers an intent "to prevent and hinder" the same persons "in their several and respective free exercise and enjoyment of every, each, all, and singular the several *rights and privileges granted and secured" to them "by the constitution and laws of the United States.*"[94]

The three defendants, Cruikshank, Hadnot, and Irwin, were found guilty of conspiring to prevent Levi Nelson and Alexander Tillman, two free black men, from the free exercise and enjoyment of the right to peacefully assemble and depriving them of life and liberty without due process of law. The two had been killed at the courthouse in Colfax. Federal officials chose to prosecute and convict Cruikshank and his codefendants for murder.

Their attorneys raised several objections to their conviction, including this argument: "Because the matters and things set forth and charged in the several counts, one to sixteen inclusive, do not constitute offences against the laws of the United States, and do not come within the purview, true intent, and meaning of the act of Congress approved 31st May 1870" (the Ku Klux Klan Act).[95] Other objections were that the circuit court did not have the legal power to try this case, and that the states were the responsible legal entities to meet the law's requirements. They also suggest that some of the 16 indictments were too vague and uncertain. Ultimately, they argued, "The verdict of the jury against the defendants is not warranted or supported by law."[96] In response to these objections, the judges of the circuit court were divided. On that basis, the ruling was sent up to the Supreme Court for a final decision.

Prior to studying the Court's findings, it is appropriate to read the sixth section of the Enforcement Act mentioned previously, described by some as the Ku Klux Klan Act.

> *That if two or more persons shall band or conspire together, or go in disguise upon the public highway, or upon the premises of another, with intent to violate any provisions of this act, or to injure, oppress, threaten, or intimidate any citizen with intent to prevent or hinder his free exercise and enjoyment of any right or privilege granted or secured to him by the constitution or laws of the United States, or shall be held guilty of felony, and, on conviction thereof, shall be fined or imprisoned, or both at the discretion of the court—the fine not to exceed $5,000, and the imprisonment not to exceed ten years; and shall, moreover, be thereafter ineligible to, and disabled from holding, any office or place of honor, profit, or trust created by the constitution or laws of the United States.*"[97]

Among the many interesting aspects of this law is its exactness regarding the newly formed group of the Klan and toward those who practiced violence and intimidation against the former slaves. The enormous financial and jail time under this act reflects its significance and importance. It is clearly intended to be a major warning to the recovering South, to abide by the new reality and not impede the rights of former slaves. Unfortunately, as mentioned previously, any law—no matter how tightly written—must be enforced. Without a sustained and ongoing enforcement, the potency of the law rapidly wanes to almost nothing.

Of course, the Court's interpretation in its first review of this law would send a powerful signal across America about the ultimate effectiveness of such provisions regarding rights and privileges. In fact, in the *Reese* case, the Court had already made a few decisions which weakened

---

94 *United States v. Cruikshank et al.*, p. 545.
95 Ibid., p. 546.
96 Ibid.
97 Ibid., p. 547.

the act. Would they continue this trend in this matter? The Court reached its decision, delivered by Chief Justice Waite.

Almost immediately, the chief justice questions the validity of the charges. "To bring this case under the operation of the statute, therefore, it must appear that the right, the enjoyment of which the conspirators intended to hinder or prevent, was one granted or secured by the constitution or laws of the United States. If it does not appear so, the criminal matter charged has not been made indictable by any act of Congress."[98] The justice next reintroduces a concept first highlighted in the *Dred Scott* case, revised in the *Slaughterhouse Cases*, and presumably addressed in the Fourteenth and Fifteenth amendments to the Constitution: "The same person may be at the same time a citizen of the United States and a citizen of a State, but his rights of citizenship under one of these governments will be different from those he has under the other."[99] This distinction between state and national powers and responsibilities is elaborated upon.

> *The government of the United States is one of delegated powers alone. Its authority is defined and limited by the Constitution. All powers not granted to it by that instrument are reserved to the States or the people. No rights can be acquired under the constitution or laws of the United States, except such as the government of the United States has the authority to grant or secure. All that cannot be granted or secured are left under the protection of the States.*
>
> *We now proceed to an examination of the indictment, to ascertain whether the several rights, which it is alleged the defendants intended to interfere with, are such as had been in law and in fact, granted or secured by the constitution or laws of the United States.*[100]

The legal potency of the Enforcement Act will be impacted in a very profound way. In a curious paragraph, the chief justice notes, "The right of the people peaceably to assemble for lawful purposes existed long before the adoption of the Constitution of the United States."[101] It is found, he suggests, wherever civilization exists. And yet, despite the universality of this right, "The government of the United States when established found it in existence, with the obligation on the part of the States to afford it protection. As no direct power over it was granted to Congress, it remains according to a prior ruling subject to State jurisdiction."[102]

Continuing with this same very limited view of the rights which people enjoy, the justice further tightens his interpretation of the enormity of states rights: "The first amendment to the Constitution prohibits Congress from abridging 'the right of the people to assemble and to petition the government for a redress of grievances.'"[103] This, like the other amendments proposed and adopted at the same time, was not intended to limit the powers of the state government in respect to their own citizens, but to operate upon the national government alone.

At this stage in the rendering of the Court's decision, the various counts of the 16 various charges are examined and dismissed by the Court for varying reasons. A few examples will

---

98   Ibid., p. 549.
99   Ibid.
100   Ibid., p. 551.
101   Ibid.
102   Ibid., p. 554.
103   Ibid., p. 552.

suffice to illustrate how the justices dismantled all of the charges facing these few defendants out of the original 96 that were charged with extreme acts of violence and ultimately murder on black citizens.

The particular amendment now under consideration assumes the existence of the right of the people to assemble for lawful purposes, and protects it against the encroachment by Congress. The right was not created by the amendment; neither was its continuance guaranteed, except as against congressional interference. For their protection in its enjoyment, therefore, the people must look to the States. The power for that purpose was originally placed there, and it has never been surrendered to the United States.[104]

The third and eleventh counts are even more objectionable. They charge the intent to have been to deprive the citizens named, they being in Louisiana, "of their respective several lives and liberty of person without due process of law." This is nothing more than alleging a conspiracy to falsely imprison or murder citizens of the United States, being within the territorial jurisdiction of the State of Louisiana. The rights of life and personal liberty are natural rights of man. "To secure these rights," says the Declaration of Independence, "governments are instituted among men, deriving their just powers from the consent of the governed." The very highest duty of the States, when they entered the Union under the Constitution, was to protect all persons within their boundaries in the enjoyment of these "unalienable rights with which they were endowed by their Creator." Sovereignty, for this purpose, rests alone with the States. It is no more the duty or within the power of the United States to punish for a conspiracy to falsely imprison or murder within a State, than it would be to punish for false imprisonment or murder itself.[105]

What the justices say is that even though the rights of life and liberty are natural ones, the governmental entity responsible for securing them is the states—the very same states, which for decades maintained and promoted slavery. The very same states which had just seceded from the Union, partly to retain their rights as states and partly to protect the institution of slavery, were now, according to the justices, supposed to be trusted with being the legal guardian and protector of newly granted rights? It hardly seems believable.

This sense of incredulousness is merited based on the justices' responses to other charges.

The fourth and twelfth counts charge the intent to have been to prevent and hinder the citizens named, who were of African descent and persons of color, in "the free exercise and enjoyment of their several rights and privilege to the full and equal benefit if all laws and proceedings, then, and there, before that time, enacted or ordained by the said State of Louisiana and by the United States; and then and there, at that time, being in force in the said State and District of Louisiana aforesaid, for the security of their respective persons and property, then and there, at that time enjoyed at and within said State and District of Louisiana by white persons, being citizens of said State of Louisiana and the United States, for the protection of the persons and property of said white citizens." There

---

104   Ibid.
105   Ibid., p. 553.

is no allegation that this was done because of the race or color of the persons conspired against. When stripped of its verbiage, the case presented amounts to nothing more than that the defendants conspired to prevent certain citizens of the United States, being within the State of Louisiana, from enjoying the equal protection of the laws of the State and of the United States.[106]

So, even in its own words, the Court acknowledges that conspiracies were present, which prevented certain citizens from enjoying their rights. Astonishingly, the Court, judging an incident that occurred a few years after the Civil War, has become color blind. They don't see race or color as a major factor. How can this be? They were aware of the Black Codes and the reality of the Klan-oriented groups that were wreaking brutality and violence on the newly forming black communities.

This surreal view is reinforced when they suggest that the recently passed Civil Rights Act has no standing in this matter, either. "No question arises under the Civil Rights Act of April 9, 1866 (14 Stat.27), which is intended for the protection of citizens of the United States in the enjoyment of certain rights, without discrimination, on account of race, color, or previous condition of servitude, because, as has already been stated, it is nowhere alleged in these counts that the wrong contemplated against the rights of these citizens was on account of their race and color."[107] What else was the catalyst for these attacks, if not race? The entire premise of the initial attacks was based on the troubled racial relations in the South. For the Court not to address that crucial issue seems ludicrous.

Even more fascinating, the case of *U.S. v. Reese* is used as a point of reference. In this case, previously discussed, the Court has done an astonishing job of reinterpreting the Fifteenth Amendment and defining it to a shadow of itself. In this opinion, the Court reminds the reader that in the *Reese* case, "We hold that the Fifteenth amendment has invested the citizens of the United states with a new constitutional right, which is, exemption from discrimination in the exercise of the elective franchise on account of race, color, or previous condition of servitude ... The right to vote in the States comes from the States; but the right of exemption from the prohibited discrimination comes from the United States. The first has not been granted or secured by the Constitution of the United States; but the last has been."[108]

With this interpretation, it is easy to see how those opposed to black enfranchisement would be applauding. The Supreme Court, in creating these legal distinctions between the powers granted by the Constitution and that held by the states, is giving the rationale for those opposed to black voting to continue on their quest.

At the end of this relatively short summation, all of the charges against these defendants have been eliminated for different reasons. The judgment of the circuit court is affirmed, the cause remanded with instructions for the defendants to be discharged. Unbelievably, of all the defendants involved and all the charges filed, nothing was found to have violated any of the rights of the now dead 50–200 black Louisiana citizens. Despite all the efforts of the Radical Republicans, the Thirteenth, Fourteenth, and Fifteenth amendments, the civil rights acts of 1866, 1870, and 1875, and the belief by thousands that a new South was rising, it was open season for violence against blacks, with the explicit approval of the Supreme Court. (Refer to Figure 3-15.)

---

106   Ibid., p. 554.
107   Ibid., pp. 555.
108   Ibid., pp. 555–556.

3-15: The Justice relief by Carlo Franzoni is found in the Supreme Court Chamber. We can think about the concept of justice and how difficult it is to fully achieve.

In light of this historic decision, it is appropriate to briefly examine the philosophies and attitudes of the justices involved to better understand their motivations in making it. Chief Justice Morrison Waite was born in Lyme, Connecticut, on November 27, 1816. After choosing law as a profession, he became a prominent attorney for the railroads. His political theories were moderate in outlook; he was antislavery, but not pro-black.[109] He represented the country in negotiations with Great Britain after the Civil War. In 1874, Waite was nominated for the chief justice position of the U.S. Supreme Court. As far as civil rights for former slaves, his record is not a strong one. In this case, he held that the Fifteenth Amendment had not granted suffrage to blacks, and therefore no federal rights for blacks had been violated by the defendants.[110] In a later case, *Strauder v. West Virginia*, Waite agreed that a statute which confined jury duty to white persons violated the "equal protection of the laws" clause of the Fourteenth Amendment.[111] Nevertheless, he voided part of the Enforcement Act of 1870 and severely qualified the Fifteenth Amendment. In perhaps his most indicative attitude toward civil rights, Waite voted with the majority in the 1883 civil rights cases, which held the Civil Rights Act of 1875 unconstitutional. "Waite was with the Court as it held that Congress could not force its code upon individuals, but could only pass 'corrective' legislation as the occasion required."[112] (See Figure 3-16.)

William Strong had a decade-long tenure on the Supreme Court, during which he made many significant decisions regarding civil rights. He was born in Somers, Connecticut, on May 6, 1808. He began his legal career as counsel for the Philadelphia and Reading Railroad Company. After being elected to the House of Representatives, in 1857 he was chosen to be on the Pennsylvania Supreme Court. He stayed on this court for 15 years, and in 1870 was nominated by President Ulysses Grant to the United States Supreme Court.

Strong dealt with many cases regarding post–Civil War rights laws passed by Congress. In the *Blyew v. United States* case, decided in 1872, he determined that the Civil Rights Act of April 1866, which gave the federal courts jurisdiction of crimes "affecting persons" (blacks) who were denied the rights secured them by the law, did not apply to those black citizens murdered in Kentucky.[113] His convoluted reasoning was that since the law stated that "the act refers to persons in existence," it could not be applied to those who had died. The jurisdiction could

---

109   Friedman and Israel, Eds., *The Justices of the Supreme Court*, vol. II, p. 613.
110   Ibid., p. 623.
111   Ibid.
112   Ibid., p. 624.
113   Ibid., p. 574.

similarly not be established because any black witnesses were also not affected by the crimes. In this case, Strong voted with the unanimous decision of the Court.

In later cases, he reflects a more liberal approach to civil rights. In an 1880 case, *Strauder v. West Virginia*, Justice Strong wrote the main opinion, which found that black defendants had the right to have juries selected impartially. He found that West Virginia's "white jury" statute violated the Fourteenth Amendment and unduly discriminated against its black citizens; it fixed "a brand upon them as ... an assertion of their inferiority and as a stimulant to that race prejudice which is an impediment to securing to individuals of the race that equal justice which the law aims to secure to all."[114] In the companion case of *Ex parte Virginia*, Strong upheld that section of the Civil Rights Act of 1875 that prohibited racial discrimination in the selection of juries. "He emphasized again that the purpose of the Fourteenth Amendment was to remove all oppression by state law because of race or color."[115] In this case, a state judge had been indicted for refusing to call blacks as jurors.

Justice David Davis, who was a close friend of President Lincoln for over 30 years, was born in Cecil County, Maryland, in 1815. After attaining his law credentials, he set up practice in Illinois. He served in the state legislature and was elected a judge for the new Eighth Circuit in 1848. In 1860, he was intimately involved in Lincoln's Republican presidential nomination. Part of Lincoln's tasks was realigning the circuit court responsibilities of the Supreme Court. In the *Dred Scott* case, five of the nine justices had been from slave states. The Judiciary Act of 1837 created nine circuits and nine places on the Supreme Court.[116] At this time, the justices regularly traveled in their various circuits, holding court. By the time of the Civil War, the proportions of the circuits were out of alignment. In 1862, Congress transformed five Southern circuits into three and created new circuits in the trans-Mississippi free states.[117] Davis was nominated to a seat on the Supreme Court in 1862.

In his opinion, the case of Ex Parte Milligan, decided in 1866, was "the most important case ever brought before the court."[118] The case revolved around the legality of military tribunals set up during the war, as opposed to civilian courts. In this case, the Court was unanimous in its verdict that the military commission was without jurisdiction, and that Milligan was entitled to a writ of habeas corpus, allowing his case to be heard in a civilian court and not a military tribunal.[119] Justice Davis was passionate about this subject." Milligan and every American citizen, Davis believed, were endowed with 'the birthright ... to be tried and punished according to law.' This, for him, was the essence of English and American constitutional development."[120] In a contemporary setting, many Radical Republicans, who felt that the conquered (and unruly) South needed to be administered by military troops, believed that the Milligan decision was on the level of the Dred Scott case in its negative ramifications. For Democrats and Southerners, many felt that the congressional program of Reconstruction was unconstitutional on the basis of Milligan.

Regarding Civil Rights, Justice Davis voted with the majority in the Slaughterhouse Cases, the *U.S. v. Reese*, and the *U.S. v. Cruikshank* cases, which invalidated parts of the enforcement act passed to implement the Civil War amendments. In 1877, he was elected to the U.S. Senate,

114 Ibid., p. 575.
115 Ibid.
116 Ibid., p. 522
117 Ibid., p. 523.
118 Ibid., p. 524.
119 Ibid.
120 Ibid.

representing Illinois. He retained a close relationship with Mrs. Lincoln and her son and secured a congressional act granting her an annual pension. It is interesting to note that this justice with such a keen sense of propriety about the law and justice did not apparently consider its extension to the former slaves who were laboring mightily to enjoy the same rights as their white counterparts. In the *Blyew* decision, he did not make any dissenting comments.

Stephen J. Field served on the Supreme Court from 1863 through 1897. He was born in Haddam, Connecticut, on November 4, 1816. While his father was a clergyman in the Congregational Church, Field chose the field of law for his life's work. In 1841, he was admitted to practice law in New York State. After working with his brother for ten years and some overseas travel, he was attracted to California for its Gold Rush in 1849. After functioning as a civil magistrate in the early Gold Rush town of Marysville, he became more involved in the new state of California's legislative and judicial arenas. Field was elected in 1857 to serve as a justice on the California Supreme Court. In 1863, he was nominated to the U.S. Supreme Court.

In his Court career, many described Field as having an unmistakable pro-business prejudice.[121] In addition to many business-related cases in 1880, he enhanced his reputation among Democrats in the South by a dissenting opinion, contending that states could properly exclude blacks from jury service in the *Ex Parte Virginia* case. In the 1880s, he thought that he might be nominated to be chief justice, but this honor was offered to another. In later cases involving such as the 1883 civil rights cases, he concurred with the majority's narrow interpretation of the congressional power to enforce an antidiscriminatory policy.[122] His stance in the area was mixed. "Field was not one of those men whose passion to protect property blinds them to all other claims of personal right. But neither was he a champion of civil liberties comparable to his contemporary, the first Justice Harlan."[123] Prior to his resigning from the Court in 1899, his total count of opinions in a majority, minority, or dissenting position was 640.

Samuel Miller was another justice who served the Court for an extended period of time, 28 years. He was born in Madison County, Kentucky, on April 5, 1816. He first earned his medical degree in 1838 and practiced as a doctor for 12 years. Over time, his interest in law became a driving force in his life. In 1847, he was admitted to the county bar. He moved west to Iowa, remarried, and set up a legal practice there. He was a believer in unrestricted immigration, liberal suffrage qualifications, broad construction of the federal Constitution, and vigorous popular democracy.[124] In light of his philosophy, Miller freed his slaves. When the Civil War began in 1861, he was an ardent believer in the need to fight to preserve the Union. He raised money to pay and equip Union troops. In 1862, after an extensive campaign on his behalf, Miller was nominated by the president and confirmed by Congress for a seat on the High Court. His support for the preservation of the Union was firm and absolute. He believed that Congress had "all the great powers essential to a perpetual Union—the power to make war, to suppress insurrection, to levy taxes, to make rules concerning captures on land and on sea."[125]

Regarding civil rights issues, Miller was no more or less liberal than most of his contemporaries. In the civil rights cases, he agreed with the majority that the Fourteenth Amendment was written to prohibit state—not individual—discrimination. In 1882, he also followed the majority in *United States v. Harris* in gutting the conspiracy clause of the Ku Klux Klan Act. However, in a later case (*Ex parte Yarbrough*), Miller gave a broader construction of the Fifteenth Amendment.

---

121 Ibid., p. 535.
122 Ibid., p. 546.
123 Ibid.
124 Ibid., p. 507.
125 Ibid., p. 511.

He further contended that there were ample constitutional provisions in regulating federal elections without recourse to state law, for suffrage is of supreme importance and is not left within the exclusive control of the states.[126] This opinion was referred to in the civil rights legislation of the 1960s. His biographer used glowing terms to describe him: "In a breathtaking achievement of will, Miller calculated the possible, measured the public good and necessity, demanded justice and common sense in the result, and only then devised the constitutional means. In short, he was generated by great power matched with enduring purpose."[127] But even this highly principled jurist voted with the majority in the *Reese* and *Cruikshank* cases, which curtailed federal enforcement of black civil rights.

Born in 1804 in northern Virginia to Quaker parents, Justice Noah H. Swayne soon turned to the practice of law. As a young attorney, he moved to Ohio as a reflection of his antislavery views. In fact, he served as legal counsel for several slave-fugitive cases. He was appointed to the U.S. Supreme Court in 1862. He was a devoted Unionist who was adamantly opposed to the Confederacy, which he viewed as an armed resistance to the rightful authority of the sovereign government.[128] In the arena of civil rights for the former slaves, Swayne's findings were mixed. On one hand, he dissented vigorously in opposing the Court's majority restriction of its meaning of the Fourteenth Amendment in the Slaughterhouse Cases.[129] Yet, "Respecting the Fifteenth Amendment, however, he supported the court's narrow approach, which had the effect of circumscribing federal enforcement of Black voting rights in U.S. v. Reese and in the Cruikshank case as well."[130] Swayne resigned from the High Court in 1881 after 19 years of service and passed away in 1884.

Nathan Clifford was born in Rumney, New Hampshire, in 1803. He decided to become an attorney and set up his law practice in York County, Maine. In 1839, he was elected to the U.S. House of Representatives. He was critical of abolitionism. In the mid-1840s, he served as attorney general of the country. Clifford was appointed by President Buchanan in 1856 to a seat on the U.S. Supreme Court. Upon this appointment, he was classified by some in the press as a "doughface," the term for a Northern man with Southern sympathies.[131] His judicial belief was that of a strict constructionist believing that the Constitution should be "sacredly maintained in all its provisions and limitations, as the best guaranty for the perpetuity of our republican institutions."[132]

While he agreed with the majority in the *Abelman v. Booth* case of 1858, Clifford in 1865 decided for the Court against slave traders. While he was sympathetic to Southern Democratic beliefs, he did not in any way condone secession or the Confederacy. He described the secession as "a wicked heresy."[133] Generally, Clifford opposed vigorous federal enforcement of the Reconstruction amendments on behalf of blacks. He voted with the majority in the *Slaughterhouse Cases*, as well as the *Reese* and *Cruikshank* cases. He died in July of 1881.

In a review of Supreme Court justices, Joseph P. Bradley is rated as one of the most prominent.[134] He was born in Fairfield, Connecticut, to a family who had been in America for over two centuries. In 1839, he was admitted to the bar. Additionally, he was a very competent

126   Ibid., p. 513.
127   Ibid., p. 518.
128   Ibid., p. 495.
129   Ibid., p. 497.
130   Ibid., p. 498.
131   Ibid., p. 482.
132   Ibid., p. 483.
133   Ibid., p. 484.
134   Ibid., p. 580.

mathematician who worked on statistics and actuarial tables for an insurance company. Bradley initiated two proposed amendments to the Constitution regarding slavery in 1860. Bradley was nominated to the Supreme Court in March 1870. In the *Slaughterhouse Cases*, he dissented from the majority opinion, which narrowly defined the rights of United States citizens. As time progressed, however, his views changed. In the *Cruikshank* case, Bradley concluded that the Enforcement Act of 1870, which made it a crime to conspire to prevent United States citizens from enjoying their constitutional rights, did not extend to an armed attack by Louisiana whites who killed sixty blacks holding a political rally, defended by various black deputies.[135] Protection of the basic rights of citizens must be left to the states and not the federal government, he wrote—a decided switch from his earlier opinions in the Slaughterhouse Cases.

Bradley also wrote the Court's decision in the civil rights cases which declared unconstitutional the Civil Rights Act of 1875. The Court held that the attempt to bar segregation in public inns was beyond the power of Congress, since the Fourteenth Amendment forbade only state action and not discrimination by private individuals.[136] The following quote from Bradley in this decision is especially telling regarding the rights of former slaves: "When a man had emerged from slavery, and by the aid of beneficent legislation has shaken off the inseparable concomitants of that state, there must be some stage in the process of his elevation when he takes the rank of mere citizen and ceases to be the special favorite of the laws, and when his rights as a citizen, or a man, are to be protected in the ordinary modes by which other men's rights are protected."[137] He died in January 1892. One author describes Bradley in exceptional terms: "Man could be perfect, Bradley felt, and his life in the law was his best attempt to attain that goal. With his powerful intellect and moral assertiveness, he surpassed all but a handful of judges who have sat upon the Court."[138]

Justice Ward Hunt had a relatively brief tenure on the Supreme Court. He was born in Utica, New York, in June of 1810. After choosing law as his vocation, he entered politics and eventually was elected to the New York Court of Appeals in 1865. He became New York State's chief justice three years later. President Grant nominated him for the U.S. Supreme Court in 1872. During his five years of active service on the High Court, Hunt wrote few major opinions. One of the major ones was his dissent on the *Reese* case, which limited the potency of the Fifteenth Amendment. Hunt said the Fifteenth Amendment was intended for the benefit of all citizens, in all elections, state and federal.[139] He further believed that when the amendment spoke about actions of the state, those acts included all of those who acted under its authority. "Therefore, the actions of state officers in denying suffrage to blacks were tantamount to state action and subject to federal restraint."[140] He concluded that the majority's opinion in the *Reese* case brought "to an impotent conclusion the vigorous amendments on the subject of slavery."[141]

Despite Hunt's obvious sentiment and beliefs, even he seemed to change his views in subsequent decisions involving civil rights. In the *Cruikshank* case, he sided with the majority in holding the indictment faulty and further crippling the rights of blacks.[142] Chief Justice

---

135   Ibid., p. 596.
136   Ibid.
137   Ibid., p. 597.
138   Ibid., p. 599.
139   Ibid., p. 603.
140   Ibid.
141   Ibid.
142   Ibid., p. 604.

Waite concluded that "we may suspect that race was the cause of the hostility; but it is not so averred."[143] In a later case involving Susan B. Anthony, who claimed that she had the right to vote according to the Fourteenth Amendment, Justice Hunt made a distinction between the rights that people held as U.S. citizens and those that were within the purview of the states. In this case, he concluded that the state of New York held ultimate rights regarding the right to vote in that state, not the federal government. He suffered a stroke in 1878, retired from the Court in 1882, and died in 1886.

After this overview of the justices involved in the *Cruikshank* case, it is difficult to draw any overarching conclusions, except one. Geographically, six of the justices had been born and educated in the New England region, especially Connecticut. The chief justice was "anti-slavery, but not pro-black." A few, such as Justices Strong and Field, had mixed votes of civil rights for the former slaves. Others such as Justice Davis who were so passionate about the "rule of law" chose not to apply this significant principle to the black citizens of America. Justice Miller, noted for his thoughts about the public good and justice, also voted to curtail federal enforcement of black civil rights. One might assume that Justice Swayne, born to a Quaker tradition and someone who had consistently advocated antislavery views, would have dissented in this case. He did in the *Slaughterhouse Cases*, but not in the *Reese* or *Cruikshank* ones. Justice Clifford voted consistently against federal enforcement of the Reconstruction amendments. Another Justice from Connecticut, Joseph Bradley, initially supported black civil rights, but within a few short years changed his views. He was described as a supreme justice in terms of his intellect and moral assertiveness, but those qualities apparently were not applied to people of color. The ninth justice involved in the *Cruikshank* case was Ward Hunt. Born in New York, where he served as a State Supreme Court justice, he initially was a prominent proponent for post–civil war rights. In the *Reese* case, he offered a strong dissent to the majority decision. Yet, within a few years, when the *Cruikshank* decision was rendered, Hunt's passionate voice fell silent.

In sum, it is appropriate to consider these four cases and review the enormous impact that they had on the post–Civil War acts and amendments. The *Blyew* case allowed extreme violence to be condoned against former slaves without any punishment, despite the presence of eyewitnesses to the crime committed. This finding, decided a mere five years after the war, was especially heinous. In many ways, it gave a legal imprimatur to the violence the Klan was initiating in the South. It should be remembered that the local federal circuit court had found the defendants guilty of murder. Instead of basing their decision on the newly ratified Fourteenth Amendment, which spoke of equal protection of the law, their finding was blithely overturned, partly based on the word "affected."

In the *Slaughterhouse Cases*, the Court used this occasion to weaken the potency and scope of the Fourteenth Amendment by creating a schism between the rights of being a citizen of the United States as compared to the rights earned as a citizen of an individual state. While the amendment used phrases such as "No state shall deny," or "No State shall abridge," the Court found that ultimately, it was the states that were the final authority for maintaining individual states' rights, not the federal government. The recent history of a nation at war exactly because many of the states had deliberately chosen to be unjust and unfair in the distribution of these rights didn't seem to be an issue. How could the justices realistically expect that the Southern states would have any inclination to give additional rights to the former slaves?

This frontal legal attack on the post–Civil War amendments continued with the *Reese* case, which again, through judicial parsing, greatly reduced the potency of the Fifteenth Amendment. This amendment and its accompanying laws were written exactly to counter incidents such as

---

143 Ibid.

those described in this case: the great difficulties encountered by black voters in their attempts to register to vote and in actually voting. The finding in this case set the stage for the successful subsequent efforts to disenfranchise black voters in the Jim Crow era.

The ultimate example of my assertion that the United States Supreme Court was a clan as dangerous as or even more so than the other Klan is based on its decision in the Cruikshank case. Dozens of accused men are indicted with multiple counts against them. They are found guilty by a federal circuit court, only to have all of the charges subsequently dropped on review by the Supreme Court. With dozens—or perhaps hundreds—of black victims and with detailed counts against the perpetrators, not one charge against one person was sustained by the nation's highest court! Thus, while one Klan helped organize brutal attacks against the former slaves and others sympathetic to their cause, this legal clan seemingly blessed such attacks by not holding any of those responsible for initiating the violence in any fashion. While there may be those who argue that these cases were decided on legal grounds alone, it seems impossible that the justices were not vividly aware of the real-life consequences of these decisions.

It is impossible to historically determine what caused the justices to turn away from their belief in the significance of post–civil war rights for the former slaves. Some historians suggest that the country as a whole was losing interest in the affairs of the South, and simply wanted the country to move on to other issues. While that may have been the case for most of the nation, one would expect justices of the Supreme Court of the land to operate on another level. Another possible explanation for the lack of conviction was that it never existed in the first place. The justices were quite comfortable in limiting the newly won rights of full citizenship for the former slaves. One can easily discern the origins of the "separate but equal" philosophy forming, as the justices, in case after case, rule against full black legal and social acceptance in post–Civil War America.

It is significant to reiterate the year that these decisions were given, 1875. The Civil War had been over for a little more than a decade. Southern governments, agreeing to the acceptance of the Thirteenth, Fourteenth, and Fifteenth amendments, had reverted rapidly to a conservative stance that included a very condescending attitude toward the former slaves. While the black community did grow in terms of schools, churches, and small businesses, they were not accepted as equal citizens by their neighbors. The Court's decisive and stunning decisions, given in the midst of Reconstruction, set the stage for continuing findings in the decades to come that were for the most part consistent with those made in the aftermath of the war. There was much prejudice, intolerance, and pain yet to come.

Discussion Questions

1. Does it matter that one factor in President Lincoln's issuance of the Emancipation Proclamation was based on military necessity?

2. What did the Black Codes, devised by the South after the Civil War, represent?

3. What was the ultimate purpose of the Thirteenth, Fourteenth, and Fifteenth amendments? Was that goal achieved during the Reconstruction period?

4. Why did the Klan arise in 1866, and why has it lasted as long as it has?

5. What are your opinions regarding the Court's decision in the *Blyew* case?

6. In the *Slaughterhouse Cases*, the justices make a distinction between the citizenship of the United States and that of individual states. What are some of the implications of that decision?

7. What can explain the deep and profound prejudices against the former slaves?

8. What was effective and what was ineffective about the Ku Klux Klan Act?

9. Should any of the defendants in the *Cruikshank* case been found guilty?

10. Did it matter that in the decade after the Civil War, cases such as those described in this chapter were decided in the manner that they were?

THE ROSA PARKS OF THE 19TH CENTURY

chapter 4

T he legal frontal attack on the civil rights of the black community continued with the conclusion of the Reconstruction period in the 1870s. The direction of the court was reflected in another little known and underappreciated case, *Hall v. DeCuir*, decided in 1877. In many ways, this case represents a "smoking gun" of sorts. It is a remarkable judgment, as it eerily mirrors the much better-known finding of *Plessy v. Ferguson*, decided in 1896. This case examined many of the same issues as in *Plessy*, with a surprising conclusion. One is left to ponder the strong possibility that the Supreme Court had by this early date (1877) laid the legal foundations and planted the seeds of the rise and rapid growth of the blatant segregation (Jim Crow) embraced by the South and accepted by most of America in the late 1800s and early to mid-1900s.

Hall v. DeCuir has an interesting origin. In 1869, the state of Louisiana voted a thirteenth article to its state constitution, which provided, "All persons shall enjoy equal rights and privileges upon any conveyance of a public character."[1] It is worthwhile to read the first section of this act.

---

1   U. S. Reports, *Hall v. DeCuir*, p. 485.

Section 1. All persons engaged within this State, in the business of common carriers of Passengers shall have the right to refuse to admit any person to their railroad cars, street cars, steamboats, or other water-crafts, stage coaches, omnibuses, or other vehicles, or to expel any person therefrom after admission, when such person shall, on demand, refuse or neglect to pay the customary fare, or when such person shall be of infamous character, or shall be guilty, after admission to the conveyance of the carrier, of gross, vulgar, or disorderly conduct, or who shall commit any act tending to injure the business of the carrier, prescribed for the management of his business, after such rules and regulations shall have been made known:

Provided, said rules and regulations make no discrimination on account of race or color; and shall have the right to refuse any person admission to such conveyance where there is not room or suitable accommodations; and except in cases above enumerated, all persons engaged in the business of common carriers of passengers are forbidden to refuse admission to their conveyance, or to expel therefrom any person whomsoever."[2]

It is breathtaking to appreciate the radical changes that occurred in post–Civil War America. In the immediate years after the war, the Southern states, in order to return to the Union, agreed to accept the Thirteenth and Fourteenth amendments as part of their process of readmission to the Union. By 1870, the Fifteenth Amendment was added to this list as well. In Louisiana, the term "public rights" was added to the 1868 state constitution. The meaning of that term in the context of the newly drafted constitution was that every citizen should enjoy "the same civil and political rights and privileges."[3] The origins of this concept included long-standing concepts of personal honor, French and Caribbean revolutionary ideas of equality and 19th-century liberal codifications of rights.[4] The words "public rights" emphasized forms of equality manifested in the public sphere, but it was a separate term from social equality, which for some meant enforced intimacy and intrusion into the private space of people.[5]

Certainly, those writing the new state laws used the term "public rights" to invoke, on the basis of individual liberty, a whole range of rights, including equal access to public accommodations and common carriers.[6] It is important to consider that these new regulations were what the post–Civil War presidents and the Radical Republicans had been hoping for—a new South dedicated to the premise of a much more fair, just, and equitable society. That included, of course, the ability to travel on public transportation without any personal limitations based on race or prior status. (See Figure 4-1.)

In this instance, a steamboat owner and operator by the name of Benson regularly transported passengers between New Orleans in the state of Louisiana to Vicksburg, in the state of Mississippi. The defendant in this case, Mrs. Josephine DeCuir, a well-dressed, highly respected member of Louisiana society and a woman of color, took passage upon the boat up the Mississippi from New Orleans to Hermitage, Louisiana. She was refused accommodations in the cabin set apart for white female passengers for which she had paid. The steward of the boat offered her a berth in the windowless "colored bureau." Mrs. DeCuir refused. Next, she was offered a place in the "saloon" area located below the "recess," a thoroughfare used by nursemaids

---

2   Ibid., pp. 485–486.
3   Rebecca Scott, *Public Rights, Social Equality. Michigan Law Review*, vol. 106, March 2008, p. 783.
4   Ibid.
5   Ibid., p. 787.
6   Ibid., p. 788.

and their charges. Again she refused.[7] The steward even offered to bring her supper in her chair. She refused. Eventually, she passed the night sitting in a chair in what was known as the recess back area of the upper (white) cabin, wrapped with her own clothes. Interestingly, for Mrs. DeCuir, this was not the first time she had been refused a spot in the white ladies' cabins. On an earlier voyage, she had experienced similar prejudice. On that occasion, she had argued with the boat captain for her right to be in the same cabin area.[8] (Refer to Figure 4-2.)

Mrs. DeCuir brought legal action against the owner of the boat in the Eighth District Court in the parish of New Orleans. Benson's defense was that the Louisiana statute was

4-1: These ships were one of the primary means of transportation in the nineteenth century.

inoperative because the state law conflicted with the federal Constitution Article 1, section 8, paragraph 3: "To regulate Commerce with foreign nations, and among the several States, and with the Indian Tribes," which notes that it is the responsibility of the Congress to regulate commerce among the states.

In this case, a district court found for Mrs. DeCuir and fined Benson one thousand dollars. He appealed to the Louisiana Supreme Court, which sustained the judgment of the lower court. The case was sent to the U.S. Supreme Court for review. In the meantime, Benson had died, and a Mrs. Hall, his administratrix, was substituted in the Court.

Chief Justice of the Court Morrison Waite delivered the Court's opinion. He immediately establishes what for him and the Court is the main question.

> *There can be no doubt but that the exclusive power has been conferred upon Congress in respect to the regulation of commerce between the several States. The difficulty has never been as to the existence of this power, but as to what is to be deemed as encroachment upon it; for, as has been often said, "Legislation may in a great variety of ways affect commerce and persons engaged in it without constituting a regulation of it within the meaning of the Constitution."[9]*

So, for example, states may regulate railroads, turnpikes, ferries, and the construction of dams and bridges, all within their respective jurisdictions, and not be considered to be interfering with the constitutional prerogative. Indeed, the Justice continues to note that, "The line which separates the powers of the States from this exclusive power of Congress is not always distinctly

---

7 Ibid., p. 792.
8 Ibid., p. 792.
9 *Hall v. DeCuir*, p. 487.

4-2: These dignified women symbolize Josephine DeCuir whose strength and resolve in the 1870s set an example of courage for later generations.

marked, and oftentimes it is not easy to determine on which side a particular case belongs."[10]

However, in this case, the state has overstepped its bounds and interfered with the national power. The justice notes that the Mississippi River passes through or along the borders of ten different states, and "If each State was at liberty to regulate the conduct of carriers while within its jurisdiction, the confusion likely to follow could not but be productive of great inconvenience and unnecessary hardship ... On one side of the river or its tributaries he might be required to observe one set of rules, and on the other another. Commerce cannot flourish in the midst of such embarrassments."[11] Justice Waite develops this line of reasoning by mentioning that in cases where Congress has not legislated its own regulations, common law, or civil law, prevails. Thus, "Congressional inaction left Benson at liberty to adopt such reasonable rules and regulations for the disposition of passengers upon his boat, while pursuing her voyage within Louisiana or without, as seemed to him most for the interest of all concerned."[12] The Court's conclusion seems apparent and is quickly offered. "We think this statute, to the extent that it requires those engaged in the transportation of passengers among the States to carry colored passengers in Louisiana in the same cabin with whites is unconstitutional and void. If the public good requires such legislation, it must come from Congress and not the States."[13] The state supreme court finding is reversed.

Most interestingly, the justice's decision made absolutely no mention of contemporary events. As noted earlier, the Thirteenth, Fourteenth, and Fifteenth amendments, as well as the civil rights acts of 1866, 1870, or 1875 were also not referenced. It is particularly significant to examine the Civil Rights Act of 1875, which directly addresses the issues raised in this case. The first section of the law seems especially clear in its purpose.

> *Section 1. That all persons within the jurisdiction of the United States shall be entitled to the full and equal enjoyment of the accommodations, advantages, facilities, and privileges of inns, public conveyances on land or water, theaters, and other places of public*

transportation by water

10   Ibid., p. 488.
11   Ibid., p. 489.
12   Ibid., p. 490.
13   Ibid.

amusement; subject only to the conditions and limitations established by law, and applicable alike to citizens of every race and color, regardless of any previous condition of servitude.[14] *(Refer to Figure 4-3.)*

Everybody have rights to sit anywhere

The next section of this 1875 act set penalties for anyone who violated this new civil rights bill. The fines ranged from $500 to $1,000. What is astonishing is that the justices gave no indication about the existence of this bill or any of the previous laws concerning the equal treatment of the newly freed slaves. The year that this case was decided, 1877, marked the end of the Reconstruction period. Perhaps

4-3: Despite the clarity and force of the 1875 Civil Rights Act, theaters and other social venues such as this Florida theater would be separated until the modern Civil Rights Movement.

this case is representative of the lack of interest by the North regarding the relationships in the South between its black and white citizens.

It is not coincidental that within a year of this decision, a new state constitution was drafted in Louisiana. In this new version, the phrase "civil, political and public rights," relating to all citizens, no longer appeared. The principle of racial separation in the schools also made a discreet appearance through the funding of an all-black university.[15]

Apparently, the real feelings and notions of the Court toward true social equality were already set forth in a lengthy and detailed concurrence authored by Justice Nathan Clifford. The justice first offers a review of the *DeCuir* case and the legal issues posed. He presented a more detailed description of the circumstances aboard the steamer than was previously given. The steamer had two cabins for its passengers. Both had staterooms, cabins, and a hall used as a dining room. White passengers were assigned seats in the upper cabin, while black passengers had seats in the lower cabin. Mrs. DeCuir, who was coincidentally accompanied on this journey with a lawyer and had lived in France for a number of years, was denied a space in the upper cabin due to her skin color and offered a spot in the lower one. As an aside, this action strikes one as a precursor to the actions of Rosa Parks 78 years later. Josephine DeCuir, like Rosa Parks, did not accept the status quo and spent the night in a chair located in the back area of the white upper berth![16]

After reviewing the legal arguments, Justice Clifford agrees with the chief justice that Congress has power to control the enrolling and licensing of sailing ships and vessels. "Few or none will deny that the power to regulate commerce among the several States is vested exclusively in Congress;

14 Barrett and Cohen, *Constitutional Law*, p. 1004.
15 Rebecca Scott, *Public Rights, Social Equality*, p. 794.
16 Ibid., 793.

and it is equally well settled that Congress has, in many instances and to a wide extent, legislated upon the subject."[17] At this stage, the concurrence might have ended. Justice Clifford reconfirms his agreement with the main decision. Yet, his opinion continues into other social and racial areas. First, he reasserted the right of the federal Supreme Court to review cases on the states' supreme courts as needed. He then makes a curious—yet powerfully revealing—statement. "Governed by the laws of Congress, it is clear that a steamer carrying passengers may have separate cabins and dining saloons for white persons and persons of color, for the plain reason that the laws of Congress contain nothing to prohibit such an arrangement ... Applicants to whom there is no such valid objection have a right to a passage, but it is not an unlimited right ... proprietors may prescribe for the due accommodation of passengers and the due arrangement of the business of the carrier."[18]

The right of the ship owners, previously not addressed as a legal issue in this case, is strongly presented and argued. Justice Clifford asserts that the proprietors "Are not bound to admit passengers on board ... who are guilty of gross and vulgar habits of conduct, or who make disturbances on board, or whose characters are doubtful, dissolute, suspicious, or unequivocally bad ... Nor are they bound to admit passengers on board whose object it is to interfere with the interests of the patronage of the proprietors, so as to make their business less lucrative or their management less acceptable to the public."[19]

This distinction is truly significant. Apparently, the justice is laying the philosophical and legal foundations of later opinions which inherently acknowledge this Jim Crow–type idea, that entry to a steamship or train does not automatically include an equal seat once onboard. Clifford cites a case decided by the Michigan Supreme Court, in which "The court says the right to be carried is one thing, and the privilege of a passenger on board as to what part of the vessel may be occupied by him is another and a very different thing."[20] The justice continues that this finding is comparable to that of an innkeeper who opens his inn to all guests: "Yet he is not only empowered to make such proper arrangements as will promote his own interests, but he is bound to regulate his house so as to preserve order, and, if practicable, prevent breaches of the peace."[21]

Clifford then cites a case decided by the Supreme Court of Pennsylvania, which granted public carriers the right to separate passengers. They deduced this right from the notion of the owner's rights to his private property and his public duty to promote the comfort and enjoyment of those traveling in his conveyance.

> *Guided by those views, the court held that it is not an unreasonable regulation to seat passengers so as to preserve order and decorum, and to prevent contacts and collisions arising from natural or well-known customary repugnancies which are likely to breed disturbances, where white and colored persons are huddled together without their consent.*[22]

What is breathtakingly important is that this language sounds very similar to what will be used in the *Plessy* case almost 20 years later. In this decision, the phrase is "to prevent contacts

---

17   *Hall v. DeCuir*, p. 498.
18   Ibid., pp. 500–501.
19   Ibid.
20   Ibid.
21   Ibid., pp. 502–503.
22   Ibid., p. 503.

and collisions arising from natural or well-known repugnancies which are likely to breed distur-bances." These phrases parallel similar ones found in the 1896 *Plessy* finding, where the justices wrote, "Legislation is powerless to eradicate racial instincts." Based on these phrases, the justices appear to be endorsing the notion that the different races were not capable of sitting together because it was repugnant and led to disturbances. Their language indicates that social equality was never embraced by the justices of the Supreme Court, and as such was never going to be the norm in America for many decades, perhaps even a century. One of the historical axioms promulgated from the Reconstruction era was that the freed slaves were legally free, but socially bound—i.e., freed from the legal aspects of being purchased, chained, and bought and sold as property, but still not accepted on a social level as being coequal citizens and neighbors. It is fair to assert that this thinking, apparently enthusiastically approved by the justices of the Supreme Court, became the standard in the entire country.

Justice Clifford, in fact, quickly confronts the notion of equality. "Substantial equality of right is the law of the State and of the United States; but equality does not mean identity, as in the nature of things identity in the accommodations afforded to passengers, whether colored or white is impossible, unless our commercial marine shall undergo an entire change."[23] So, just as male passengers are never allowed a passage in the ladies' cabin, the laws of the United States do not require the master of a steamer to put persons in the same compartment who would be repulsive or disagreeable to each other.[24] Thus, according to the justice, despite the battles of the Civil War, various civil rights acts, as well as other constitutional amendments focus on equality, at the end of the day, sitting together on a steamboat traveling to a common destination would be an action best described as disagreeable and repulsive!

Clifford is not complete in his justification of this stance. He goes on to describe the situa-tion around the country involving boards of education and segregation. The first example he cites was in Ohio, where separate schools were created for black and white students. "Under that law, colored children were not admitted as a matter of right into the schools for white children, which gave rise to contest, in which the attempt was made to set aside the law as unconstitutional; but the Supreme Court of the State held that it worked no substantial inequal-ity of school privileges between the children of the two classes in the locality of the parties."[25] He concludes—again, eerily reminiscent of the *Plessy* decision 20 years in the future—"Any classification which preserves substantially equal school advantages is not prohibited by either State or Federal Constitution, nor would it contravene the provisions of either."[26]

The next case Clifford cites was rather well known, *Roberts v. City of Boston*, which had been decided by the Massachusetts Supreme Court. In this instance, separate primary schools were maintained for white and black children. Upon a legal challenge to that system by a black plaintiff, the court concluded, "Distinguished counsel insisted that the separation tended to deepen and perpetuate the odious distinction of caste; but the court responded, that they were not able to say that the decision was not founded on just grounds of reason and experience, and in the results of a discriminating and honest judgment."[27] The justice is emphatic in his thinking when he proposes that the creation of separate schools based on race is acceptable and in no way was in violation of the Fourteenth Amendment. (Refer to Figure 4-4.)

---

23 Ibid.
24 Ibid., pp. 503–504.
25 Ibid., p. 504.
26 Ibid.
27 Ibid., p. 505.

4-4: It would take generations for schools to integrate due to decisions such as those made in this case, and others, claiming that separation of children was appropriate.

After citing cases that backed his thinking, Clifford reviews and then dismisses a case decided by the Iowa Supreme Court (*Coger v. Packet Company*, 37 Iowa, 145), which was somewhat similar to this case. In that instance, a black woman had been removed from the whites-only dining room after her protestations that she was entitled to be there. "Hearing was had, and the court decided that persons of color were entitled to the same rights and privileges, when traveling, as white persons, and that they cannot be required by any rule or custom based on distinction of color or race to accept other or different accommodations than those furnished to white persons."[28] Clifford proceeds to declare that are were four reasons why this case is not applicable to that of *DeCuir*.

The third and fourth indicate the Court's understanding of the cases' differences. "3. Because the decision was rested entirely upon other and different grounds. 4. Because the facts of the two cases are widely and substantially different."[29]

As his concurrence continues, Clifford makes passing references to major laws and amendments that have been written regarding civil rights. It is apparent that his enthusiasm for these laws is limited: "Colored persons, it is admitted, are citizens."[30] The rights they enjoy are then listed by him. Interestingly, these are rights of a legal nature: "The ability to make a contract, to sue, inherit, convey real property, and to full and equal benefit of all laws and proceedings for the security of personal property, as is enjoyed by white citizens."[31] In his curt and almost cryptic listing of legal rights, no reference is made to social rights or acts of violence perpetrated against people of color. He then, in an almost condescending manner, speaks about vague references made to the Civil Rights Act and the Fourteenth Amendment. Again, his view severely limits the potency of those laws. "Enough appears in the language employed in those provisions to show that their principal object was to confer citizenship, and the rights which belong to citizens as such, upon the colored people, and in that manner to abrogate the rule previously adopted by this court in the Dred Scott case."[32] In Clifford's view, the right of Congress to regulate the enrollment and licensing of ships and vessels absolutely outweighs any injustice shown to people of color.

It is important to pause for a moment and reflect upon the larger historical events of the day. While the "official years" of the Reconstruction period were from 1865 through 1877, it is easily possible to suggest that for most Northerners, the time and energy devoted to Southern concerns was less than that. For example, in 1873, a mere eight years after the conclusion of the

28 Ibid., p. 508.
29 Ibid.
30 Ibid.
31 Ibid.
32 Ibid., p. 509.

war, a major depression gripped the country. Fueled by 25 railroads defaulting on their interest payments, the country entered a six-year period of abject depression. It was a period marked by widespread bankruptcies, chronic unemployment, and a drastic slowdown in railroad building. It is easy to postulate that for people unemployed and worried about surviving through this downturn, outrages occurring in the South would certainly not be a concern for most. The end of the Reconstruction period in 1877 concluded rather inauspiciously. A political deal was formulated between Southern Democrats and Republicans at Wormley House, a Washington hotel, based on the contested outcome of the 1876 presidential election. There it was agreed that the Democrats would support the Republican candidate, Rutherford B. Hayes, who was in a struggle with Samuel J. Tilden for congressional votes for president. In return for their support, Hayes agreed to remove federal troops from Louisiana and South Carolina. Upon his election by the House, Hayes followed through on his promise and withdrew troops from the two states, thus concluding the Reconstruction era.[33]

In some ways, it is appropriate to briefly consider how many years would have been enough for a Reconstruction period. The responses to this question run the gamut by my students at Kennesaw State University. In general, however, the replies gravitate to around a generation, at least. Most students are astute enough to realize that the transition in post–Civil War Southern society involving the reality of the former slaves becoming fully accepted citizens would take longer than eight or 12 years. With the depression of 1873 and the political deals made in 1877, it is possible to surmise, as many historians do, that most of Northern society was simply weary and anxious to end all concerns with the Civil War and move on with other issues such as new inventions, Indian wars, and the expansion of the West.

Nevertheless, it is my contention that this void of morality and concern is exactly the role that the Supreme Court must step into and embrace. The justices represent the institution that is aware of the history of slavery in America. They are aware of the provisions in the Constitution regarding slavery. They understand the significance of the three civil war amendments, as well as the various civil rights acts, whose purpose was to recalibrate American society. In the end, they do not fulfill these expectations. In fact, due to the body of decisions they made, such as *Hall v. DeCuir*, one could suggest that race relations between blacks and whites suffered greatly. (See Figure 4-5.)

Thus, in the same year that the Reconstruction period ended, 12 years after the Civil War, much of the legal foundation that the former slaves were attempting to stand on in terms of their newly won personal freedoms was being eroded and neutralized by a supremely intolerant court.

Even when the Court decided cases presumably in favor of the black community and their equal rights, the apparent victory was deceptive. In three cases decided in 1880, the rights of the former slaves, specifically regarding the Fourteenth Amendment, were scrutinized with interesting results. In *Strauder v. West Virginia*, the state of West Virginia had convicted Strauder, a black man, of murder. The case was appealed to the state supreme court, which affirmed the verdict. Strauder petitioned that the case be moved to a federal circuit court because, "By virtue of the laws of the state of West Virginia no colored man was eligible to be a member of the grand jury or to serve on a petit jury in the State; that white men are so eligible, and that by reason of his being a colored man and having been a slave, he had reason to believe, and did believe, he could not have the full and equal benefit of all laws and proceedings in the state of West Virginia for the security of his person as is enjoyed by white citizens."[34] The West Virginia

---

33   Tindall and Shi, *The Essential America*, p. 305.
34   U. S. Reports, *Strauder v. West Virginia*, p. 304.

4-5: Despite such artistic representations of Justice found in Washington, D.C., it would take almost a century, or longer, for people of color to receive a measure of justice and equality.

law in question was enacted March 12, 1873: "All white male persons who are twenty-one years of age and who are citizens of this State shall be liable to serve as jurors, except as herein provided."[35]. It is sadly interesting to note that eight years after the Civil War, states still wrote and enforced laws with such blatant racism as "all white male persons."

After briefly reviewing the Fourteenth Amendment, the Court, via Justice William Strong, gives its own interpretation of the amendment.

This is one of a series of constitutional provisions having a common purpose; namely, securing to a race recently emancipated, a race that through many generations had been held in slavery, all the civil rights that the superior race enjoy. At the time when they were incorporated into the Constitution, it required little knowledge of human nature to anticipate that those who had long been regarded as an inferior and subject race would, when suddenly raised to the rank of citizenship, be looked upon with jealousy and positive dislike, and that State laws might be enacted or enforced to perpetuate the distinctions that had before existed ... The colored race, as a race, was abject and ignorant, and in that condition was unfitted to command the respect of those who had superior intelligence. Their training had left them mere children, and as such they needed the protection which a wise government extends to those who are unable to protect themselves. They especially needed protection against unfriendly action in the States where they were resident.[36] (See Figure 4-6.)

After presenting this very condescending view of the black community 14 years after the Civil War, the Court embraces the Fourteenth Amendment and its goals. They argue that the purpose of the amendment and its accompanying enforcing legislation was "What is this but declaring that the law in the States shall be the same for the black and the white; that all persons, whether colored or white, shall stand equal before the laws of the State, and, in regard to the colored race, for whose protection the amendment was primarily designed, that no discrimination shall be made against them by law because of their color?"[37] The Court contends that the state of West Virginia was discriminatory in excluding people of color from grand and petit juries.

The very fact that colored people are singled out and expressly denied by a statute all right to participate in the administration of the law, as jurors, because of their color, though they are citizens, and may be in other respects fully qualified, is practically a brand

35 Ibid., p. 305.
36 Ibid., p. 306.
37 Ibid., p. 307.

upon them, affixed by the law, an assertion of their inferiority, and a stimulant to that race prejudice which is an impediment to securing to individuals of the race that equal justice which the law aims to secure to all others.[38]

The decision continues with the justification of the amendment and an unambivalent statement: "Any State action that denies this immunity to a colored man is in conflict with the Constitution."[39] As the decision reaches its conclusion, reference is made to legislation, specifically Section 641, whose purpose is clear from its language. This statute will figure prominently in a follow-on case also decided in the same 1879 session.

Sect. 641 is such a provision. It enacts that "when any civil suit or criminal prosecution is commenced in any State court for any cause whatsoever against any person who is denied, or cannot enforce, in the judicial tribunals of the State, or in the part of the state where such prosecution is pending, any right secured to him by any law providing for the equal civil rights of citizens of the United States, or of all persons within the jurisdiction of the United States, such suit or prosecution may, upon the petition of such defendant, filed in said State court at any time before the trial, or final hearing of the case, stating the facts, and verified by oath, be removed before trial into the next Circuit Court of the United States to be held in the district where it is pending."[40]

4-6: The title of this artwork is Justice Versus Prejudice. One can decide which concept prevailed in America.

---

38 Ibid., p. 308.
39 Ibid., p. 310.
40 Ibid., p. 311.

At the conclusion of the decision, the supreme court of West Virginia is reversed, and the case is returned to the Circuit Court of Ohio County, with instructions to reverse that decision as well.

In the second case concerning people of color serving on grand or trial (petit) juries, the Court renders a second ruling. In *Ex Parte Virginia*, J. D. Coles, a judge in Virginia in 1878, was indicted for excluding and failing to select as grand jurors and petit jurors black citizens, who were otherwise qualified for those roles. The judge argued that he should be discharged and the case dismissed, as it was unconstitutional and that the issue was one governed by the state of Virginia, not the federal government. The Court utilizes two separate acts and amendments as their legal framework on this case. First was an 1876 act entitled, "An Act to protect all citizens in their civil and legal rights."[41] The act seems fairly straightforward in its intent: "No citizen, possessing all other qualifications which are or may be prescribed by law, shall be disqualified from service as grand or petit juror in any court of the United States, or of any state, on account of race, color, or previous condition of servitude."[42] Any officer or person charged with summoning jurors who failed to summon a qualified citizen was liable to be fined $5,000.

The second legal reference is the Fourteenth Amendment, which speaks of no state depriving any person of life, liberty, or property without due process of law. The Court quickly determines that in this case, the judge was acting in an official capacity as a representative of the state, which directly conflicted with the above act and the Fourteenth Amendment. The first point made in this case, delivered by Justice William Strong, is that the Supreme Court, according to the provisions of the 1875 act, had the appropriate authority to judge this case. "And the Fifth section enacts that all cases arising under the provisions of the Act shall be reviewable by the Supreme Court of the United States."[43]

The Court then focuses on the post–Civil War Amendments and their core purpose. "To raise the colored race from that condition of inferiority and servitude in which most of them had previously stood into perfect equality of civil rights with all other persons within the jurisdiction of the states. They were intended to take away all possibility of oppression by law because of race or color."[44] The Court reiterates its support for the Fourteenth Amendment and the Act of 1875 as it offers a direct response to the contention of Judge Coles, that this is a state and not a federal issue. "We do not perceive how holding an office within a state, and claiming to act for the state, can relieve the holder from obligation to obey the Constitution of the United States, or take away the power of congress to punish his disobedience ... Upon the whole, as we are of [the] opinion that the act of Congress upon which the indictment against the petitioner was founded is constitutional, and that he is correctly held to answer it, and, as therefore no object would be secured by issuing a writ of habeas corpus, the petitions are denied."[45]

Justices Field and Clifford offer a minority dissenting opinion. They suggest that the 1875 act regarding the choosing of jurors is unconstitutional. They also believe that the actions of Judge Coles in his choosing of eligible jurors are acceptable under the law. "Although he may have exercised at all times his best judgment in the selection of qualified persons, unless he could prove what in most cases would be impossible—that in a county of many thousand inhabitants, there

---

41   http://supreme.justia.com/cases, *Ex Parte Virginia*, p. 2.
42   Ibid.
43   Ibid., p. 4.
44   Ibid., p. 7.
45   Ibid., p. 9.

was not a colored person qualified to serve as a juror," their final point being that the disposition of the entire case was a state, not a federal, issue. "But the control of matters of purely local concern, not coming within the scope of the powers granted or the restraints mentioned, was left where it has always existed—with the States."[46]

Justice Nelson offers a separate dissent, where he strongly disagrees with the majority opinion. He reinforces the point made above about the relationship between the federal and state powers: "I cannot think I am mistaken in saying that a change so radical in the relation between the Federal and State authorities as would justify legislation interfering with the independent action of the different departments of the State governments in all matters over which the States retain jurisdiction was never contemplated by the recent amendments."[47]

The justice continues to make a distinction between the various rights that the black community is entitled to experience.

> *Civil rights are absolute and personal. Political rights, on the other hand, are conditioned and dependent upon the discretion of the elective or appointing power, whether that be the people acting through the ballot or one of the departments of their government. The civil rights of the individual are never to be withheld, and may be always judicially enforced. The political rights which he may enjoy, such as holding office and discharging a public trust, are qualified because their possession depends on his fitness, to be adjudged by those whom society has clothed with the elective authority.* "[48]

The justice feels quite strongly that the consequences of the Court's decision are quite harmful for the viability of the states. "The proceeding is a gross offence to the state; it is an attack upon her sovereignty in matters over which she has never surrendered her jurisdiction. The doctrine which sustains it, carried to its logical results, would degrade and sink her to the level of a mere local municipal corporation."[49]

It seems the Supreme Court has made two major decisions that bolster the legal rights of the black community. In the *Strauder* and *Ex Parte Virginia* cases, the Court's main criterion appeared to be the blatancy of the state offenses. In the first case, the state law—still in effect years after the Civil War—clearly was discriminatory in identifying only whites as grand jurors. In the *Ex Parte* case, a judge had systematically excluded all potential jurors of color. From the outcomes of these two decisions, one might conclude that the Court was beginning to support the aspirations of the black community, albeit in this limited arena, of being called as jurors for trials. This was not to be the case. In one day, three decisions were offered by the Court. The final one was *Virginia v. Rives*. (Refer to Figure 4-7.)

This case is fairly straightforward; Burwell Reynolds and Lee Reynolds, two men of color, were indicted for murder in Patrick County, Virginia. The case was removed into the circuit court of the state and brought for trial. At that stage, the defendants petitioned the court that the venire (the process by which jurors are summoned to try a case) be modified so as to allow one-third of the jury to be composed of black men. This motion was overruled, on the grounds that the court had no authority to change the venire, as the court was satisfied that the venire had been drawn from the jury pool, according to law. Before the trial, Burwell and Lee Reynolds filed a

---

46   Ibid., p. 17.
47   Ibid., p. 22.
48   Ibid., p. 27.
49   Ibid., p. 29.

4-7: The goal of black citizens was to have representation on such juries as this 1914 one.

petition requesting that their case be moved to the Circuit Court of the United States for the Western District of Virginia. The petition made a very compelling presentation. The two men were 17 and 19 years old. They were charged with murdering a white man. The Reynolds Brothers' basic argument was that the grand jurors who had voted an indictment against them, as well as the jurors summoned to try them, were white. They also wrote in their petition that they had appealed to the judge of the court and the prosecuting attorney that a portion of the jury should be composed of black jurors. This request was denied. They also alleged that a strong prejudice existed in the local county against them, and they were certain that they would not be able to obtain a fair trail.[50]

Burwell and Lee Reynolds further noted in their petition that people of color had never been allowed to serve as jurors, either in criminal or civil cases in Patrick County. The state court denied their request, and they were convicted. The verdicts were set aside, and they were retried. One was convicted, and in the other case, the jury disagreed about guilt. At this point in the process, the circuit court ordered that a United States marshal take the defendants from Patrick County custody to that of the circuit court. The Commonwealth of Virginia applied to the U.S. Supreme Court to issue a writ of mandamus, literally "we command" (an extraordinary writ issued from a court to an official, compelling performance of an act that the law recognizes as an absolute duty) to the judge of the Western District Court, Alexander Rives, to cause him to have the men retransferred back to Virginia. The questions before the Court are whether or not the case should be held under the auspices of the state or the federal circuit court, and did the case meet the criteria set forth in Section 641 of the Revised Statutes, as noted previously, regarding these legal rights. The law seems clear,

> *When any civil suit or prosecution is commenced in any state court, for any cause what-soever, against any person who is denied or cannot enforce in the judicial tribunals of the State, or in the part of the State where such suit or prosecution is pending, any right secured to him by any law providing for the equal civil rights of citizens of the United States.*[51]

The High Court decided to adjudicate the case. First, it spends some time clarifying and qualifying the legal situation and offering some context for the Fourteenth Amendment and its accompanying legislation. "The plain object of these statutes, as of the Constitution which authorized them, was to place the colored race, in respect of civil rights, upon a level with whites. They made the rights and responsibilities, civil and criminal, of the two races exactly the same."[52] One qualifying judgment which figured prominently in the civil rights cases yet to

---

50   http://supreme.justia.com/cases, *Virginia v. Rives*, p. 3.
51   Ibid., p. 4.
52   Ibid.

be decided was the concept well established by the Court that the amendment is directly against state actions, not individual ones. "Sect. 641 was also intended for their protection against State action and against that alone."[53] After they agree that there were cases where moving them from the state to the federal level was justified, the Court makes an important distinction.

> But it is still a question whether the remedy of removal of cases from State courts into the courts of the United States, given by sect. 641, applies to all cases in which equal protection of the laws may be denied to a defendant. And clearly it does not ... The statute authorizes a removal of the case only before trial, not after the trial has commenced. It does not, therefore, embrace many cases in which a colored man's right may be denied. It does not embrace a case in which a right may be denied by judicial action during the trial, or by discrimination against him in the sentence, or in the mode of executing the sentence.[54]

The justices continue to give a very convoluted explanation about when someone's rights might be violated. "But the violation of the constitutional provisions, when made by the judicial tribunals of a State, may be, and generally will be, after the trial has commenced. It is then, during or after the trial that denials of a defendant's right by judicial tribunals occur. Not often until then. Nor can the defendant know until then that the equal protection of the laws will not be extended to him. Certainly until then he cannot affirm that it is denied, or that he cannot enforce it, in the judicial tribunals."[55]

The justices go on to expound that, prior to a case, even though a person feels that their rights are being violated, they have no recourse, because, "When he has only an apprehension that such rights will be withheld from him when his case shall come to trial, he cannot affirm that they are actually denied, or that he cannot enforce them.[56] There must be verifiable facts before someone can complain of mistreatment. The Court limits the scope of the legislation of Section 641 by stating, "The statute was not, therefore, intended as a corrective of errors or wrongs committed by judicial tribunals in the administration of the law at the trial."[57]

Astonishingly, as the decision nears its end, the justices balance this decision with that of *Strauder* given in the same term.

> Now, conceding as we do, and as we endeavored to maintain in the case of Strauder v. West Virginia, that discrimination by law against the colored race, because of their color, in the selection of jurors, is a denial of the equal protection of the laws to a negro when he is put upon trial for an alleged criminal offence against a State, the laws of Virginia make no such discrimination. If, as was alleged in the argument, though it does not appear in the petition or record, the officer to whom was entrusted the selection of the persons from whom the juries for the indictment and the trial of the petitioners were drawn, disregarding the statute of the State, confined his selection to white persons, and refused to select any persons of the colored race, solely because of their color, his action was a gross violation of the spirit of the State's laws, as well as the act of Congress of March 1, 1875, which

---

53 Ibid., p. 5.
54 Ibid.
55 Ibid.
56 Ibid., p. 6.
57 Ibid.

prohibits and punishes such discrimination. He made himself liable to punishment at the instance of the state and under the laws of the United States. In one sense, indeed, his act was the act of the state, and was prohibited by the constitutional amendment. But inasmuch as it was a criminal misuse of the State law, it cannot be said to have been a "denial or disability to enforce on the judicial tribunals of the State" the rights of the colored men, as is contemplated by the removal act. Sect 641. It has to be observed that act gives the right of removal only to a person "who is denied, or cannot enforce, in the judicial tribunals of the State his equal civil rights." And this is to appear before trial. When a statute of the State denies his right, or interposes a bar to his enforcing it, in the judicial tribunals, the presumption is fair that they will be controlled by it in their decisions; and in such a case a defendant may affirm on oath what is necessary for a removal. Such a case is clearly within the provisions of Sect. 641. But when a subordinate officer of the state, in violation of State law, undertakes to deprive an accused party of a right which the statute law accords to him, it can hardly be said that he is denied, or cannot enforce, "in the judicial tribunals of the State" the rights which belong to him. In such a case it ought to be presumed the court will redress the wrong. If the accused is deprived of the right, the final and practical denial will be in the judicial tribunal which tries the case, after the trial has commenced. If, as in this case, the subordinate officer whose duty it is to select jurors fails to discharge that duty in the true spirit of the law; if he excludes all colored men solely because they are colored; or if the sheriff to whom a venire is given, composed of both white and colored citizens, neglects to summon the colored jurors only because they are colored; or if a clerk whose duty it is to take the twelve names from the box rejects all the colored jurors for the same reason,—it can with no propriety be said that the defendant's right is denied by the state and cannot be enforced in the judicial tribunals. The court will correct the wrong, will quash the indictment or the panel, or, if not, the error will be corrected in a superior court. We cannot think such cases are within the provisions of sect. 641. Denials of equal rights in the action of the judicial tribunals of the state are left to the revisory powers of this court.[58] *(Refer to Figure 4-8.)*

The above text reads like a blueprint for the subsequent denial of rights to men of color, with the apparent blessing of the nation's highest court. The justices continue this theme about denials of defendants' rights with more explicitness.

The assertions in the petition for removal, that the grand jury by which the petitioners were indicted, as well as the jury summoned to try them, were composed wholly of the white race, and that their race had never been allowed to serve as jurors in the County of Patrick in any case in which a colored man was interested, fall short of showing that any civil right was denied or that there had been any discrimination against the defendants because of their color or race ... Nor did the refusal of the court and of the counsel for the prosecution to allow a modification of the venire, by which one-third of the jury, or a portion of it, should be composed of persons of the petitioners own race, amount to any denial of a right secured to them by any law providing for the equal civil rights of citizens of the United States ... was not a right given or secured to them, or to any person, by the law of the State, or by an act of Congress, or by the Fourteenth Amendment of the Constitution. It is a right to which every colored man is entitled that, in the selection of jurors to pass upon his life,

---

58   Ibid., pp. 6–7.

liberty, or property, there shall be no exclusion of his race, and no discrimination against them because of their color. But this is a different thing from the right which is asserted was denied to the petitioners by the state court, viz., a right to have the jury composed in part of colored men. A mixed jury in a particular case is not essential to the equal protection of the laws, and the right to it is not given by any law of Virginia or by any Federal status. It is not, therefore, guaranteed by the Fourteenth Amendment, or within the purview of sect. 641.[59]

4-8: This jail cell symbolizes the fears of generations of black citizens: They would not receive a fair trial or justice in America.

Based on this very lengthy, convoluted, and almost tortured explanation (which almost provides a detailed formula for the legal denial of rights for black voters), the Court concludes that the circuit court has no authority to hold the men in question and that they should be remanded back to the state to carry out their sentence. Furthermore, any errors regarding possible denial of equal rights are to be dealt with by higher courts. The *Rives* decision, publicly given at the same time as the *Strauder* and *Ex Parte* ones, seems to have a very apparent meaning to those interested in severely limiting the political participation of the black community in criminal and civil trials: Don't be so blatant as to have state-sanctioned discrimination, but beyond that, the right of blacks to have fellow blacks on their juries was nothing for states to concern themselves with. Not only that, but the proving of an injustice had to occur *before* the trial commenced, not during or after. What an astoundingly difficult process to achieve justice!

As time passed, it is significant to point out the nexus between the decisions of the Court and the increasingly violent reality for many blacks on the ground. One of my primary premises is that this linkage has been ignored historically. The following case, *United States v. Harris*, decided in 1883, aptly illustrates this phenomenon. In 1876, the Circuit Court of the United

---

59   Ibid., p. 7.

4-9: This photograph illustrates the large broad-based community support that organizations devoted to violence, such as the Klan, enjoyed at these times. Law enforcement, often supportive of such groups, were unwilling or unable to maintain law and order.

States for the Western District of Tennessee returned an indictment against R. G. Harris and 19 others. Harris led an armed lynch mob into a Tennessee jail and captured four black prisoners. A deputy sheriff on duty unsuccessfully attempted to protect the prisoners. One of the prisoners, P. M. Wells, died as a result of this action. The United States government brought criminal charges against Harris and others under Section 2 of the 1871 Force Act, also known as the Ku Klux Klan Act (previously mentioned in a Chapter 3). It is worthwhile to review the law in question. (See Figure 4-9.)

That if two or more persons shall band or conspire together, or go in disguise upon the public highway, or upon the premises of another, with intent to violate any provision of this act, or to injure, oppress, threaten, or intimidate any citizen with intent to prevent or hinder his free exercise and enjoyment of any right or privilege granted or secured to him by the Constitution or laws of the United States, or because of his having exercised the same, such persons shall be held guilty of felony, and, on conviction thereof, shall be fined or imprisoned, or both, at the discretion of the court, the fine not to exceed five thousand dollars, and the imprisonment not to exceed ten years.[60]

The defendants made an argument that was becoming a familiar refrain for the High Court. Harris and the others contended that the indictment against them was unconstitutional and not within the jurisdiction of the federal courts, and should be solely handled by the state's justice systems. When circuit court and district court judges were unable to decide the merits of this question, it was referred to the Supreme Court. Justice William B. Woods delivered the opinion of the Court. First, he deals with the technical question of whether the Court is the appropriate legal venue to decide this case. The Court affirms that it is. Justice Woods writes, "There are only four paragraphs in the Constitution which can in the remotest degree have any reference to the question in hand. These are Section 2 of Article IV of the original Constitution and the Thirteenth, Fourteenth and Fifteenth Amendments."[61] These are to be considered in inverse order.

As these four paragraphs are considered, the importance of cases covered in previous chapters will be readily apparent. According to Justice Woods, the Fifteenth Amendment has no relevancy to this case, as the Court decided in the *United States v. Reese* and *United States v. Cruikshank* cases, that the amendment "Does not confer the right of suffrage on anyone. It merely invests

60   Barrett and Cohen, *Constitutional Law*, p. 1049.
61   http://supreme.justia.com/us, *United States v. Harris*, p. 6.

citizens with the constitutional right of exemption from discrimination in the enjoyment of the elective franchise on account of race, color, or previous condition of servitude."[62]

In a similar finding, the justice continues to assert that the Fourteenth Amendment, which speaks of equal protection of the laws, is not relevant in this instance.

> *It is a guarantee of protection against the acts of the state government itself. It is a guarantee against the exertion of arbitrary and tyrannical power on the part of the government and legislature of the state, not a guarantee against the commission of individual offenses, and the power of Congress, whether express or implied, to legislate for the enforcement of such a guarantee does not extend to the passage of laws for the suppression of crime within the states ...*
>
> *The duty of protecting all its citizens in the enjoyment of an equality of rights was originally assumed by the states, and it remains there. The only obligation resting upon the United States is to see that the states do not deny the right. This the Amendment guarantees, and no more. The power of the national government is limited to this guarantee."[63]*

Justice Woods proceeds to affirm that the state of Tennessee was not at fault in that the brutal offenses in this case were the result of individuals, not an officially sanctioned state action. The next point of law concerns the Thirteenth Amendment and its enforcement through the Sections of the Enforcement Act of 1871.

> *Even if the amendment is held to be directed against the action of private individuals as well as against the action of the States and United States, the law under consideration covers cases both within and without the provisions of the amendment. It covers any conspiracy between two free white men against another free white man to deprive the latter of any right accorded him by the laws of the state or of the United States. A law under which two or more free white private citizens could be punished for conspiring or going in disguise for the purpose of depriving another free white citizen of a right accorded by the law of the state to all classes of persons—as, for instance, the right to make a contract, bring a suit, or give evidence—clearly cannot be authorized by the amendment which simply prohibits slavery and involuntary servitude. Those provisions of the law, which are broader than is warranted by the article of the Constitution by which they are supposed to be authorized, cannot be sustained."[64]*

As the decision proceeds, the potency of the Thirteenth Amendment receives more discussion. It is acknowledged that private citizens can conspire together and by violence, arson, assault, and murder, deprive others of the equal protection of the laws. This is, of course, exactly what had happened in this case. But according to the Court's logic, "We should by virtue of the Amendment (13th) accord to Congress the power to punish every crime by which the right of any person to life, property, or reputation is invaded. Thus, under a provision of the Constitution which simply abolished slavery and involuntary servitude, we should, with few

---

62 Ibid.
63 Ibid., p. 7.
64 Ibid., p. 9.

exceptions, invest Congress with power over the whole catalogue of crimes. A construction of the amendment which leads to such a result is clearly unsound."[65]

The final item, which is fairly quickly dispensed with, is the second section of Article IV of the Constitution: "The citizens of each state shall be entitled to all the privileges and immunities of citizens of the several states." The point of reference for this article is the *Slaughterhouse Cases*, in which the Court deemed that it

> *did not create those rights which it called privileges and immunities of citizens of the states. It threw around them in that clause no security for the citizen of the state in which they were claimed or exercised. Nor did it profess to control the power of the state govern-ments over its citizens. Its sole purpose was to declare to the several states that whatever those rights, as you grant or establish them to your own citizens, or as you limit or qualify or impose restrictions on their exercises, the same, neither more nor less, shall be the measure of the rights of citizens of other states within your jurisdiction.*
>
> *It was never supposed that the section under consideration conferred on Congress the power to enact a law which would punish a private citizen for an invasion of the rights of his fellow citizen conferred by the State of which they were both residents on all its citizens alike."*[66]

The finding concludes rather tersely that the original disagreement about the enforcement acts being applicable in this case is not a valid argument. Interestingly, no dissent is given in this case. The structure and meaning of this decision, especially the latter half, is overwhelming. By 1883, the justices of the Supreme Court—in a case where a mob entered a jail, attacked a local sheriff, and proceeded to brutally attack, maim, and even kill men of color—decide that these men were not protected by the three post–Civil War amendments, the laws which ac-companied them, and even by an article in the Constitution. The formula repeated throughout these decades is that the responsibility for justice was to come from the states. The only problem, of course, is that the violence and killing originated from those very states. It is apparent that the direction the Court is offering to those thinking about violence is to proceed, as there is very little that the federal government will do to help the besieged black community.

In the same year that the *Harris* case was decided, 1883, another significant case was decided that once again was not in favor of the black community. This continuing erosion of rights accelerated greatly when the Court decided the case, known as the Civil Rights Cases, in 1883. A number of instances alleging prejudice in various public settings were brought to the Court for final decision.

These cases dealt with discrimination that was easily recognizable. They were based on the Civil Rights Act of 1875 (noted previously). The first two sections of the act seem explicitly clear,

> *Section 1. That all persons within the jurisdiction of the United States shall be entitled to the full and equal enjoyment of the accommodations, advantages, facilities, and privileges of inns, public conveyances on land or water, theaters, and other places of public amusement; subject only to the conditions and limitations established by law, and*

---

65   Ibid., p. 10.
66   Ibid.

applicable alike to citizens of every race and color, regardless of any previous condition of servitude.

Section 2. That any person who shall violate the forgoing section by denying to any citizen, except for reasons by law applicable to citizens of every race and color, and regardless of any previous condition of servitude, the full enjoyment of any of the accommodations, advantages, facilities, or privileges in said section enumerated, or by aiding or inciting such denial, shall for every such offence forfeit and pay the sum of five hundred dollars to the person aggrieved thereby, to be recovered in an action of debt, with full costs; and shall also, for every offence, be deemed guilty of a misdemeanor, and, upon conviction there of, shall be fined not less than five hundred nor more than one thousand dollars, or shall be imprisoned not less than thirty days not more than one year: Provided, That all persons may elect to sue for the penalty aforesaid, or to proceed under their rights at common law and by State statutes; and having so elected to proceed in the one mode or the other, their right to proceed in the other jurisdiction shall be barred. But this provision shall not apply to criminal proceedings, either under this act or the criminal law of any State: And provided further, that a judgment for the penalty in favor of the party aggrieved, or a judgment upon an indictment, shall be a bar to either prosecution respectively.[67]

Civil Rights Cases

Under this act, real-life instances of discrimination were brought to the courts for justice. In two of the cases, people of color were denied entry into inns and hotels. In another case, a person was denied entrance into a theater based on his skin color, while in a parallel incident, a person was not allowed to enter the Grand Opera House in New York City. In a final case, a man's wife, who was black, was prevented by the train conductor to sit in the ladies' car on a train. The legal enormity of these cases cannot be overstated. (Refer to Figure 4-10.)

These cases reflect a minute fraction of the daily and ongoing acts of discrimination that people of color were experiencing, albeit almost 20 years removed from the end of the Civil War. Once again, Congress had passed a law which seemed extraordinarily explicit, both in its purpose and penalties. The Court's findings about these cases would have enormous and immediate impact on the lives of almost every American, and quite possibly could be seen as preparing the legal foundations for the subsequent Jim Crow period.

The reasons against the discrimination are many—the

4-10: The inability or unwillingness of the High Court in the late 1800s to integrate public venues such as theaters, led to separate facilities such as this 1939 movie theater in Waco, Texas.

---

67   United States Reports, *Civil Rights Cases*, p. 9.

Thirteenth and Fourteenth amendments, as well as the Civil Rights Act of 1875, quoted above. The solicitor general of the United States argues that these acts of discrimination violated the Thirteenth and Fourteenth amendments. He further argues that the right of locomotion is a personal liberty, and that when people are deprived of this liberty, it is a federal issue. "Restraint upon the right of locomotion was a well known feature of the slavery abolished by the Thirteenth Amendment. A first requite of the right to appropriate the use of another man was to become the master of his natural power of motion, and, by a mayhem therein of the common law to require the whole community to be on the alert to restrain that power."[68] He ends with an obvious conclusion based on the 1875 act: "Therefore, the above act of 1875, in prohibiting persons from violating the rights of other persons to the full and equal enjoyment of the accommodations of inns and public conveyances, for any reason turning merely upon the race or color of the latter, partakes of the specific character of certain contemporaneous solemn and effective action by the United states to which it was a sequel—and is constitutional."[69]

William Randolph, a lawyer for some of the plaintiffs in the *Civil Rights Cases*, added his arguments to the Court. He begins with a powerful premise. Where the Constitution guarantees a right, Congress is empowered to pass the legislation appropriate to give effect to that right. The lawyer asserts that governments may regulate the conduct of its citizens toward each other, and that when an owner of property devotes his property to a use in which the public has an interest, such as a ferry or an inn, which are utilized by the public, it is then appropriate for these public-type facilities to be regulated for the common good.

Justice Joseph P. Bradley delivers the Court's finding and immediately presents the issue in the following manner: "It is obvious that the primary and important question in all the cases is the constitutionality of the law: for if the law is unconstitutional none of the prosecutions can stand."[70] So, rather quickly, the foundation of the law itself is questioned. As part of their examination, the Court turns to a review of the Fourteenth Amendment. The first response of the justice is to address the strength of the amendment. After reviewing it, Justice Bradley acknowledges that, while the Congress has the constitutional imperative to pass such laws, it is the ultimate responsibility of the High Court to make an independent judgment about its validity.

The amendment reads, "No State shall make or enforce any law which shall abridge the privileges or immunities of citizens of the United States; nor shall any State deprive any person of life, liberty, or property without due process of law; nor deny to any person within its jurisdiction the equal protection of the laws." Immediately, a major restriction of the amendment is made: "It is State action of a particular character that is prohibited. Individual invasion of individual rights is not the subject-matter of the amendment."[71] The focus of this interpretation becomes apparent. "It does not authorize Congress to create a code of municipal law for the regulation of private rights; but to provide modes of redress against the operation of State laws, and the action of State officers executive or judicial, when these are subversive of the fundamental rights specified in the amendment."[72] In the following pages, this distinction between state and private rights is made in a very strong manner.

---

68   Ibid., p. 7.
69   Ibid., p. 8.
70   Ibid., p. 9.
71   Ibid., p. 11.
72   Ibid.

An inspection of the law shows that it makes no reference whatever to any supposed or apprehended violation of the Fourteenth Amendment on the part of the states. It is not predicated on any such view. It proceeds ex directo to declare that certain acts committed by individuals shall be deemed offences, and shall be prosecuted and punished by proceedings in the courts of the United States. It does not profess to be corrective of any constitutional wrong committed by the States; it does not make its operation to depend upon any such wrong committed. It applies equally to cases arising in the States which have the justest laws respecting the personal rights of citizens, and whose authorities are ever ready to enforce such laws, as to those which arise in States that may have violated the prohibition of the amendment. In other words, it steps into the domain of local jurisprudence, and lays down rules for the conduct of individuals in society toward each other, and imposes sanctions for the enforcement of those rules, without referring in any manner to any supposed action of the State or its authorities."[73]

To press this argument further, that this issue was one of local authority, and not within the purview of the Congress to override local authorities, the justice proceeds, "It is repugnant to the Tenth Amendment of the Constitution, which declares that powers not delegated to the United States by the Constitution, nor prohibited by it to the States, are reserved to the States respectively or to the people."[74]

Justice Bradley then emphatically makes a clear distinction between the acts of individuals and the actions of a state government: "The wrongful act of an individual, unsupported by any such authority, is simply a private wrong, or a crime of that individual: an invasion of the rights of the injured party, it is true, whether they affect his person, his property, or his reputation; but if not sanctioned in some way by the state, or not done under State authority, his rights remain in full force, and may presumably be vindicated by resort to the laws of the State for redress."[75]

So, despite the detailed and expressly written language of the amendment, the ruling by the justices greatly limits the power of the amendment. Even while they acknowledge the damaging effects of such prejudice, they will not hold individuals responsible for such actions.

The decision then proceeds to reiterate the notion that Congress does not possess the legal authority to pass the amendment if it will supersede state authority. At this juncture, the justices pose a provocative question.

We have discussed the question presented by the law on the assumption that a right to enjoy equal accommodation and privileges in all inns, public conveyances, and places of public amusement, is one of the essential rights of the citizen which no State can abridge or interfere with. Whether it is such a right, or not, is a different question which, in the view we have taken of the validity of the law on the ground already stated, it is not necessary to examine.[76]

---

73 Ibid., p. 14.
74 Ibid., p. 15.
75 Ibid., p. 17.
76 Ibid., p. 21.

The justices now proceed to discuss this case from the perspective of the Thirteenth Amendment. An issue arises in the course of the deliberations that denial to an inn or theater equaled a form of slavery or a badge of servitude, which was banned by the amendment. The justices do not believe there are connections between slavery or servitude and being denied entry into an establishment.

But is there any similarity between such servitudes and a denial by the owner of an inn, a public conveyance, or a theatre, of its accommodations and privileges to an individual, even though the denial be founded on the race or color of an individual? Where does any slavery or servitude, or badge of either, arise from such an act of denial? Whether it might be a denial of a right which, if sanctioned by state law, would be obnoxious to the prohibitions of the Fourteenth Amendment, is another question. But what has it to do with the question of slavery?[77]

4-11: In his "Letter from a Birmingham Jail," Martin Luther King Jr. wrote about traveling in his car and having to sleep in it because, "... no motel will accept you; when you are humiliated day in and day out by nagging signs reading 'white' and 'colored'; when your first name becomes 'nigger,' and your middle name becomes 'boy' (however old you are)."

The Court then gives a very surprising and somewhat incredible interpretation of the Black Codes, which arose after the Civil War in the South. "It may be that by the Black Code (as it was called) in the times when slavery prevailed, the proprietors of inns and public conveyances were forbidden to receive persons of the African race, because it might assist slaves to escape from the control of their masters. This was merely a means of preventing such escapes, and was no part of the servitude itself."[78] (Refer to Figure 4-11.)

Now the Court goes on to give a fascinatingly limited view of what the cessation of slavery meant. First, they defined slavery in fairly mild terms: "The long existence of African slavery in this country gave us very distinct notions of what it was, and what were its necessary incidents. Compulsory service of the slave for the benefit of the master, restraint of his movements except by the master's will, disability to hold property and more."[79]

The Court continues by offering its version of the rights that the former slaves were entitled to as a result of Congress passing the Thirteenth Amendment and the Civil Rights Act of 1866. "Those fundamental rights which

---

77   Ibid.
78   Ibid., pp. 21–22.
79   Ibid., p. 22.

are the essence of civil freedom, namely, the same right to make and enforce contracts, to sue, be parties, give evidence, and to inherit, purchase, lease, sell, and convey property, as is enjoyed by white citizens."[80] It is significant to note how narrowly the Court chooses to define the newly won rights of the former slaves. What they see as the definition of freedom was clearly different from what the slaves themselves envisioned. To clarify this very point, Justice Bradley continues, "Congress did not assume, under the authority given by the thirteenth amendment, to adjust what may be called the social rights of men and races in the community; but only to declare and vindicate those fundamental rights which appertain to the essence of citizenship, and the enjoyment or deprivation of which constitutes the essential distinction between freedom and slavery."[81]

What the Court, of course, neglects to mention is the subsequent Fourteenth and Fifteenth amendments and the many laws passed by Congress to make the lives of the former slaves as equal as possible for all citizens. What is chilling about their definition of slavery is that by this time, the Civil War had been over for almost 20 years, but the view of the justices toward the former slaves or the generation born from them is nothing even close to social equality. By making these distinctions, the justices are able to help foster and maintain a belief that the laws and definition of freedom will not be applied equally and fairly to all Americans. Sadly, the Court remains steadfast in making this kind of separation a part of the fabric of America for decades.

Once again, near the conclusion of its decision, the Court raises the issue of the nature of discrimination. "Can the act of a mere individual, the owner of the inn, the public conveyance or place of amusement, refusing the accommodation, be justly regarded as imposing any badge of slavery or servitude upon the applicant, or only as inflicting an ordinary civil injury, properly cognizable by the laws of the State, and presumably subject to redress by those laws until the contrary appears? ... we are forced to the conclusion that such an act of refusal has nothing to do with slavery or involuntary servitude, and that if it is violative of any right of the party, his redress is to be sought under the laws of the State."[82] (Refer to Figure 4-12.)

In fact, this prejudice stood until the 1964 case of *Heart of Atlanta Motel v. United States* (379 US 241), when the Court found that Title II of the Civil Rights Act of 1964, which forbade racial discrimination in places of public accommodation that affected commerce, was constitutional. The Court held that the Commerce Clause allowed Congress to regulate local incidents of commerce ... The Court concluded that places of

4-12: The unfortunate social response to the 1883 rulings was the creation of separate existences, on many levels, for white and black Americans.

80 Ibid.
81 Ibid., p. 24.
82 Ibid., p. 27.

public accommodation had no "right" to select guests as they saw fit, free from governmental regulation.[83]

In effect, what the 19th century justices are recommending is that people who have suffered discrimination in various localities utilize the justice system of those same places for any legal remedies. In fact, they advance this argument further, by suggesting that it would be "running the slavery argument into the ground," to look at every act of discrimination as one related to slavery. Indeed, near the conclusion of the decision, the justices almost appear to indicate that there will not be full equality regarding people of color for some time to come. The Court writes about the thousands of free blacks who lived in America prior to the end of slavery.

> *There were thousands of free colored people in this country before the abolition of slavery, enjoying all the essential rights of life, liberty, and property the same as white citizens; yet no one, at that time, thought that it was any invasion of his personal status as a freeman because he was not admitted to all the privileges enjoyed by white citizens, or because he was subjected to discriminations in the enjoyment of accommodations in inns, public conveyances and places of amusement. Mere discriminations on account of race and color were not regarded as badges of slavery.[84]*

Thus, by these words, the Court acknowledges prejudice of the past—even for free blacks—as their standard. There is no apparent move to find full social equality anywhere or any time soon. In effect, if life with some legal freedoms was good enough for these already free blacks, it should be good enough now. It is significant that this attitude of blacks not being perceived as full equals in American society would contaminate the whole arena of race relations in our country. It is on this sad note of twisted history that the majority opinion ends.

Justice John Marshall Harlan offers an impassioned and extensive dissent to the Court's findings. While his opinion did not affect the outcome, it is offered as a historical perspective to these cases. He essentially challenges all the assertions of his fellow justices. For example, he believed that in passing the civil rights act, Congress had a specific purpose: "To prevent race discrimination in respect of the accommodations and facilities of inns, public conveyances, and places of public amusement."[85] In a brilliant strategy, turning the arguments of his fellow justices completely around, Harlan lists the many cases involving slavery such as the 1793 Fugitive Slave Law and the decision in *Prigg v. Commonwealth of Pennsylvania*, where the Court decided that the national government has the right and authority to act in the individual states to fulfill a constitutional clause regarding slaves. He then proceeds to detail the Fugitive Slave Act of 1850, which also empowered the national government to enforce the rights of the slave owners. "They placed at the disposal of the master seeking to recover his fugitive slave, substantially the whole power of the nation."[86] His logic is impeccable; if the government could enforce these laws in favor of slavery, it could certainly act now with the same authority to eradicate it and its practices.

Next, Justice Harlan reviews the racial theories expressed by Justice Taney almost 30 years earlier in the *Dred Scott* case. He repeats the conclusions reached in that case: "They had been for more than a century before been regarded as beings of an inferior race, and altogether unfit

---

83   http://oyez.org, *Heart of Atlanta Motel v. United States.*
84   Ibid., p. 27. (Pagination is somewhat out of order at this point in the decision)
85   Ibid., p. 24.
86   Ibid., p. 30.

to associate with the white race, either in social or political relations, and so far inferior that they had no rights which the white man was bound to respect, and that the negro might justly and lawfully be reduced to slavery for his benefit."[87] He believes that "The national government has the power, whether expressly given or not, to secure and protect rights conferred or guaranteed by the Constitution."[88] He reiterates this idea: "Congress, therefore, under its express power to enforce that amendment [the Thirteenth], by appropriate legislation, may enact laws to protect that people against deprivation, because of their race, of any civil rights granted to other freemen in the same State; and such legislation may be of a direct and primary character, operating upon States, their officers and agents, and, also, at least, such individuals and corporations as exercise public functions and world power and authority under the State."[89]

Next, in a detailed and penetratingly insightful manner, Harlan directly addresses the real-world issues of discrimination and the legal rights of people of color on public conveyances, inns, and places of public amusement. First, he mentions travel on land and water. His interpretation is that these institutions are state functionaries. "In Olcott v. Supervisors, 16 Wall 678, it was ruled that railroads are public highways, established by authority of the state for public use; that they are none the less public highways, because controlled and owned by private corporations; That it is a part of the function of government to make and maintain highways for the convenience of the public; that no matter who is the agent, or what is the agency, the function performed is that of the State."[90] Harlan concludes, "Such being the relations these corporations hold to the public it would seem that the right of a colored person to use an improved public highway, upon the terms accorded to freemen of other races, is as fundamental, in the state of freedom established in this country, as are any of the rights which my brethren concede to be so far fundamental as to be deemed the essence of civil freedom."[91]

The next area he examines is the Fourteenth Amendment. It is crystal clear to Harlan that the provisions of the amendment, which call upon Congress to enforce by appropriate legislation the provisions of the article, are absolutely in order. He then addresses the question of the rights of the former slaves in the context of the Fourteenth Amendment and the Constitution. His passion is apparent, as are his beliefs.

First, Harlan examines the opening words of the amendment. "'All persons born or naturalized in the United States, and of the State wherein they reside'—is of a distinctly affirmative character … It introduced all of that race, whose ancestors had been imported and sold as slaves at once, into the political community known as the 'People of the United States.' They became, instantly, citizens of the United States, and of their respective states. Further, they were brought by this supreme act of the nation, within the direct operation of that provision of the Constitution which declares that 'the citizens of each State shall be entitled to all privileges and immunities of citizens in the several states.'"[92]

The primary question asked by Justice Harlan is, what rights or privileges do people of color have as citizens in the states in which they reside? In his opinion, it is the role of Congress to expand its authority to ensure that all citizens are treated equally in whatever state they live. He then repeats an argument previously made. If the fugitive slave laws were legitimate powers

---

87 Ibid., p. 31.
88 Ibid., p. 34.
89 Ibid., pp. 36.
90 Ibid., pp.37-38.
91 Ibid., p. 39.
92 Ibid., p. 46.

recognized by the Constitution, why he asked, should the hands of Congress now be tied in inaction?

He continued his line of reasoning: "It was perfectly well known that the great danger to the equal enjoyment of their rights, as citizens, as to be apprehended not altogether from unfriendly State legislation, but from the hostile action of corporations and individuals in the States. If the rights intended to be secured by the act of 1875 are such as belong to the citizen, in common or equally with other citizens in the same State, then it is not to be denied that such legislation is peculiarity appropriate to the end which Congress is authorized to accomplish, viz., to protect the citizen, in respect of such rights, against discrimination on account of his race."[93]

It is well worth reading Justice Harlan's entire dissent. These few concluding paragraphs are masterful.

> But the Court says that Congress did not, in the act of 1866, assume, under the authority given by the Thirteenth Amendment, to adjust what may be called the social rights of men and races in the community. I agree that government has nothing to do with social rights of men and races in the community. I agree that government has nothing to do with social, as distinguished from technically legal, rights of individuals. No government ever has brought, or ever can bring, its people into social intercourse against their wishes. Whether one person will permit or maintain social relations with another is a matter with which the government has no concern. ... What I affirm is that no State, nor the officers of any State, nor any corporation or individual wielding power under State authority for the public benefit or the public convenience, can, consistently either with the freedom established by the fundamental law, or with that equality of civil rights which now belongs to every citizen, discriminate against freemen or citizens, in those rights, because of their race, or because they once labored under the disabilities of slavery imposed upon them as a race. The rights which Congress, by the act of 1875, endeavored to secure and protect are legal, not social rights. The right, for instance, of a colored citizen to use the accommodations of a public highway, upon the same terms as are permitted white citizens, is no more a social right than his right, under the law, to use the public streets of a city or a town, or a turnpike road, or a public market, or a post office, or his right to sit in a public building with others, of whatever race, for the purpose of sharing the political questions of the day discussed. Scarcely a day passes without our seeing in this court-room citizens of the white and black races sitting side by side, watching the process of our business. It would never occur to any one that the presence of a colored citizen in a court-house, or court-room, was an invasion of the social rights of white persons who may frequent such places. And yet, such a suggestion would be quite as sound in law—I say with all respect—as is the suggestion that the claim of a colored person to use, upon the same terms as is permitted to white citizens, the accommodations of public highways, or public inns, or places of public amusement, established under the license of law, is an invasion of the social rights of the white race.[94]

In this dissent's last paragraph, his passion and prophetic views about our country and its future deserve reading and thought.

> At every step, in this direction, the nation has been confronted with class tyranny, which a contemporary English historian says is, of all tyrannies, the most intolerable, "for it is

---

93   Ibid., pp. 54.
94   Ibid., pp. 59–60.

ubiquitous in its operation, and weighs, perhaps, most heavily on those whose obscurity or distance would withdraw them from the notice of a single despot." Today, it is the colored race, which is denied, by corporations and individuals wielding public authority, rights fundamental in their freedom and citizenship. At some future time, it may be that some other race will fall under the ban of race discrimination. If the constitutional amendments be enforced, there cannot be, in this republic, any class of human beings in practical subjection to another class, with power in the latter to dole out to the former just such privileges as they may chose to grant. The supreme law of the land has decreed that no authority shall be exercised in this country upon the basis of discrimination, in respect of civil rights, against freedmen and citizens because of their race, color, or previous condition of servitude. To that decree—for the due enforcement of which, by appropriate legislation, Congress has been invested with express power—every one must bow, whatever may have been, or whatever now are, his individual views as to the wisdom or policy, either of the recent changes in the fundamental law, or of the legislation which has been enacted to give them effect.[95]

Sadly, despite such magnificent words and sentiments, the reality on the ground was set.

Discrimination against people of color had been sanctioned by the Supreme Court. Note the year, 1883. Less than two decades after the Civil War, black social rights seem to have been forfeited, at the very least. In addition to social rights not given, basic human rights were at risk as well. The period between 1883 and 1933 was viewed by the black community as a time of great danger, as the reality of lynching became part of their American experience. "The growing consciousness that lynching was a problem in the 1880's was reflected by the annual publication of lynching statistics by the Chicago Tribune, beginning with the year 1882 when 113 were recorded. The number had more than doubled by 1892, when the peak of 230 lynchings was recorded."[96] It is appropriate to suggest that the number of lynchings was much higher than those recorded.

The linkage back to the High Court's decisions is apparent. "This abandonment of Blacks was reflected by the Supreme Court when it voided the Civil Rights Act of 1875, thereby absolving the federal government of concern for the increasing racial segregation then under way and thus encouraging an increase in the frequency of lynching."[97]

The reality of lynching may be difficult, if not impossible, for this generation to envision, but for folks living at this time, it was very real. Two contemporary examples about this phenomenon will help reflect the deep emotions associated with lynching. In the latter decades of the 1800s, the *Atlanta Constitution* hired Charles Henry Smith, who wrote under the pen name of Bill Arp, as a correspondent who wrote about Southern topics. "Throughout his twenty-five year career as a columnist … Bill Arp's idea about the Negro remained the same. Blacks, he thought, were an inferior race, endowed by God with certain traits and needing at all times close contact with whites, not only for supervision but for moral guidance as well."[98] Arp's attitude toward lynching speaks for itself,

At the same time he urged the enfranchising of qualified Negroes, however, Arp advocated the lynching of black brutes. "Outrage and murder combined removes the brute at once

---

95 Ibid., p. 62.
96 Grant, *The Anti-Lynching Movement: 1883–1932*, p. 20.
97 Ibid., pp. 20–21.
98 Parker, alias Bill Arp, pp. 127–128.

from the human code and places him along with the wild beasts, with mad dogs and hyenas." "Lynching for that crime is the law of nature, and will go on. When juries are organized to try hyenas and wolves and gorillas, maybe then these brutes in human form will be tried, but not before. The argument is exhausted, and we stand by our wives and children."[99]

Arp's views are explicitly and harshly expressed. "I would lynch every brute who assaulted a white woman. I could see him massacred or burned or hanged, drawn and quartered … As for lynching, I repeat what I have said before, 'Let the good work go on. Lynch 'em! Hang 'em! Shoot 'em! Burn 'em!'"[100]

To express the depth of these social beliefs, another well-known member of that Southern society, Rebecca L. Felton, is examined. A politically active and influential journalist, Felton had an advice column for the *Atlanta Journal*. Despite the fact that she advocated tirelessly for women's right to vote, her views on lynching were quite conservative and parallel those of Arp. "In an 1897 speech she said that the biggest problem facing women on the farm was the danger of black rapists." If it takes lynching to protect women's dearest possession from drunken, ravening beasts, she said, "then I say lynch a thousand a week."[101]

This drumbeat of antiblack equal and social rights continues unabated in the next decade. In fact, some of the Court's findings seemed inconsistent with those it had made a few years earlier. In a case decided in 1890, named *Louisville, New Orleans, and Texas Railway Co. v. Mississippi*, the foundation for "separate but equal" was established. The case seems simple enough; a statute in the state of Mississippi dated March 2, 1888, required all railroads carrying passengers in that state (other than streetcars) to provide equal—but separate—accommodations for the white and colored races, having been construed by the supreme court of the state to apply solely to commerce within the state, therefore not being in conflict with the commerce clause of the Constitution of the United States.[102] In this case, the Louisville, New Orleans & Texas Railway Company was indicted for neglecting to provide the separate seating.

Justice David Brewer delivered the opinion of the Court. First, he examines prior cases that were similar to this one. The case of *Hall v. DeCuir*, discussed above, seemed on point with this case. In that case, the state of Louisiana had passed a law that forbade seating discrimination on steamboats. As noted, the High Court held that the Louisiana law was invalid and strove to differentiate the two cases.

The Supreme Court of the State of Louisiana held that the act applied to interstate carriers, and required them, when they came within the limits of the state, to receive colored passengers into the cabin set apart for white persons. This Court, accepting that construction as conclusive, held that the act was a regulation of interstate commerce, and therefore beyond the power of the state … In this case, the Supreme Court of Mississippi held that the statute applied solely to commerce within the state, and that construction, being the construction of the statute of the state by its highest court, must be accepted as conclusive here.[103]

---

99 Ibid.
100 Ibid.
101 http://georgiaencyclopedia.org, Mrs. Rebecca Felton.
102 hppt://supreme.justia.com/cases, *Louisville, New Orleans & Texas Ry. Com. v. Mississippi*, p. 1.
103 Ibid., pp. 3–4.

Interestingly, the Court addresses the cost of having extra trains in a rather casual manner, "its provisions are fully complied with when trains within the state are attached to a separate car for colored passengers. This may cause an extra expense to the railroad company, but not more than state statutes requiring certain accommodations at depots, compelling trains to stop at crossings of other railroads, and a multitude of other matters confessedly within the power of the state."[104] It is, once again, Justice Harlan who writes a spirited defense based on the *Hall v. DeCuir* case. In fact, one might understand the incredulity underlying his words.

> *In its application to passengers on vessels engaged in interstate commerce, the Louisiana enactment forbade the separation of the white and black races while such vessels were within the limits of that state. The Mississippi statute, in its application to passengers on railroad trains employed in interstate commerce, requires such separation of races while those trains are within that state. I am unable to perceive how the former is a regulation of interstate commerce and the other is not. It is difficult to understand how a state enactment of commerce among the states, while a similar enactment forbidding such separation is not a regulation of that character.*[105]

So, in brief, in the *Hall* case, the Court concludes that the state of Louisiana could not make a law requiring equal accommodations. The result was segregation and unequal seating and lodging. With the *Mississippi* case, they allowed the segregation, even though the railroad in this case, like the steamboat, was involved in interstate commerce. The result was, sadly, the same: segregation and unequal seating and accommodations.

The final case to be studied in this chapter is perhaps one of the better-known ones, *Plessy v. Ferguson*, decided in 1896. There are certain ironies associated with this case that deserve analysis. First is the state involved, Louisiana. The same state that in the post–Civil War years had passed a state law calling for integration of its steamboats, as discussed above in the *Hall v. DeCuir* case, only to have that law overturned by the High Court. In this case, they were following the practice of Mississippi, and decided to fully segregate their passengers by race. It is fair to consider the question of how a state that passed a law urging integration is able to turn around so relatively quickly and now require the opposite. (See Figure 4-13.)

Another irony of the *Plessy* case is that the issue of race is discussed in a surreal manner. Homer Plessy, the plaintiff in this case, is described in the Court record as, "That petitioner was a citizen of the United States and a resident of Louisiana, of mixed descent, in the proportion of seven eighths Caucasian and one eighth African blood; that the mixture of colored blood was not discernible in him, and that he was entitled to every recognition, right, privilege and

4-13: This is a photograph of Homer Plessy, the key figure in the case that carries his name. Ultimately, his only goal was to be able to sit on a train or boat in any open seat.

Surreal- not normal

104   Ibid., p. 5.
105   Ibid., p. 7.

immunity secured to the citizens of the United States of the white race by its Constitution and laws."[106] John Ferguson was a judge in the criminal district court for the parish of New Orleans.

The gist of the case is fairly straightforward. "He (Plessy) took possession of a vacant seat in a coach where passengers of the white race were accommodated, and was ordered by the conductor to vacate this coach and take a seat in another assigned to persons of the colored race, and having refused to comply with such demand he was forcibly ejected with the aid of a police officer, and imprisoned in the parish jail to answer a charge of having violated the above act."[107]

As with most of these cases, there is much more background to them that precedes the case. In this instance, a committee of 18 prominent men of color from Louisiana formed a group called "A Citizen's Committee to Test the Constitutionality of the Separate Car Law."[108] They also engaged a leading legal authority, Albion W. Tourgée, who served them at no cost, to assist them with all legal issues involved. Very much like Rosa Parks, decades later in Montgomery, the committee was waiting for the right person to be arrested to test the law.

Interestingly, some of the early discussions about this issue centered on the complexion of the person to be arrested. Many conversations were held about this item. This may explain the seven-eighths Caucasian aspect of the case. Also of interest is that the railroads were part of this understanding to make a test case of this new law: "The first railroad provided the Jim Crow car and posted the sign required by law, but told its conductors to molest no one who ignored instructions ... The extra expense of separate railroad cars was one reason for railroad opposition to the Jim Crow law."[109]

The test case was set up, including the white passenger who would object to the black traveler. Everything was in place. On February 24, 1892, Daniel F. Desdunes—not Homer Plessy,—bought a ticket to Mobile, Alabama, boarded the Louisville and Nashville train, and took a seat in the white coach. All went according to plan. Desdunes was arrested, and a trial date was set to test the constitutionality of the Jim Crow law. The Desdunes case was unexpectedly resolved, when the Louisiana Supreme Court, ruling in another case, decided (based on a plea from the Pullman Railroad Company) that the law was unconstitutional as it applied to interstate passengers. In that regard, the Louisiana court was following the U.S. Supreme Court's ruling in the *Hall v. DeCuir* case, that individual states could not pass laws that would impact interstate commerce.

Ironically, this was a shallow victory, if at all, as the law was still being applied to intrastate passengers, and the states adjacent to Louisiana had similar or identical Jim Crow laws.[110] Within a week, Homer A. Plessy boarded the East Louisiana Railroad bound for Covington, Louisiana, and took a seat in the white coach. Since Plessy described himself as "seven-eighths Caucasian and one-eighth African blood" and swore that the admixture of colored blood is not discernible, it may be assumed that the railroad had been informed of the plan and agreed to cooperate.[111] It might be worthwhile to contemplate this blood mixture of Plessy's. Were the originators of the test case trying to send a not-so-subtle message that the person "breaking" the law was, by blood, seven-eighths white?

---

106   United States Reports, *Plessy v. Ferguson*, p. 538.
107   Ibid., pp. 541–542.
108   Woodward, *American Counterpoint*, p. 217.
109   Ibid., p. 220.
110   Ibid.
111   Ibid.

As the case made its way up to the U.S. Supreme Court, Albion Tourgée, the prominent attorney, filed a brief with the Court on behalf of Mr. Plessy. His thoughts would be echoed later in the dissent of Justice Harlan. First, he notes that the statute in question did not apply to black nurses attending white children. "The exemption of nurses shows that the real evil lies not in the color of the skin but in the relation the colored person sustains to the white. If he is a dependent, it may be endured: if he is not, his presence is insufferable."[112]

Speaking about the future regarding the separating of the races, Tourgée posits the following verses, which are very prophetic and most likely the source of Justice Harlan's comments about the same theme.

> *Why not require all colored people to walk on one side of the street and the whites on the other? Why not require every white man's house to be painted white and every colored man's black? ... Why not require every white business man to use a white sign and every colored man who solicits customers a black one ... The question is not as to the* equality *of the privileges enjoyed, but the* right of the State to label one citizen as white and another as colored *in the common enjoyment of a public highway as this court has decided a railway to be.*[113]

It may seem apparent after studying the group of previous cases, especially the last one about the railroads in Mississippi, how the Court would vote a mere eight years later. Nevertheless, the significance in this case is not necessarily the finding, but the aftermath of the decisions. The constitutionality of this case is based on the fact that it conflicts with both the Thirteenth Amendment, abolishing slavery, and the Fourteenth, which prohibits certain restrictive legislation on the part of the states. Justice Henry B. Brown, born in Massachusetts, a resident of Michigan, delivered the opinion of the Court. First, he presents an interesting view of the notion of slavery and involuntary servitude. "Slavery implies a state of bondage, the ownership of mankind as a chattel ... and the absence of a legal right to the disposal of his own person, property and services."[114] In this regard, the justice continues with the realization that even though blatant slavery had been outlawed, there existed other areas of concern,

> *It was intimated, however, in that case that this amendment was regarded by the statesmen of that day as insufficient to protect the colored race from certain laws which had been enacted in the Southern States, imposing upon the colored race onerous disabilities and burdens, and curtailing their rights in the pursuit of life, liberty and property to such an extent that their freedom was of little value; and that the Fourteenth Amendment was devised to meet this exigency.*[115]

While this statement is accurate historically, the Court seemingly ignores that reality. There is a distinction made between slavery and the "badge of servitude" with social inequality. The finding in the Civil Rights Cases is quoted to affirm the decision that the act of an individual owner of an inn, a steamboat, or theater in refusing accommodations to people of color, "cannot

112 Ibid., p. 225.
113 Ibid., p. 226.
114 *Plessy v. Ferguson*, p. 542.
115 Ibid.

be justly regarded as imposing any badge of slavery or servitude upon the applicant."[116] In other words, "A statute which implies merely a legal distinction between the white and colored races—a distinction which is founded in the color of the two races, and which must always exist so long as white men are distinguished from the other race by color—has no tendency to destroy the legal equality of the two races, or reestablish a state of involuntary servitude."[117] This first distinction is not a new one for the Court. The prejudice displayed toward people of color is not slavery, just a valid form of legal discrimination—based, as they write, on skin color.

Next, Justice Henry Billings Brown considers the argument that the Fourteenth Amendment should benefit Homer Plessy. "The object of the amendment was undoubtedly to enforce the absolute equality of the two races before the law, but in the nature of things it could not have been intended to abolish distinctions based upon color, or to enforce social, as distinguished from political equality, or a commingle of the two races upon terms unsatisfactory to either. Laws permitting, and even requiring, their separation in places where they are liable to be brought into contact do not necessarily imply the inferiority of either race to the other, and have been generally, if not universally, recognized as within the competency of the state legislatures in the exercise of their police power."[118]

After a review of prior cases that concerned this issue, the Court reaches a conclusion that warrants close reading and analysis.

> In determining the question of reasonableness it is at liberty to act with reference to the established usages, customs and traditions of the people, and with a view to the promotion of their comfort, and the preservation of the public peace and good order. Gauged by this standard, we cannot say that a law which authorizes or even requires the separation of the two races in public conveyances is unreasonable, or more obnoxious to the Fourteenth Amendment than the acts of Congress requiring separate schools for colored children in the District of Columbia, the constitutionality of which does not seem to be questioned, or the corresponding acts of state legislatures.[119]

It is fascinating to reflect on the words above. Is it a reasonable premise to suggest, as the justices do, that people should be legally kept apart because it is the established custom? This separation also promotes the people's comfort. Whose comfort? Certainly not those being told that they can't sit in certain seats on a train or ship. Furthermore, once folks are separated, does this increase public peace and good order? The assumption is that peace and good order would not prevail if people of different colors sat together on a steamship or train. This type of thinking very much lays the legal and social foundations for the Jim Crow era, which was about to explode on the national scene. In this regard, the High Court is giving explanations, almost casually, to justify separation.

To make matters worse, the Court's decision continues with a further affront to the black community. In effect, suggesting that enforced separation should not be considered a badge of inferiority, "If this be so, it is not by reason of anything found in the act, but solely because the colored race chooses to put that construction on it."[120] The Court then makes a fanciful assertion, that if the black race were in the majority and that whites were made to sit in designated seats, they would not see this as a mark of inferiority. This sounds like a classic example of

---

116 Ibid.
117 Ibid., p. 543.
118 Ibid., p. 544.
119 Ibid., pp. 550–551.
120 Ibid.

blaming the victim. What an ironic twist of thinking to blame the black community for their legitimate feelings, by telling them that in a parallel situation, whites wouldn't have those very same feelings!

The Court finishes this finding with a fairly major assertion that I quote to students regarding the role of law. "The argument also assumes that social prejudices may be overcome by legislation, and that equal rights cannot be secured to the Negro except by the enforced commingling of the two races. We cannot accept this proposition ... Legislation is powerless to eradicate social instincts or to abolish distinctions based upon physical differences, and the attempt to do so can only result in accentuating the difficulties of the present situation."[121]

This powerful statement makes a few odious points. First, the nation's highest legal tribunal is telling the black community, in plain language, that the law cannot help them meet their aspirations of equality—despite the prior amendments and civil rights acts due to the feelings of the white community. They state this emphatically, as they quote a case from the Court of Appeals of New York in another case: "this end can neither be accomplished nor promoted by laws which conflict with the general sentiment of the community upon which they are designed to operate."[122]

The second obnoxious point is that the power of resolving this issue is in the hands of the dominant white community. What incentive do those who oppose integration have to resolve this at all? The highest Court has agreed with them, that their views are the most important ones regarding their society. And, as long as they desire to have separation, that is what they should do. It is easy to see how many read this case as an imprimatur for the reality of almost total social, religious, political, and daily separation of the races.

As a final insult, the Court concludes its finding for the state to have segregated cars on the railroads, with a brief discussion about proportionality of blood. "It is true that the question of the proportion of colored blood necessary to constitute a colored person, as distinguished from a white person, is one upon which there is a difference of opinion in the different States, some holding that any visible admixture of black blood stamps the person as belonging to the colored race ... others that it depends upon the preponderance of blood ... and still others that the predominance of white blood must only be in the proportion of three fourths."[123] The High Court chooses not to be involved in this issue, leaving it to the States to make their own laws.

Justice Harlan, as in the prior case, offers a stirring and strangely prophetic dissent,

If a State can prescribe, as a rule of civil conduct, that whites and blacks shall not travel as passengers in the same railroad coach, why may it not so regulate the use of the streets of its cities and towns as to compel white citizens to keep on one side of a street and black citizens to keep on the other? Why may it not, upon like grounds, punish whites and blacks who ride together in street cars or in open vehicles on a public road or street? Why may it not require sheriffs to assign whites to one side of a court room and blacks to the other? And why may it not also prohibit the commingling of the two races in the galleries of legislative halls or in public assemblages convened for the consideration of the political questions of the day?[124]

---

121 Ibid.
122 Ibid.
123 Ibid., p. 552.
124 Ibid., p. 557–558.

Sadly, much of what Harlan wrote about in giving exaggerated social examples of separation in making his argument became the reality of Jim Crow, when areas of society that had never been separated became so.

The next few paragraphs are so significant that they should be required reading for every American. Justice Harlan's vision for America parallels some of the lofty and profound writing of Dr. Martin Luther King, who may have been influenced by Harlan.

> *The white race deems itself to be the dominant race in this country. And so it is, in prestige, in achievements, in education, in wealth and in power. So, I doubt not, it will continue to be for all time, if it remains true to its great heritage and holds fast to the principles of constitutional liberty. But in view of the Constitution, in the eye of the law, there is in this country no superior, dominant, ruling class of citizens. There is no caste here. Our Constitution is color-blind, and neither knows nor tolerates classes among citizens. In respect of civil rights, all citizens are equal before the law. The humblest is the peer of the most powerful. The law regards man as man, and takes no account of his surroundings or of his color when his civil rights as guaranteed by the supreme law of the land are involved.*[125]

> *The destinies of the two races, in this country, are indissolubly linked together, and the interests of both require that the common government of all shall not permit the seeds of race hate to be planted under the sanction of law. What can more certainly arouse race hate, what more certainly create and perpetuate a feeling of distrust between these races, than state enactments, which, in fact, proceed on the ground that colored citizens are so inferior and degraded that they cannot be allowed to sit in public coaches occupied by white citizens? … The sure guarantee of the peace and security of each race is the clear, distinct, unconditional recognition by our governments, National and State, of every right that inheres in civil freedom, and of the equality before the law of all citizens of the United States without regard to race.*[126]

Despite these majestic words from Harlan, the majority of the Court not only accepted the separate but equal doctrine on the Louisiana railroads, it opened up a racial Pandora's Box known as Jim Crow. Much of the post–Civil War South had areas of society that had already been segregated such as schools, churches, hotels, and rooming houses. Yet, in other public places such as trains, depots, theaters, and soda fountains, segregation was more sporadic.[127] With the *Plessy* decision, the principle of statutory racial segregation extended into every area of Southern life, including street railways, hotels, restaurants, hospitals, recreations, sports, and employment.[128]

However it occurred, the infamy of *Plessy* is what resulted from it, a movement that rapidly grew into almost total separation of whites and blacks. Perhaps it was the logic of the Court that it was natural that the races should be separated, and that the role of the law was not to force that issue. The Court also verified that local customs and mores should prevail when setting

---

125   Ibid., p. 559.
126   Ibid., p. 560.
127   Tindall and Shi, *The Essential America*, p. 312.
128   Ibid., p. 314.

the social standards for local communities. The intricate reality of Jim Crow should be a must-study for every American student. As the new 20th century began, city ordinances, local rules, and regulations were often accompanied by unofficial Jim Crow rules that had to be rigidly followed. "For up and down the avenues and byways of Southern life appeared with increasing profusion the little signs: 'Whites Only' or 'Colored' ... Many appeared without requirement by law—over entrances and exits, at theaters and boarding houses, toilets and water fountains, waiting rooms and ticket windows."[129] (Refer to Figure 4-14.)

The depth and breadth of the Jim Crow era are not appreciated by most students of history. A South Carolina law in 1915,

> *Prohibited textile factories from permitting laborers of different races from working together in the same room, or using the same entrances, pay windows, exits, doorways, or windows at the same time, or the same lavatories, toilets, drinking water buckets, pails, cups, dippers or glasses at any time.*[130]

Areas in society that had not been involved in segregation were now swept up in it. "Segregation of the races now became standard procedure for the following, hospitals, mental hospitals, penal institutions, homes for the aged and the blind, the deaf and dumb, and more."[131] The separation evolved into areas that most today would just shake their heads at in disbelief. The races were separated in amusements, diversions, recreations, and sports. Thus, when the circus came to town, in much of the South, that event involved creating separate entrances, exits, ticket windows, and ticket sellers that would be kept at least 25 feet apart.[132] One would think that the various businesses would protest some of these changes such as the circus, as the extra waiting lines, ticket sellers, etc., would cost extra money to accomplish. There is very little evidence that such protests were made, if at all.

4-14: This sign signifies the reality of Jim Crow across America. Separation in almost every aspect of life became the norm for generations.

Some final items about the perversity, depth, and extent of these laws are apparent in these examples. "It was unlawful for whites and blacks to play pool or billiards together. All persons licensed to sell beer or wine could only serve whites or blacks exclusively and not sell it to the races together. Textbooks shall not be interchangeable between white and black schools. Libraries shall set up separate places in the library for black patrons."[133]

Finally, Jim Crow permeated into social contact between blacks and whites. Following are some examples of the so-called Jim Crow etiquette that was communicated to both blacks and whites. Failure to adhere to these rules might trigger being forced to leave town, violent attacks, and, in some cases, lynching. (See Figure 4-15.)

- A Black male could not offer his hand [to shake hands] with a White male because it implied being socially equal. Obviously, a Black male could not offer his hand or any other

---

129   Woodward, *The Strange Career of Jim Crow*, p. 98.
130   Ibid.
131   Ibid., p. 99.
132   Ibid., p. 100.
133   http://nps.gov/malu, for teachers/Jim Crow laws.

4-15: Lynching was a stark and tragic consequence of Jim Crowism. Racism, which existed across America, as this 1920 event in Minnesota indicates, led many law-abiding citizens to take actions that they never would have otherwise considered. Their hatred must have been intense!

part of his body to a White woman, because he risked being accused of rape.

• Blacks were not allowed to show public affection toward one another in public, especially kissing, because it offended Whites.

• White motorists had the right-of-way at all intersections.

• When conversing with Whites, the following rules applied:
  ▪ Never assert or even intimate that a White person is lying.
  • Never suggest that a White person is from an inferior class.
  • Never laugh derisively at a White person.
  • Never comment upon the appearance of a White female.[134]

While this book is not about the Jim Crow era, once again, as a learning process, log onto a reputable site such as the Martin Luther King Jr. National Historic Site for a more detailed background and history of these laws.

In conclusion, the Supreme Court cases between 1877 and 1896 seem, for the most part, to legally establish the notion of separate but equal and the legal acceptance of Jim Crow. In *Hall v. DeCuir*, Josephine DeCuir was denied the opportunity to sit where she wanted on a steamboat. Despite the apparent clarity of the Civil Rights Act of 1875, which spoke directly about equal accommodations on public conveyances, the Court deemed that the state had no need to integrate its steamship passengers.

While the *Strauder* and the *Ex Parte Virginia* cases seemed to back up the ideals of the Fourteenth Amendment regarding equal protection of the law, the decision in *Virginia v. Rives* easily negated those decisions, and in some ways offered a blueprint to be followed that denied to black citizens the ability to serve as jurors. In the *Harris* case, violence against blacks was condoned. A much more significant case was also decided in 1883, the *Civil Rights Cases*. As mentioned in our discussion, this case involved many instances of real discrimination across the country. Despite the explicit dicta written in the 1875 Civil Rights Act against such discrimination based on color, the justices decided that while the State governments could not discriminate, individuals could. In the eyes of the Court, this type of prejudice did not rise to the level of a "badge of slavery." Nevertheless, while not a badge of slavery, it certainly was a clear act of intolerance and prejudice and the perfect foundation for separate but equal beliefs.

In both railroad cases, the pretense—if there ever was one—about equal rights had disappeared. The Court, in either case, allowed the railroads, despite the extra expense involved, to maintain separate but equal accommodations for blacks and whites. As mentioned above, the *Plessy* case became the official launching pad for at least six decades of blatant racism represented by the term Jim Crow. At this stage, almost at the end of the 19th century, one might think that

---

134   www.Tdblues.com

the Court had done enough damage to the post–Civil War rights due the black community. Unfortunately, there were more rights to be threatened.

Discussion Questions

1. How do you imagine Josephine DeCuir felt when she was refused a berth in the white ladies' cabin that she had paid for? Is the comparison between Rosa Parks and her a valid one?

2. When the Court cited a finding from the Pennsylvania Supreme Court, they quoted this line: "it is not an unreasonable regulation to seat passengers so as to preserve order and decorum, and to prevent contacts and collisions arising from natural or well-known customary repugnancies which are likely to breed disturbances, where white and colored persons are huddled together without their consent." In plain English, what are the justices implying?

3. Reread the Civil Rights Act of 1875. Are the writing and intent clear? Why didn't the Justices simply follow the dictates of the act?

4. Do you believe that by this early date, the Court began formulating the concept of "separate but equal?"

5. How many years do you think were necessary for a successful Reconstruction?

6. In the *Strauder* case, Justice Strong wrote, "The colored race, as a race, was abject and ignorant, and in that condition was unfitted to command the respect of those who had superior intelligence." How do you interpret this sentence?

7. In the *Harris* case, which laws do you think would have been applicable? What were some of the on-the-ground consequences about this case's finding?

8. Have you ever been denied entry into a restaurant, theater, or any other public place? How did you feel? Why were you not allowed to enter?

9. What are your reactions to the *Plessy* case? What were the reasons given by the Court in their decision? Do you agree with any or all of those reasons?

10. What are your reactions to the Jim Crow era in its many aspects? Of all that you have read, what is the most disturbing to you? Is that era over forever? Could it happen again? To another group?

JUSTICE HARLAN: COME GET YOUR NIGGER NOW!

chapter 5

B y the end of the 19th century and into the 20th, despite the reality of Jim Crow, new difficulties arose for people of color. That community suffered increased discrimination and prejudice from a variety of fronts, including a reduction of voting rights, diminished educational possibilities, the corrosive effects of nativism, a decrease of work opportunities, and ultimately, the loss of life itself. In fact, the status and social worth of blacks were waning at a great rate. The role of the Supreme Court was a continuing decisive factor in creating and fostering this situation.

This era, prior to the Second World War, might be seen as the worst in our nation's history in terms of race relations, excepting slavery. Regarding the High Court, it was reaping what it had sown in the previous century. Many hate-filled Americans, based partially on the judgments of the Court, felt that the life of a black citizen was not worth the life of any white person. Certainly, it seemed that the legal and justice system in place for most Americans was not appropriate for its black members. It was, in many ways, "open season" on people of color, without any thought of possible punishment.

During the 1890s, the political leaders of the South, named Bourbons by some, began to consider the possibility of eliminating or diminishing the black vote.[1] Obviously, laws and constitutional changes such as the Fifteenth Amendment made this a difficult goal to achieve. Nevertheless, those individuals dedicated to the diminution of the black vote devised an ingeniously deceptive system to dilute black votes. The state of Mississippi led this movement in 1890, when it called a state constitutional convention to change the suffrage provisions of the 1868 constitution, written under the influence of the Radical Republicans. This new voting process devised by Mississippi set the pattern that seven more states would follow over the next two decades.[2]

The plan created four impediments prior to a person's voting. It is instructive to briefly quote the laws verbatim to indicate the level of sophistication and thought that went into creating and implementing these obstacles to voting for the black community.

Section 241—Every male inhabitant of this State except idiots, insane persons and Indians not taxed, who is a citizen of the United States, twenty-one years old and upwards, who has resided in this State two years, and one year in the election district, or in the incorporated city or town in which he offers to vote, and who is duly registered as provided in this article, and who has never been convicted of bribery, burglary, theft, arson, obtaining money or goods under false pretences, perjury, forgery, embezzlement or bigamy, and who has paid, on or before the 1st day of February of the year in which he shall offer to vote, all taxes which may have been legally required of him, and which he has had an opportunity of paying according to law for the two preceding years, and who shall produce to the officer holding the election satisfactory evidence that he has paid said taxes, is declared to be a qualified elector; but any minister of the Gospel in charge of an organized church shall be entitled to vote after six months' residence in the election district, if otherwise qualified.

Section 244—On after the first day of January, A.D. 1892, every elector shall, in addition to the foregoing qualifications, be able to read any section of the constitution of this state; or he shall be able to understand the same when read to him, or give a reasonable interpretation thereof. A new registration shall be made before the next ensuing election after January the first A.D. 1892.[3]

Imagine that a person has to undertake these steps prior to voting. First, a residency requirement eliminated some black voters who were migrant workers living part of the year out of their area. The second requirement was the petty crimes disqualification, which was also utilized to remove potential voters who may have been accused of minor offenses. The third obstacle to voting was the poll, or head, tax. This tax, initially called for in Article One, Section Nine of the U.S. Constitution, was a fixed amount tax per individual based on a state's census data. It provided a stream of revenue for the various states. Elections were funded utilizing this tax.

In the context of the post–Civil War South, these taxes became weapons used against black voters. For instance, once this tax had been paid by eligible black voters, local town authorities often "lost" the receipt of a tax payment, requiring that it be paid again. This "poll tax" became so embodied in American culture that it remained part of Southern federal voting procedures

---

1   Tindall and Shi, *America: A Narrative History*, p. 567.
2   Ibid.
3   United States Reports, vol. 170, *Williams v. Mississippi*, pp. 217–218.

until the mid-1960s, when it was finally eliminated via the Twenty-Fourth Amendment to the Constitution. Over time, poll taxes for state elections were gradually eliminated.

The final, and perhaps most challenging, obstacle for voting was the requirement in Section 244, mentioned above, where the voter had to read and interpret sections of the state constitution in front of an election official. It is easy to imagine how this requirement especially served as a deterrent for potential voters. I'm sure that voters today, if informed that they had to pay a poll tax or stand in front of a state official and read and interpret the state constitution, would, most likely, not vote. At the same time, exemptions were made in the various election laws that granted so called "grandfather clauses" for adult white males whose fathers or grand-fathers had voted before the abolition of slavery. (See Figure 5-1.)

In June of 1896, the little known case of *Williams v. Mississippi* changed the reality of voting for generations of black voters. Henry Williams was indicted by a grand jury for murder in Washington County, Mississippi. He made a motion to quash the indictment based on the allegation that the grand jury which indicted him was unconstitutional and repugnant to the Fourteenth Amendment of the Constitution. As part of his appeal, Williams attacks the new voting system,

5-1: This 1876 drawing, critical of the usage of literacy tests for African-Americans to vote shows a man, "Mr. Solid South," barely literate himself, writing on a wall, "Eddikashun Qualifukasin," (Education Qualification).

> *It is further alleged that there is no statute of the State providing for the procurement of any registration books of voters of said county, and [it is alleged in detail] the terms of the constitution and the section of the code mentioned, and the discretion given to the officers, "is but a scheme on the part of the framers of that constitution to abridge the suffrage of the colored electors in the State of Mississippi on account of the previous condition of servitude by granting a discretion to the said officers as mentioned in the several sections of the constitution of the State and the statute of the state adopted under the said constitution, the use of said discretion can be and has been used in the said Washington County to the end complained of.*[4]

The allegation also notes that the Mississippi constitutional convention that had devised the voting impediments "was composed of 134 members, only one of whom was a negro ... the makers of the new constitution arbitrarily refused to submit it to the voters of the State for approval, but ordered it adopted, and an election to be held immediately under it ... but for that the 'defendant's race would have been represented impartially on the grand jury which presented the indictment,' and hence he is deprived of the equal protection of the laws of the State."[5]

Justice Joseph McKenna delivered the unanimous decision of the court in this very short case, involving a dozen pages focused on this issue. After briefly reviewing the purpose of the Fourteenth Amendment, he proceeds to mention past decisions which limited the potency of that amendment.

---

4   Ibid., p. 214.
5   Ibid., p. 215.

... but it has also been held, in a very recent case, to justify a removal from a state court to a Federal court of a cause in which such rights are alleged to be denied, that such denial must be the result of the constitution or laws of the State, not of the administration of them.[6]

As the decision continues, the justice offers a detailed understanding of the various sections of the newly rewritten Mississippi voting codes which so adversely affected black voters.

Under section 244 it is left with the administrative officer to determine whether the applicant reads, understands or interprets the section of the constitution designated. The officer is the sole judge of the examination of the applicant, and even though the applicant is qualified, it is left with the officer to so determine; and the said officer can refuse him registration.[7] *(Refer to Figure 5-2.)*

STATE OF LOUISIANA--PARISH OF JEFFERSON.

Office of Sheriff and Tax Collector.

191

Received of *A. S. White*
resident of *Second* (2) Ward, the sum of ONE DOLLAR, Poll Tax for the year 191 7, for the support of the PUBLIC SCHOOLS.

Lewis L. Coventhem
Sheriff and Ex-Officio Tax Collector.

5-2: Pictured is a standard poll tax receipt from the state of Louisiana in 1917.

The High Court also recognizes that the new codes included the payment of a poll tax, which had to be paid before men were allowed to vote. In the discussion about these taxes, the High Court refers to a case decided by the Mississippi Supreme Court, which it now utilized as legal ammunition. The state court refers to its black citizens in the following manner.

And further the court said, speaking of the Negro race: "By reason of its previous condition of servitude and dependencies, this race had acquired or accentuated certain peculiarities of habit, of temperament, and of character, which clearly distinguished it as a race from the whites. A Patient, docile people: but careless, landless, migratory within narrow limits, without forethought: and its criminal members given to furtive offences, rather than the robust crimes of the whites. Restrained by the Federal Constitution from discriminating against the Negro race, the convention discriminates against its characteristics, and the offences to which its criminal members are prone.[8]

So, the High Court is quoting from the state court as legal verification and justification for the limitations to black voters. The above paragraph is incredible, given the time that had passed since the end of slavery and the political and economic development of the black community. Even black criminals are found less than acceptable compared to white ones!

One of the conclusions of the Court is that the laws "reach weak and vicious white men as well as weak and vicious black men, and whatever is sinister in their intention, if anything,

6   Ibid., p. 219.
7   Ibid., p. 221.
8   Ibid., p. 222.

can be prevented by both races by the exertion of that duty which voluntarily pays taxes and refrains from crime."[9] The Court makes an astonishing assertion next: "There is an allegation of the purpose of the [constitutional] convention to disenfranchise citizens of the colored race, but with this we have no concern, unless the purpose is executed by the constitution or laws or by those who administer them."[10] What a wonderful "legal fiction"—people are denied basic voting rights, but because the state has found a way to circumvent the Fourteenth Amendment, it is of no concern to the nation's Highest Court!

The Court makes a curious reference near the end of this decision. The 1886 case of *Yick Wo v. Hopkins* was cited. In that case, the Court ruled in favor of Chinese businessmen who it believed had experienced prejudice in the granting of licenses for laundries in San Francisco. The verbiage used is impressive: "Though the law itself be fair on its face and impartial in appearance, yet, if it is applied and administered by public authority with an evil eye and an unequal hand, so as to practically to make unjust and illegal discriminations between persons in similar circumstances, material to their rights, the denial of equal justice is still within the prohibition of the Constitution."[11] One might conclude that these criteria apply to this case, but the Court reaches an opposite finding. "This comment is not applicable to the constitution of Mississippi and its statutes. They do not on their face discriminate between the races, and it has not been shown that their actual administration was evil, only that evil was possible under them."[12]

The judgment of the Mississippi court is upheld and all the objections to the elimination of blacks to participate in the case of Henry Williams, and, most especially, the four newly written state requirements for voting are reconfirmed. The final phrase of the Court, "it has not been shown that their actual administration was evil, only that evil was possible under them," deserves examination. It certainly could be posited that this Court, which two years earlier had decided the *Plessy* case, knew full well what the real-life consequences were with these obstacles against black voters.

Throughout the South, states followed the 1890 Mississippi plan, with some variations. In 1898, Louisiana devised the "grandfather clause," which allowed illiterates to register to vote if their fathers or grandfathers had been eligible to vote on January 1, 1867, when African Americans were still disenfranchised.[13] By the early 1900s, every Southern state had adopted a statewide Democratic primary, which, with some exceptions, effectively excluded black voters. As an example of the "evil" that the Supreme Court hadn't seen, in Alabama in 1900, 121,159 black men over 21 years of age were literate and eligible to vote, but only 3,742 were registered.[14] These low numbers obviously reduced the effectiveness of the black community's vote and political power. (Refer to Figure 5-3.)

In 1899, there was one more case, the *Cumming v. Richmond County (GA) Board of Education*, which clearly reflected the downward trend experienced by the black community in the latter half of the 1800s. In this instance, monies had been collected at the local level to maintain a separate white high school. The complaint that the black citizens held was clear. "That the petitioners interposed no objections to so much of the tax as was for primary, intermediate and grammar schools, but the tax for the support of the system of high schools was illegal and

---

9   Ibid.
10   Ibid., p. 223.
11   Ibid., p. 225.
12   Ibid.
13   Tindall and Shi, *America: A Narrative History*, p. 568.
14   Ibid.

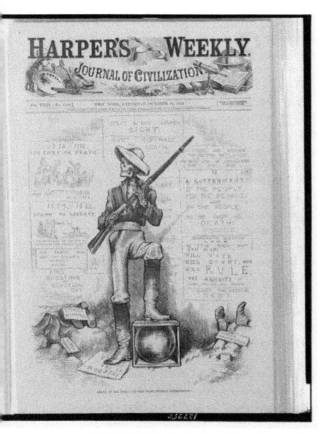

5-3: This 1879 drawing depicts a skeleton representing Southern Society holding a shotgun at a polling place, preventing African-Americans from voting.

void for the reason that that system was for the use and benefit of the white population exclusively."[15]

The response of the local education board: "it would be unwise and unconscionable to keep up a high school for sixty students and turn away three hundred little negroes who are asking to be taught their alphabet and to read and write."[16] The black high school students were advised that their educational needs could be met in Augusta, a neighboring Georgia city.

Justice Harlan delivered the relatively short opinion of the Court. First, he reviews the findings of the Supreme Court of Georgia concerning this case. That court had not been able to decide if the Fourteenth Amendment's clauses about "equal rights and immunities of citizens of the United States" had been abridged by the decision of the local school board. The constitution of the state of Georgia was clear about one point, however, in regard to the elementary school education of its youngsters. "The schools shall be free to all children of the State, but separate schools shall be provided for the white and colored races."[17] Ultimately, the justice is unable to determine whether or not the local school board had acted for economic reasons or in bad faith.

Under the circumstances disclosed, we cannot say that this action of the state court was, within the meaning of the Fourteenth Amendment, a denial by the State to the plaintiffs and to those associated with them of the equal protection of the laws or of any privileges belonging to them as citizens if the United States. We may add that while all admit that the benefits and burdens of public taxation must be shared by citizens without discrimination against any class on account of their race, the education of the people in schools maintained by state taxation is a matter belonging to the respective states, and any interference on the part of the Federal authority with the management of such schools cannot be justified except in the case of a clear and unmistakable disregard of rights secured by the supreme law of the land. We have here no such case to be determined.[18]

---

15 *Cumming v. Richmond*, United States Reports, vol. 175, Banks and Brothers, 1899, p. 529.
16 Ibid., p. 533.
17 Ibid., p. 543.
18 Ibid., p. 545.

Interestingly, the Georgia state constitution, which clearly mandated that separate schools be maintained for black and white students, did not appear to be any concern for the Supreme Court, even though it seems to be in direct contradiction to the Fourteenth Amendment, which called for "equal protection of the law."

Unfortunately, in addition to this type of ongoing racism against people of color, the country began to reconnect with the concept of nativism. This belief, in place in America since the mid-1800s, focused on a mistrust of immigrants. Nativism is defined by John Higham as "intense opposition to an internal minority on the ground of its foreign [i.e., "un-American"] connections." Antiforeign parties in the mid-1800s were known as "Know-Nothing" parties.[19] Nativists believed that the nationalities of the initial immigrations to America of British, French, German, and other Nordic groups were superior to the Slavs, Italians, Greek, and Jewish people coming to America.

Beginning in the 1890s, proponents of this belief advocated limiting immigration for these various groups. Presidents Cleveland, Taft, and Wilson overrode proposed laws devised by the nativists to limit immigration to America. Nevertheless, groups such as the Chinese suffered from this type of thinking. "They were not white; they were not Christian; many were not literate."[20] In 1882, Congress passed a bill authorizing a ten-year suspension of Chinese immigration. This act ensured that about one-third of those Chinese attempting to come to America were not able to do so.[21] (See Figure 5-4.)

As the new century dawned, the racism of the last one continued unabated. The case of *James v. Bowman*, decided in 1903, is such an example. In December 1900, an indictment was found by the United States District Court for the District of Kentucky against Henry Bowman and Harry Weaver, based on section 5507 of the Revised Statutes of the United States.[22] The indictment charged that certain "men of African descent, colored men, negroes, and not white men, being citizens of Kentucky and the United States, were, by means of bribery, unlawfully and feloniously intimidated and prevented from exercising their lawful right of voting in November of 1898 at a Congressional election."[23]

As with previous cases, it is helpful to view the actual law involved to determine what legal context the justices were considering. Section 5507 is connected to the Fifteenth Amendment as legislation supporting the right to vote.

5-4: The ideology of nativism had a corrosive effect on many ethnic groups, especially the Chinese.

Every person who prevents, hinders, controls, or intimidates another from exercising or in exercising the right of suffrage, to whom that right is guaranteed by the Fifteenth Amendment to the Constitution of the United States, by means of bribery or threats of depriving such person of employment or occupation, or of ejecting such person from a

---

19 John Higham, *Strangers in the Land*, p. 4.
20 Tindall and Shi, p. 628.
21 Ibid., p. 629.
22 *James v. Bowman*, United States Reports, vol. 190, Banks and Brothers, 1902, p. 127.
23 Ibid.

rented house, lands, or other property, or by threats of refusing to renew leases or contracts for labor, shall be punished as provided in the preceding section."[24]

The solicitor general argued the case representing the United States. He referenced the Fourteenth and Fifteenth Amendments to the Constitution and made the following assertion: "Whether section 5507 relates to bribery pure and simple, or to bribery committed because of race, color, or previous condition of the voter, it is entirely within the power of congress over Federal elections. The power to punish bribery per se being conceded, no question can be raised as to the power to punish bribery for any cause."[25]

Those attorneys representing Henry Bowman then quoted from a new decision offered by the Circuit Court of Appeals for the Sixth District, *Karem v. United States*. In that case, Karem was indicted and charged "with conspiring with others to injure, oppress, threaten, and intimidate certain negroes in the free exercise of the right of suffrage at a state election on account of their race, color, and previous condition of servitude."[26] The Court held that section 5508, one of the legal provisions that was part of the Enforcement Act of 1870 that was written to enforce the Fifteenth Amendment, "ha[s] been held to have been in excess of the jurisdiction of the Congress under the Fifteenth Amendment, and therefore null and void."[27] The attorneys concluded, "The appellee contends that section 5507 is unconstitutional, and while Congress may provide for the punishment of bribery by an individual at Congressional elections, it has not constitutionally done so, and that the judgment of the District Court be affirmed."[28]

Justice David J. Brewer delivered the opinion of the Court. He immediately addresses the provisions written to enforce the post–Civil War Amendments. He relies on prior decisions to quickly reach his conclusions. A major postwar legal distinction was that the Fifteenth Amendment "relates solely to action 'by the United States or by any State,' and does not contemplate wrongful individual acts."[29] The same distinction is made, as previously studied, to the Fourteenth Amendment as well, "The provisions of the Fourteenth Amendment of the Constitution we have quoted all have reference to state action exclusively, and not to any action of private individuals."[30]

The justice continues with a litany of cases previously studied that greatly limit the potency of the amendments. The parsing and limiting of the amendments, which in many ways neutralized them, is also applied by the justice to the acts of this case.

In passing it may be noticed that this indictment charges no wrong done by the State of Kentucky, or by any one acting under its authority. The matter complained of was purely an individual act of the defendant. Nor is it charged that the bribery was on account of race, color or previous condition of servitude. True, the parties who were bribed were alleged to be "men of African descent, colored men, negroes, and not white men," and again, that they were "persons to whom the right of suffrage and the right to vote was then and there

24 Ibid., p. 128.
25 Ibid., p. 131.
26 Ibid., pp. 132–133.
27 Ibid.
28 Ibid., p. 135.
29 Ibid., p. 136.
30 Ibid.

guaranteed by the Fifteenth Amendment to the Constitution of the United States." But this merely describes the parties wronged as within the classes named in the amendment. They were not bribed because they were colored men, but because they were voters. No discrimination on account of race, color or previous condition of servitude is charged.[31]

The above distinction is one that has been made before by the High Court. While they acknowledge that the discrimination is directed toward "men of African descent," they find a way to circumvent any legal penalties toward those acting against the black community. The final comment in this decision is directed toward Congress. "Congress has no power to punish bribery at all elections."[32] The judgment of the District Court is affirmed, and Henry Bowman's attempt to challenge the constitutionality of section 5507 of the law supporting the Fifteenth Amendment is successful.

In addition to intimidation and violence against people of color, some cases brought before the Court reflect an almost surreal reality for blacks living in a new American century. The case of *Clyatt v. United States*, decided in 1905, is another of the little-known cases in our country's civil rights history. In November 1901, the Circuit Court of the United States for the Northern District of Florida returned a two-count indictment against Samuel Clyatt.[33] He was indicted for "unlawfully and knowingly returning one Will Gordon and one Mose Ridley [men of color] to a condition of peonage, by forcibly and against the will of them, returning them … to work out a debt claimed to be due them."[34]

A trial resulted in a guilty verdict, and Clyatt was sentenced to confinement at hard labor for four years. The verdict was challenged through the Court of Appeals for the Fifth Circuit and ultimately was heard by the Supreme Court.[35] The attorneys representing Clyatt argue that the term "peonage" is something created and authorized by a state or territory, and a single person could not create it.[36] Any wrongs committed by a person should be corrected by the state, not the federal government. They further argue that any legislation such as the Thirteenth, Fourteenth, and Fifteenth amendments did not relate to this case regarding peonage. "But that does not mean that the person depriving him of his liberty can be punished by the National Government. The offense is against the State."[37] (Refer to Figure 5-5.)

Assistant Attorney General Purdy represented the government and gave a very short argument in favor of Clyatt's conviction. His argument focuses on the idea of what peonage is. "The system of Mexican peonage and the holding of a person to a condition of peonage is involuntary servitude within the meaning of the Constitution."[38] Justice David Brewer delivered the Court's findings in a brief response. First, he discusses the definition of peonage and involuntary servitude. He acknowledges that the Thirteenth Amendment established "an absolute declaration that slavery or involuntary servitude shall not exist in any part of the United States."[39] He continues to support the potency of the Thirteenth Amendment: "Under the Thirteenth Amendment, the legislation, so far as necessary or proper to eradicate

---

31 Ibid., p. 139.
32 Ibid., p. 142.
33 *Clyatt v. United States*, p. 209.
34 Ibid.
35 Ibid.
36 Ibid., p. 210.
37 Ibid., p. 212.
38 Ibid., p. 214.
39 Ibid., p. 217.

U.S. INDICTS SUGAR PLANTERS FOR HOLDING NEGRO LABORERS IN PEONAGE...... NEWS ITEM

"AND WHILE YOU'RE IN THERE, FIND OUT SOMETHING ABOUT A FELLOW NAMED ABE LINCOLN"

5-5: Apparently, this practice of capturing and holding laborers against their will went on for decades, as this 1940s picture suggests.

all forms and incidents of slavery and involuntary servitude, may be direct and primary, operating upon the acts of individuals, whether sanctioned by state legislation or not."[40]

The next line of reasoning for the justice is to examine the specific section of law in question.

Section 5526 punishes "every person who holds, arrests, returns, or causes to be held, arrested, or returned." Three distinct acts are mentioned— holding, arresting, and returning. The disjunctive "or" indicates the separation between them, and shows that either one may be the subject of indictment and punishment."[41]

After defining the word "return," the justice explains, "It was essential, therefore, under the charge in this case to show that Gordon and Ridley had been in a condition of peonage, to which, by the act of the defendant, they were returned."[42]

In fact, the justice seems to have a clear picture of what had occurred in this case.

The testimony discloses that the defendant with another party went to Florida and caused the arrest of Gordon and Ridley on warrants issued by a magistrate in Georgia for larceny, but there can be little doubt that these criminal proceedings were only an excuse for securing the custody of Gordon and Ridley and taking them back to Georgia to work out a debt.[43]

Yet, despite this understanding, Justice Brewer reaches a totally different conclusion based on the notion of peonage. He notes that, "there is not a scintilla of testimony to show that Gordon and Ridley were ever theretofore in a condition of peonage."[44] He acknowledges that they were in debt and had left the state of Georgia with that debt unpaid. Yet, this situation did not meet the formal criteria of peonage that the justices employed in their decision. So, because they had not been held in peonage, they couldn't be charged with this crime. Despite the fact that the defendants forcibly went to another state and basically kidnapped two black men, the

---

40 Ibid.
41 Ibid., pp. 218–219.
42 Ibid., p. 219.
43 Ibid., p. 222.
44 Ibid.

Court decides that the judgment should be reversed and the case remanded for a new trial. What is especially troubling is that the federal courts on the local level, in this case a circuit court, enforced the law correctly, with the indictment and guilty charge against Clyatt. All of this work was undone by the High Court. Justice Harlan offers a brief dissent, in which he suggests that there was sufficient evidence to make a case within the statute regarding peonage.

In the case of *Hodges v. United States*, decided in 1906, it was apparent that the daily abuses and tribulations suffered by people of color were quite real and devastating. This situation is one that most people can readily understand.

5-6: This photograph shows young boys, black and white, at their jobs working hard. As adults they all deserved equal chances to succeed.

The owners of a lumber company were charged with threatening and intimidating a number of black men who had signed labor contracts to work at the lumber mill. The situation, as described in the Court's finding, is certainly explicit (Figure 5-6).

> The said defendants did knowingly, willfully, and unlawfully conspire to injure, oppress, threaten and intimidate them in the free exercise of said right [to work] ... because they were citizens of African descent ... they must abandon said contracts and their said work at said mill and cease to perform any further labor thereat, or receive any further compensation for said labor ... the said defendants being then and there armed with deadly weapons, threatening and intimidating the said workmen there employed, with the purpose of compelling them by violence and threats and otherwise to remove from said place of business, to stop said work and to cease the enjoyment of said right and privilege and by then and there willfully, deliberately and unlawfully compelling said Berry Winn, Dave Hinton, Percy Legg, Joe Mardis, Joe McGill, Dan Shelton, Jim Hall and George Shelton to quit said work and abandon said place ... because they were colored men and citizens of African descent ... [45]

Initially, the men charged with these violent acts were found guilty, sentenced to imprisonment and fined. They were found guilty of violating a number of laws based on enforcing the Thirteenth and Fourteenth amendments. One in particular, Section 1977, seems to directly address this circumstance.

> All persons within the jurisdiction of the United States shall have the same right in every State and territory to make and enforce contacts, to sue, to be parties, give evidence, and

45   *Hodges v. United States*, pp. 3–4.

to the full and equal benefit of all laws and proceedings for the security of persons and property as is enjoyed by white citizens, and shall be subject to like punishment, pains, penalties, taxes, licenses, and exactions of every kind, and no other.[46]

If ever there was an instance where the law seems unequivocal, this is that case. The attorneys representing the men charged with these violations make some familiar-sounding arguments. First, they ask, "is the right of a citizen of African descent to make or enforce a contract a right granted by the Constitution or laws of the United States?"[47] They answer this question with the notion that it was local state and city governments that granted this aspect of citizenship, not the federal government. In fact, their view of the former slaves and the post Civil War Amendments is telling as well. "The Thirteenth Amendment did nothing more than to create or make a freeman of a slave. Since he became a freeman the municipal laws of the land give to him the right to contract, to sue and be sued in the State or municipality in which he resides."[48]

They continue their argument by reducing the strength of the Thirteenth Amendment. In a piece of argumentation marked by moxie, the attorneys acknowledge the wrongs their clients have committed, but they argue that even if the black men were threatened and intimidated with the loss of their work contracts, "it does not follow that the conspiracy upon a part of certain individuals to intimidate or interfere with a Negro citizen in the performance of his contract fastens upon the Negro any badge of slavery any more than it would be held to fasten a badge of slavery upon a white man if his right to contract should be interfered with by intimidations or threats."[49] They brazenly suggest that any laws broken were state laws, not federal ones, and that the ultimate definition of the Thirteenth Amendment is that it "has respect not to distinction of race or class or color, but to slavery."[50]

An assistant attorney general, Milton D. Purdy, as well as a special assistant to the attorney general, Otis J. Carlton, offers powerful arguments for the men who had been deprived of their contracts and livelihood by violence. They base much of their presentation on the Thirteenth Amendment. "The Thirteenth Amendment was intended to secure to the colored race practical freedom."[51] The consequences of limiting this amendment and the laws which enforce it are blatantly apparent,

The Government contends that the people, having clear notions of the status of the colored race and of what attempts would be made to return it to its servile condition, intended by the Thirteenth Amendment to grant and secure practical freedom. It outrages our feelings of humanity to believe that the men who had fought to free the slaves merely intended to sever the legal ligament which bound the slave to his master, leaving the latter at liberty to cut him off from the fundamental rights which white men enjoyed. Such a narrow construction leaves the black race in a state made worse by their emancipation by the breaking of the cord of self-interest which bound the slaveholder to take care of his property.[52]

---

46 Ibid., p. 4.
47 Ibid., p. 6.
48 Ibid.
49 Ibid., p. 7.
50 Ibid.
51 Ibid., p, 10.
52 Ibid., p. 11.

The attorneys continue with a spirited defense of the amendment: "That was done by the Thirteenth Amendment, and because, under that Amendment Congress may enact legislation acting primarily upon individuals, it may punish those who attempt by concerted action to deprive the Negro of his right to contract solely for the reason that he is a Negro."[53] These men end their arguments with passion and prophecy for those people of color who had violently been forced to give up their vocations.

If the Negro who is in our midst can be denied the right to work, and must live on the outskirts of civilization, he will become more dangerous than the wild beasts, because he has a higher intelligence than the most intelligent beast. He will become an outcast lurking about the borders and living by depredation.

There is but one refuge from that condition, and that is to put himself back under some chosen master in the condition of slavery itself. If the Nation has not the power at the very threshold to say to those who declare against this or other races, that as a race it shall not have one of the most essential rights of a free man, it is powerless indeed. It was given to the Nation by the Thirteenth Amendment, and this case is brought within it.[54]

Justice David Brewer delivers the opinion of the Court in this case. First, he eliminates the Fourteenth and Fifteenth amendments as points of legal reference by stating, "That the Fourteenth and Fifteenth Amendments do not justify the legislation [Sections 1977 and 5508 mentioned above] is also beyond dispute, for they, as repeatedly held, are restrictions upon state action, and no action on the part of the State is complained of."[55] His decision continues with a reference to the Slaughterhouse Cases, which undertook to address the question of what exactly were the privileges and immunities of citizens of the several states. The Court quotes the earlier decision and provides the following answer: "Protection by the Government, the enjoyment of life and liberty, with the right to acquire and possess property of every kind, and to pursue and obtain happiness and safety; subject, nevertheless, to such restraints as the Government may prescribe for the general good of the whole."[56] The opinion follows with an amplification of the rights guaranteed by the federal and state governments.

It would be the vainest show of learning to attempt to prove by citations of authority, that up to the adoption of the recent Amendments no claim or pretence was set up that those rights depended on the Federal Government for their existence or protection, beyond the very few express limitations which the Federal Constitution imposed upon the States—such, for instance, as the prohibition against ex post facto laws, bills of attainder, and laws impairing the obligation of contracts. But with the exception of these and a few other restrictions, the entire domain of the privileges and immunities of citizens of the States, as above defined, lay within the constitutional and legislative power of the States, and without that of the Federal Government.[57]

53 Ibid., p. 13.
54 Ibid., p. 14.
55 Ibid.
56 Ibid., p. 15.
57 Ibid.

This paragraph deserves closer examination. First, it is highly significant to note that at the beginning of a new century, the potency of the post–Civil War amendments seems to be almost completely nullified. Except for a few generalized rights, the role of the federal government is nonexistent when it comes to loss of rights by the actions of individuals within the states. Of course, if the states are the loci of the ongoing loss of various rights and privileges by people of color, how can the Court—with a straight face—maintain that the vehicle for legal remedy is within those same states? In a final irony, the Court itself enumerates one of the few general laws seemingly protected by the federal government as "laws impairing the obligation of contracts." That principle is the legal center of this case, and even that is not enough to offer any protection for the men who had been attacked, intimidated, and violently forced to lose their work contracts.

Next in his opinion, the justice uses Webster's dictionary to define the term slavery as "the state of entire subjection of one person to the will of another."[58] In this regard, the justice concludes that, "no mere personal assault or trespass or appropriation operates to reduce the individual to a condition of slavery."[59] So, the fact that a person was assaulted and deprived of their right to work, is, technically, for this Court, not a "badge of slavery" and not subject to intervention by federal authorities. (Refer to Figure 5-7.)

At this point, Justice Brewer might have concluded his opinion. He, instead, continues with an astounding and sadly insightful interpretation of his and the Court's true visions of race relations in early-20th-century America. First, he offers a somewhat strange definition of the badges of slavery by noting that, "In slave times in the slave States not infrequently every free Negro was required to carry with him a copy of a judicial decree or other evidence of his right to freedom or be subject to arrest."[60] He then notes that the High Court in *Fong Yue Ting v. United States* had no issue with an act passed by Congress in May of 1892, which required all Chinese laborers residing in the United States to apply for a certificate of identity that they had to carry with them at all times. Failure to have this certificate resulted in an arrest. For

5-7: *A question to reflect upon is how to define a "badge of slavery." Does that mean being chained as these Africans are, or can it also be a "badge" when a person is not allowed to work at their job, or pray at the church of their choice, or attend the show or play that they want and to sit where they want?*

58   Ibid., p. 17.
59   Ibid., p. 18.
60   Ibid., p. 19.

Justice Brewer, the fact that the Chinese were made to carry such certificates was not related in any way to badges of slavery. One might wonder if the justice is suggesting that it would be acceptable if slaves or free blacks were required to carry such papers. (Refer to Figure 5-8.)

In a final paragraph which deserves further study and analysis, the Justice writes the following.

One thing more: At the close of the civil war, when the problem of the emancipated slaves was before the nation, it might have left them in a condition of alienage, or established them as wards of the Government like the Indian tribes, and thus retained for the Nation jurisdiction over them, or it might, as it did, give them citizenship. It chose the latter. By the Fourteenth Amendment it made citizens of all born within the limits of the United States and subject to its jurisdiction. By the Fifteenth it prohibited any State from denying the right of suffrage on account of race, color or previous condition of servitude, and by the Thirteenth it forbade slavery or involuntary servitude anywhere within the limits of the land. Whether this was or was not the wiser way to deal with the great problem is not a matter for the courts to consider. It is for us to accept the decision, which declined to constitute them wards of the nation or leave them in a condition of alienage where they would be subject to the jurisdiction of Congress, but gave them citizenship, doubtless believing that thereby in the long run their best interests would be subserved, they taking their chances with other citizens in the states where they should make their homes. For these reasons we think the United States court had no jurisdiction of the wrong charged in the indictment.[61]

Disengenuis

5-8: In a speech given in 1891, the well-educated and cultured justice David Brewer spoke about the joys of acquiring property as, "the pursuit of happiness is one of the unalienable rights," referred to in the Declaration of Independence as a goal for Americans. His thoughts about the validity and legal standing of the Black community indicated that this "pursuit of happiness" didn't apply to them.

Gosopel slaves

---

61   Ibid., pp. 19–20.

The judgments were reversed and the case remanded with instructions to release the men initially convicted in the indictment. In other words, no one was held responsible for the black men losing their job contracts.

Most significantly, it seems highly appropriate to take a few of the phrases employed by Justice Brewer at the onset of a new century to appreciate some of his apparent feelings (and those of the Court, as well) about the former slaves over 40 years after the conclusion of the Civil War. His first phrase is most revealing and disappointing: "the problem of the emancipated slaves," hardly indicates a sense that slavery was wrong, and that now, decades later, it is well past time that people two and three generations removed from slavery be finally fully accepted as equal citizens. So, instead of fellow citizens who have had their rights abused and violated, the justice wrote about the "problem of the emancipated slaves," as if they were newly freed without any rights! How profoundly discouraging this phrase must have been to anyone advocating equality at the turn of the century.

A second area of concern found in this paragraph is the idea that the former slaves might have been better served if they had been treated as wards of the government, like the Native Americans. The only appropriate word here is "Wow." This must have been disconcerting for people of color, to read that a Supreme Court justice felt that the government would care for them. Since the Civil War, the country had witnessed decades of fighting and battles in the various Indian wars. In 1887, the U.S. government passed the Dawes Act, which forever changed Native American culture in a highly negative way. In fact, the origin of this notion of tutelage for the freed slaves was not a dominant one after the war. Why raise it now? Apparently, Justice Brewer felt that at one time it had merit.

Another deflating sentence is, "Whether this was or was not the wiser way to deal with the great problem is not a matter for the courts to consider." So, in 1905, the Court is having doubts about the efficacy of granting the former slaves legal rights. The term "great problem" is a fascinatingly depressing choice of words. What is this problem? People of color merely desire the same rights as every other citizen, no more, no less. So the nation's highest Court, while saying that it is not the Court's place to make judgments, has indeed made a very substantial judgment about the attainment of full civil rights for people of color.

In a final pessimistic and negative view of the rights of the black community, the justice writes that Congress, after declining to keep the black community in a condition of alienage, "gave them citizenship, doubtless believing that thereby in the long run their best interests would be subserved, they taking their chances with other citizens in the state where they should make their homes." The words "taking their chances" are frightening. Here is a justice of the country's highest legal body suggesting that people's lives are a matter of chance. What happened to the rights guaranteed by the Constitution, its amendments, and the many civil rights acts? In fact, Brewer's words imply that black citizens had rolled the dice of social and political equality in America, by trying to live fully as whites, and had lost that gamble.

Two justices, Harlan and Day, dissented from the above decision. Their argument, made in a prior case, is straightforward: "Congress may not only prevent the reestablishing of the institution of slavery, pure and simple, but may make it impossible that any of its incidents or badges should exist or be enforced in any State or Territory of the United States."[62] To bolster this dissent, the justices quote from the Civil Rights Act of 1866, passed after the ratification of the Thirteenth Amendment that ended slavery and offered citizenship to the former slaves. " ... and that such citizens, of every race and color, without regard to any previous condition of slavery or involuntary servitude, should have the same right in every State and Territory to make and enforce contracts,

---

62   Ibid., p. 27.

to sue, be parties, ... as is enjoyed by white citizens ... Congress then had the right to go further and to enforce its declaration by passing laws for the prosecution and punishment of those who should deprive, or attempt to deprive, any person of the rights thus conferred upon them."[63]

Near the end of his opinion, Justice Harlan states what to him is obvious about this majority finding,

> *The court does adjudge that Congress cannot make it an offense against the United States for individuals to combine or conspire to prevent, even by force, citizens of African descent, solely because of their race, from earning a living. Such is the import and practical effect of the present decision, although the court has heretofore unanimously held that the right to earn one's living in all legal ways, and to make lawful contracts in reference thereto, is a vital point of freedom established by the Constitution ... These general principles, it is to be regretted, are now modified, so as to deny to millions of citizen-laborers of African descent, deriving their freedom from the Nation, the right to appeal for National protection against lawless combinations of individuals who seek, by force, and solely because of the race of such laborers, to deprive them of the freedom established by the Constitution of the United States.*[64]

The condescending and disparaging remarks mentioned above by Justice Brewer barely reflect the depth of the hatred held toward people of color. This mean-spiritedness was illustrated by the 1906 case, *United States v. Shipp.* The details of this case indicate that 50 years after the Civil War, living a life based on American fairness and justice was often a fantasy for many people of color. In this instance, a 21-year-old white woman, Nevada Taylor, from Chattanooga, Tennessee, was attacked and raped on January 23, 1906. The next day, the attack was described in the local paper as, "the most fiendish crime in the history of Chattanooga."[65] After a sizable reward was offered for information, a white citizen stepped forward to indicate that Ed Johnson, a young black man, was near the scene of the crime. The local sheriff, Joseph Shipp, arrested Johnson. Despite three hours of interrogation and the existence of a dozen alibi witnesses, the public fervor against Johnson rose.

Recognizing that Johnson's life was in dire danger from a mob, the sheriff and a local judge moved him by train to Nashville. Within two weeks, lawyers were appointed for Ed Johnson's defense, and a trial was held in Chattanooga. During this trial, 17 witnesses were called by the defense, with a dozen swearing that Ed Johnson was with them at the Last Chance Saloon, potentially giving him an ironclad alibi. At the request of jurors, Miss Taylor (the rape victim), was recalled to the witness stand and asked if Ed Johnson was the man who raped her. Her response was, "I will not swear that he is the man, but I believe that he is the Negro who assaulted me."[66] She was once again asked if he was the guilty party. Her response was, "Listen to me. I would not take the life of an innocent man. But before God, I believe this is the guilty Negro."[67]

---

63   Ibid., p. 29.

64   Ibid., pp. 36–37.

65   http://abajournal, p. 2. The civic mood across the South was raw regarding black and white relations. During September 22–24, 1906, the city of Atlanta experienced four days of rioting, with white mobs killing dozens of blacks, wounding others, and destroying property. The immediate spark for these actions was unsubstantiated newspaper accounts of black men assaulting white females. (www.Georgiaencyclopedia. org/articles/history. Atlanta race riot 1906.)

66   Ibid., p. 3.

67   Ibid.

Despite Johnson's compelling testimony and that of many others, he was found guilty. The trial judge, Samuel McReynolds, scheduled Johnson to be hanged on March 13 in the basement of the county jail.

Within days of Johnson being found guilty, two black attorneys, Noah W. Parden and his partner, Styles L. Hutchins, leading lawyers in Chattanooga, began planning possible appeals to his guilty verdict. On February 20, they filed an appeal with the Tennessee Supreme Court; the appeal was denied within a week. On March 7, they continued this process on the federal level with a petition in U.S. District Court in Knoxville. Their legal arguments were formidable,

> The nine-page petition pointed out that Johnson's original lawyers were denied the right to file pretrial motions, that the trial was unfairly influenced by the threat of mob violence, that only white people were summoned to jury service, that Johnson's lawyers abandoned their client by advising him to waive his rights to appeal, and that there were numerous irregularities during the trial, including the fact that a juror tried to attack the defendant in the middle of the trial.[68]

After deliberating for a number of hours, Judge C. D. Clark agreed with many of the assertions made by Johnson's new attorneys. He issued a ten-day stay of execution and permitted Johnson's lawyers to appeal directly to the U.S. Supreme Court.[69] In the days following this decision, a group of men set fire to the law office of Parden and Hutchins. In the middle of the night, shots were fired through the windows of Parden's home while his wife, Mattie, was there alone.[70] Mattie stayed with a local minster while her husband traveled to Washington, D.C., to make an appeal to Supreme Court justice John Marshall Harlan, a Kentuckian, who was assigned to hear emergency appeals from the 6th Circuit.[71]

In the petition, Parden "pointed to specific violations of the Fourth, Fifth, Sixth and Fourteenth Amendments. The atmosphere in the community was so poisoned that there was no way Ed Johnson could have received a fair trial from an impartial jury," Parden said. "Everybody in that courtroom knew going in what they were going to do. They were there to give Ed Johnson a trial, and then they were going to hang him."[72]

Justice Harlan, who had written a powerful dissent to the *Plessy v. Ferguson* majority opinion, granted the appeal, followed a few days later by the entire Court accepting a hearing about the case. Telegrams were sent from the High Court, informing the various authorities in Chattanooga about the granting of the appeal from Justice Harlan and the entire Court. Sadly, the High Court's intervention was not enough to overcome a frenzy of mob hatred.

As news of the Court's involvement spread throughout the city, dozens of armed men stormed the county jail holding Johnson. Sheriff Shipp gave all his deputies the night off with the exception of a 72-year-old jailer. Other inmates had been removed to another floor. A siege of the jail began the evening of March 19; within a few hours, the locks to the jail and cell of Ed Johnson had been broken, and he was grabbed up and taken by a mob of hundreds to the county bridge that spanned the Tennessee River.[73] (Refer to Figure 5-9.)

---

68 Ibid., p. 4.
69 Ibid., p. 5.
70 Ibid.
71 Ibid.
72 Ibid.
73 Ibid., p. 6.

As a noose was placed around his neck, Ed Johnson was afforded the opportunity to say a few final words. According to newspaper accounts, the following were his words: "I am ready to die. But I never done it. I am going to tell the truth. I am not guilty. I am not guilty. I have said all the time that I did not do it and it is true. I was not there." Then his uttered his last words. "God bless you all. I am innocent."[74] (See Figure 5-10.)

At that point, Ed Johnson was lifted into the air by his neck. Since death didn't happen quickly enough, the mob opened fire on his swinging body—he was shot more than 50 times. A bullet pierced the rope holding him, and he fell to the wooden planks of the bridge. Someone from the group yelled, "He's not dead yet."

5-9: *While there are no known photographs of the Ed Johnson lynching, others that capture the brutality and unbelievability of these incidents do exist. Pictued here are the bodies of Laura Nelson and her teenage son who had been jailed to stand trial for the shooting of a deputy in Okemah, Oklahoma, in May 1911. They never had their day in court as they were taken out of their cells and lynched, as shown, from a local bridge. Laura had an infant baby with her that was left on the banks of the river. His fate is unknown.*

A man later identified as a deputy sheriff shot Johnson five more times at point-blank range. He then pinned a note onto Johnson's chest that read, *To Justice Harlan. Come get your nigger now.*[75]

This act of defiance brought reactions from the administration of President Theodore Roosevelt. Two Secret Service agents came and investigated the incident. Their conclusion was fairly apparent: There was a conspiracy between the sheriff, his deputies, and leaders of the lynch mob to kill Johnson. The U.S. attorney general, William Moody, filed a petition on May 28 charging Sheriff Shipp, six deputies, and 19 leaders of the lynch mob with contempt of the Supreme Court for ignoring the Court's instructions when it had granted the appeal of the case.

Beginning in February 1907 and lasting over two years, evidence was heard in the federal courthouse in Chattanooga, within blocks of the bridge from which Ed Johnson had been murdered. In March of 1909, Charles Bonaparte, the new attorney general (William Moody had been appointed to the High Court), argued,

> *This proceeding is unique in the history of court ... Its importance cannot be overestimated. Lynchings have occurred in defiance of state laws and state courts without attempt, or at most with only desultory attempt, to punish the lynchers ... never in its history has an order of this court been disobeyed with such impunity. Justice is at an end when orders of the highest and most powerful court in the land are set at naught. Obedience to its mandates is essential to our institutions.*[76]

For the Court in its 1906 decision about the case, its authority was the main point of attention and concern: "But even if the circuit court had no jurisdiction to entertain Johnson's

---

74   Ibid.
75   Ibid.
76   Ibid., p. 7.

petition, and if this Court had no jurisdiction of the appeal, this Court and this Court alone, could decide that such was the law. It and it alone necessarily had jurisdiction to decide to permit argument, and to take the time required for such consideration as it might need."[77]

Ultimately, on May 24, 1909, by a five-to-three vote, Sheriff Shipp, one of his deputies, and four leaders of the lynch mob were found guilty of contempt of the Supreme Court. Chief Justice Fuller's statements reflect his thoughts,

5-10: Pictured is the grave marker of Ed Johnson. His final words reverberate through history, speaking for himself and countless others treated so illegally and immorally— "I am innocent!"

It is apparent that a dangerous portion of the community was seized with the awful thirst for blood which only killing can quench, he stated. The persons who hung and shot this man were so impatient for his blood that they utterly disregarded the act of Congress as well as the order of this court … When anyone in custody, "is at the mercy of a mob", the administration of justice becomes a mockery. When this court granted a stay of execution on Johnson's application, it became its duty to protect him until his case should be disposed of. And when its mandate, issued for his protection, was defied, punishment of those guilty of such attempt must be awarded.[78]

On November 15, 1909, the sheriff and two others were ordered to serve 90 days in jail, while the others were sentenced to 60 days, all at the U.S. jail in the District of Columbia. Upon their return to Chattanooga, Shipp and the others were welcomed by over 10,000 cheering supporters. Later, a monument was erected in Shipp's honor. Judge Mc Reynolds, the trial judge, went on to serve in Congress for 18 years.[79]

---

77   http://supreme.justia.com. *United States v. Shipp*, p. 4.
78   http://abajournal.com, p.8.
79   Ibid.

This hearing marks the only time in its history that the High Court held a criminal trial. In an interview for the *Atlanta Independent*, Noah Parden made the following comment, "We are at a time when many of our people have abandoned the respect for the rule of law due to the racial hatred deep in their hearts and souls. Nothing less than our civilized society is at stake."[80] The final words about this horrible issue rightfully belong to the victim, Ed Johnson. On the back of his headstone, found in a

5-11: Leo Frank's lynching reflects the power of hate-filled words. The racism spewed out by Thomas Watson and others led to Frank's death. Families, with children, had their pictures taken near the hanging bodies to create family post-cards to share with friends and relatives.

dilapidated cemetery on Missionary Ridge above Chattanooga, is the phrase, *Farewell until we meet again in the sweet by and By*, and on the front are his last words: *God Bless you all. I AM A Innocent man.*[81] (Refer to Figure 5-11.)

It is worthwhile to analyze this entire event. From an overall historical view, these types of brutal events reflected the reality of fear that prevailed for many in the black community about this type of violence. Lynchings were so pervasive in America that in 1892, Alabama's Tuskegee University devised a specific definition for a slaying that qualified it as a lynching. "A racially motivated hate crime was not a lynching unless the group participating in the killing numbered three or more, and its members had acted under the pretext of service to justice, race or tradition."[82] Between 1882 and 1951, Tuskegee documented 4,730 lynchings that met that definition. Approximately one-quarter of these lynchings were in the western part of the country and involved white victims. Nevertheless, the relative ease and coordination that it took to organize the murder of Ed Johnson reflect a lack of civility, an extreme disregard for the rule of law, and—most significantly—the deeply held belief that the life and value of a person of color were not important.

These hangings such as in Chattanooga involved thousands of everyday citizens, who, as a mob, concluded that this type of vigilantism was the American way. What a frightening prospect for people of color and for the country as a whole. The various amendments such as the Fourteenth, which speaks about equal protection under the law and a Constitution that promotes Life, Liberty, and the Pursuit of Happiness, seemed to be make-believe, imaginary phrases that have no place in the real world of threats, intimidation, and ultimately an unjustly brutal death at the hands of a mob. It is a sad conclusion to lay much of the blame for this at

---

80   Ibid.
81   Ibid.
82   Ibid.

the feet of the Supreme Court, who even at this time were apparently more concerned about holding people in contempt rather than a man's existence. Furthermore, it is fair to suggest that the host of decisions made by the Court in the previous century—denying blacks true equality and acceptance as citizens—had now created this poisonous environment, giving people the sense that mob vigilantism could prevail where people of color were concerned.

Based on the above, it seems apparent that race relations in America at the beginning of this new century were at a new low point. As an example of this phenomenon, William P. Pickett, a lawyer, wrote a book published in 1909 entitled, *The Negro Problem: Abraham Lincoln's Solution.* This almost-six-hundred-page volume lays out in a systematic manner the myriad of problems supposedly caused by people of color in America and a solution to this issue: colonization. As the title implies, the notion of colonization was proposed by Lincoln. Speeches by President Lincoln offered prior to the Emancipation Proclamation are presented to bolster his argument. In a speech given in August 1862, Lincoln expresses his thoughts on the subject.

> *I suppose one of the principal difficulties in the way of colonization is that the free colored man cannot see his comfort would be advanced by it … This is (I speak in no unkind sense) an extremely selfish view of the case. … There is an unwillingness on the part of our people, harsh as it may be, for you free colored people to remain with us … If intelligent colored men, such as are before me, would move in this matter, much might be accomplished. It is exceedingly important that we have men at the beginning capable of thinking as white men, and not those who have been systematically oppressed. There is much to encourage you.*[83]

In his proposed solution to the Negro problem, Pickett lays out a detailed set of principles and ideas to work from. The primary one being, "There is, after all, but one way to extirpate an evil. The cause of the evil must be removed."[84] He then reveals a number of principles that he claims would have been embraced by President Lincoln if he had been in charge of the Reconstruction of the South.

- The absolute and unequivocal recognition and declaration of the fact that the Negro race is, as a matter of present condition, alien, inferior, and inassimilable, and is therefore not qualified to constitute an element of future American citizenship.
- In recognition of this fact, the adoption of a policy for the gradual removal of the negro race from the country, not in a spirit of hostility to the negro, but as a measure necessary for the permanent welfare of both races, and in which each will co-operate in carrying the project into execution.
- The adoption of the following provisions is recommended: The modification of the first section of the Fourteenth Amendment to the constitution of the United States, so as to provide that all persons of the negro race born after the year 1925 shall be excluded from national citizenship, and until that time conferring upon each state the power of regulation over the subject of state citizenship.
- The repeal of all civil rights acts, state and national and of all other provisions of law designed to confer upon the negro privileges other than those based upon his intrinsic merit and demonstrated service to society.

---

83 Pickett, *The Negro Problem*, p. 467.
84 Ibid., p. 336.

- The enactment in all the states of laws prohibiting the intermarriage of the white and Negro races.
- The absolute prohibition of the immigration of persons of Negro blood.
- A carefully devised and generously assisted plan to induce the voluntary emigration of all persons of African blood.[85]

What is jaw-dropping about the contents of this book is the myriad of details that Pickett has proposed. In many ways, it reminded me of some of the Nazi-era laws that would be directed against members of the Jewish community a few decades later. So, nearly 50 years after the conclusion of the Civil War, Pickett's writings reveal an astounding attempt to essentially strip blacks of their legal standing as Americans and force them to immigrate to another continent, all allegedly for their own good!

One might consider that Pickett was some sort of loner, not really representing the thinking of the times. Unfortunately, the reviews of his work by various journals representing prestigious universities and associations indicate that his views were considered mainstream—and quite legitimate of consideration. In January 1910, his work was reviewed by the University of Chicago Press. The reviewer, after giving a synopsis of the work, concluded, "At least his book is earnest and interestingly shows how apparently insurmountable obstacles shrink before a conviction of the wisdom of a radical plan."[86] In December of 1909, Pickett's work was reviewed by the American Economic Association. In this case, the reviewer finds that Pickett is quite a moral person.

He doesn't hate them, but he just wants them out of town

Eugenics

> *But if Mr. Pickett is somewhat severe in his estimate of the situation and in his plans for dealing with it, it must be said for him that he exhibits not the slightest trace of race animosity as such. His conclusions are based on the high ground of social utility as he sees it. One by one he rejects the plans proposed since emancipation: amalgamation, "extermination", and the subject race-theory ... That Mr. Pickett is an earnest, dispassionate student of the problem and that he makes an effective plea for his case is sufficiently clear.*[87]

At the same time, Pickett's work was analyzed by the Annals of the American Academy of Political and Social Science. In this instance, the reviewer suggests the following, "That there are tremendous difficulties the author sees—he may even consider them insuperable—if so, he will agree with the reviewer. Nevertheless, the plan deserves some consideration. The author's tone is balanced, his attitude very fair. He deprecates, as does every student, certain great and obvious evils in our life as a result of the Negro's presence. His statements are generally accurate, though lack of personal observation leads him into some errors of judgment."[88]

These attitudes of prejudice passed on in the veneer of respectability reflect the ongoing belief that the black citizen in America—fully a half century after the Civil War—is not a worthwhile member of society and quite vulnerable to the dictates of the white majority. These attitudes led to occurrences such as the *Shipp* case, leading to the death of Ed Johnson and an incident in Florida with a tragically similar outcome.

---

85 Ibid., pp. 337–338.
86 http://jstor.org/stable
87 Ibid.
88 Ibid.

A 1911 confrontation in Tallahassee, Florida, illustrates the bleak realities of life for people of color. A group of ten blacks had been arrested on questionable charges regarding a racial attack on a white man. Of the ten, six were charged with murder.

> *A crowd gathered in Tallahassee, and talk of lynching increased. Six of the men were smuggled out of Tallahassee and taken to Lake City for safekeeping. A few evenings later several men drove to Lake City and got the blacks out of jail on a forged release order, took them to the edge of town, and riddled all six with bullets for more than a half hour. No one in Lake City went to investigate the shooting until the assassins were driving away, thus there were no witnesses to the crime. Governor Albert Gilchrist offered a $250 reward for information about the lynching, but a cursory investigation was shortly abandoned without success.*[89]

A parallel situation—of a mob mentality flaunting the rule of law—prevailed in the 1915 case of Leo Frank, a Jewish man, convicted of raping and murdering a young girl in Marietta, Georgia. Frank's trial was held surrounded by an atmosphere of intense public pressure and the intimidation of all involved in the case. Even though his death sentence was commuted, Frank was taken from a jail cell, transported over hundreds of miles, and hanged in a very public and festive manner. In fact, in a landmark case, *Frank v. Mangum*, the lack of fairness on a state level was so profound that Frank's attorneys felt their final chance at justice would be a writ of habeas corpus to the nation's highest court. A federal writ is used to test the constitutionality of a state criminal conviction.[90]

In April 1915, the High Court heard the case of *Frank v. Mangum*, mentioned above. Frank requested the Court to recognize the poisonous atmosphere that surrounded his case, from its inception through the sentencing. Part of the argument reads,

> *And shortly before the presiding judge began his charge to the jury, the judge privately conversed with two of the prisoner's counsel, referred to the probable danger of violence to the prisoner if he were present when the verdict was rendered ... in the same conversation the judge expressed the view that even counsel might be in danger of violence should they be present at the reception of the verdict, and under these circumstances they agreed that neither they nor the prisoner should be present.*[91]

In this case, the Court set up the criterion that would be used to grant the appeal. "In dealing with these contentions, we should have in mind the nature and extent of the duty that is imposed upon a Federal court on application for the writ of habeas corpus ... Under the terms of that section, in order to entitle the present appellant to the relief sought, it must appear that he is held in custody in violation of the Constitution of the United States.[92]

At one point in the decision, the justices offer a description of a situation that approximated what Frank experienced.

---

89   Hall, Ed., *Race Relations and the Law*, pp. 291–292.
90   Gifis, *Legal Terms*, p. 213.
91   *Frank v. Mangum*, p. 2.
92   Ibid., p. 4.

> *We, of course, agree that if a trial is in fact dominated by a mob, so that the jury is intimidated and the trial judge yields, and so that there is an actual interference with the course of justice, there is, in that court, a departure from due process of law in the proper sense of the term. And if the state, supplying no corrective process, carries into execution a judgment of death or imprisonment based upon a verdict thus produced by mob domination, the state deprives the accused of his life or liberty without due process of law.*[93]

While the Court gives this definition of an apparent miscarriage of justice, its next paragraph greatly nullifies the thrust of the justices' meaning.

> *But the state may supply such corrective process as to it seems proper. Georgia has adopted the familiar procedure of a motion for a new trial, followed by an appeal to its supreme court, not confined to the mere record of conviction, but going at large, and upon evidence adduced outside of that record, into the question of whether the processes of justice have been interfered with in the trial court.*[94]

In the end, by a majority vote (7–2), the Court found, "he is not shown to have been deprived of any right guaranteed to him by the 14th Amendment or any other provision of the Constitution or laws of the United States; on the contrary, he has been convicted, and is now held in custody, under 'due process of law' within the meaning of the Constitution."[95]

The dissenters, Justices Holmes and Hughes, have a differing view of the realities of such a trial. Justice Holmes authored the dissent.

> *The single question in our minds is whether a petition alleging that the trial took place in the midst of a mob savagely and manifestly intent on a single result is shown on its face unwarranted, by the specifications, which may be presumed to set forth the strongest indications of the fact at the petitioner's command ... But supposing the alleged facts to be true, we are of [the] opinion that if they were before the supreme court, it sanctioned a situation upon which the courts of the United States should act; and if, for any reason, they were not before the Supreme Court, it is our duty to act upon them now, and to declare lynch law as little valid when practiced by a regularly drawn jury as when administered by one elected by a mob intent on death.*[96]

In the *Frank* case, there are a few elements that deserve consideration as historical background. The first are the writings of Thomas Watson, a social leader of Marietta society in the early 1900s. His weekly magazines, the *Jeffersonian* and *Watson's Magazine*, provide a glimpse into the prevailing racism and level of emotions which surrounded a case such as that of Leo Frank. Watson's attitudes toward blacks and slavery are clear,

---

93 Ibid., p. 8.
94 Ibid.
95 Ibid., p. 12
96 Ibid., p. 14.

He is an inferior being: is not any more our brother than the apes are, and we don't intend that he shall ever live on a footing of equality with us. That might as well be understood. The "Fatherhood of God" does not put every created being on the same racial level. Slavery took a lawless savage and made an intelligent useful worker out of him. And the noblest tribute to the benevolent character of Southern slavery is that nowhere else on earth is the negro race so well as in these United States.[97]

This kind of vile prejudice was directed toward blacks and Jews alike. The following illustrates the degree of anti-Semitism that Watson helped create that led to the tragic consequences of the *Frank* case.

The "factory girl," as the rich Jews and the rich Peachtree people contemptuously call her, is turning to dust in her grave—her blood yet crying vainly to high heaven for vengeance— and the lecherous Simian who marked her for his enjoyment, pursued her like a wolf after its prey; assaulted her and choked her to death, disports himself lightly at the State farm, in his new blue serge suit, his patent leather shoes, his insolent arrogance of successful dandyism. How much more of it can we stand? How much MORE will the rich Jews RUB IT IN ON US?

There is a God's lavish of "Georgia's shame," but it does not cling to the bold, true men of Cobb County who executed upon a legally tried and thrice condemned murderer, the mandate of the Law. The Law had said, three times, "Hang Leo Frank by the neck, until he is dead:" the vigilantes did just that, and no more.[98]

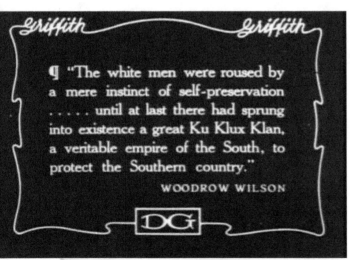

5-12: As one can imagine, having the endorsement of U.S. president Woodrow Wilson helped bolster the acceptance of much of the movie's prejudical and stereotypical themes and ideas.

Based on this type of relentless race baiting, it is easy to see how some of Marietta's most prominent citizens on the night of August 16, 1915, devised a sophisticated, illegal plan that included 25 men driving across the state, brazenly entering a state prison, overpowering the guards, and transporting Frank back to Marietta, where he was hanged in an oak grove. News spread quickly of the lynching, and a large crowd quickly gathered. "The mood was festive, with women and children present to view the body, still hanging from the oak tree. Some of the crowd tore small strips of cloth from Frank's clothes, and others snipped strands of the rope. Photographs were taken, and these were available

97   http://thomaswatsonmustgo.org, p. 2.
98   Ibid., p. 6.

for sale in Marietta for several years afterwards."[99] (Refer to Figure 5-12.)

Watson's Southern-based raw prejudice was mirrored on a national level by the introduction of the movie *The Birth of a Nation*, directed by D. W. Griffith. This film is based on a novel written by Thomas Dixon, called *The Clansman*. Both the book and the movie, which utilizes many new cinematic techniques, describe blacks as, "brutish, lazy and morally degenerate and dangerous." In the film's climax, the Ku Klux Klan rises up to save the South from the Reconstructionist era prominence of African Americans.[100]

When the film was released nationwide in 1915, the National Association for the Advancement of Colored People (NAACP) protested about the historical accuracy and themes of the film, calling it "three miles of filth."[101] One of the initial triumphs of Griffith was having his movie be the first ever shown at the White House, where it was viewed and endorsed by Woodrow Wilson, himself a former political science professor, as "It is like writing history with lightning."[102] Despite the organized actions of the NAACP, Griffith, the director, claimed that it was based on historically accurate records, and used it as a vehicle to influence an entire generation about their attitudes toward people of color, the Reconstruction period, the Klan, and the South. (See Figures 5-13 and 5-14.)

The general racist beliefs inherent in nativism soon were transformed into a new social phenomenon called eugenics. Devised by Sir Francis Galton, a leading Darwinian scientist, the recommendation was that humanity would be uplifted by breeding from the best and restricting the offspring of the worst.[103] In the early 1900s, this movement soon spread across America. The racial and nativistic implications of eugenics quickly became apparent. "From the eugenicist's point of view, the immigration question was at heart a biological one, and to them admitting 'degenerate breeding stock' seemed one of the worst sins the nation could commit against itself."[104]

The ultimate ramifications of this movement were the Emergency Immigration acts of 1921 and 1924, which greatly limited the numbers of ethnic groups from western Europe, i.e., Poles, Italians, Irish, Jews, and others who were deemed undesirable into the country. While the focus of this work is not on the subject of eugenics, it is something very worthwhile to study.

In many ways, the early 20th century represented a "perfect storm" of intolerance, racial animosity, and prejudice. The hatred radiated toward those coming to America, as well as those people

This scene from the movie The Birth of a Nation *encapsulates its themes: The person of color will be intimidated, dominated, and ultimately subservient to white people.*

5-13: The Klan apparently felt powerful and comfortable enough to proudly march through the capital of America in 1926, espousing their racist and nativist agenda. Imagine a person of color or new immigrant observing such a parade. What must have been their thoughts?

99   http://trutv.com, 1.
100 http://history.com, p. 1.
101 http://chnm.gmu.edu/episodes/the-birth-of-a-nation
102 Ibid.
103 Higham, *Strangers in the Land*, p. 150.
104 Ibid, p. 151.

of color already residing here. In fact, in a perverse way, the prejudices often merged together and created new, more toxic forms of hatred. The best example of this is the Ku Klux Klan. In the early decades of the 1900s, it added new dimensions of racism to its agenda. "The new Klan was determined to protect its warped version of the American way of life not only from blacks, but also from Roman Catholics, Jews, and immigrants."[105] In fact, the Klan had grown so much as a social force in 1925 that it staged a 40,000-man parade down Pennsylvania Avenue in Washington, D.C.[106] (Refer to Figure 5-15.)

The pervasive nature of the Klan in Southern life and culture can be illustrated by Hugo Black, a future Supreme Court justice, noted for his fairness to people of all color. Black joined the Klan in Birmingham, Alabama, in 1923. He was a member for two years, when he resigned to run for the United States Senate. When, in 1937, after being confirmed to the High Court, evidence arose that he had been a Klan member, Black made a national radio address, where he explained that, "he abhorred racial and religious intolerance while acknowledging that he once belonged to the Klan."[107] In the 1954 *Brown v. Board of Education* landmark case, he voted with the rest of his colleagues to outlaw the "separate but equal" doctrine regarding education.

Unfortunately, there seemed to be few white individuals or institutions that were advocating for the black community at this time. Presidents such as Woodrow Wilson, as previously mentioned, who created insightful and prophetic visions for a League of Nations as part of the peace treaty process after World War I, were at the same time racists, with little regard for the rights of American blacks.

> *Woodrow Wilson showed little interest in the plight of African Americans. In fact, he shared many of the racist attitudes prevalent at the time ... He also opposed giving the vote to uneducated whites, and he detested the enfranchisement of blacks, arguing that Americans of Anglo-Saxon origin would always resist domination by "an ignorant and inferior race." He believed that white resistance to black rule was "unalterable." ... Many of the southerners he appointed to his cabinet were uncompromising racists who systematically began segregating the employees in their agencies. When black leaders protested these actions, Wilson replied that such racial segregation was intended to eliminate, "the possibility of friction" in the federal workplace.[108]*

With attitudes and actions such as those exhibited by the president, it is not difficult to imagine how bleak everyday living had become for much of the black community. Ironically, many young black men had served their country honorably in the First World War, where they had been treated in France with full equal and social rights. Upon returning home, they would be reminded quickly that they were no longer overseas.

Even when there were cases that apparently bolstered black legal rights, such as in *Guinn & Beal v. United States*, those victories were illusory. Since the end of the Civil War and the passage of the Fifteenth Amendment and its accompanying statutes, blacks in the South had the legal right to vote. As mentioned above, however, various states instituted obstacles which

---

105   Tindall and Shi, *The Essential America*, vol. 2, W. W. Norton, 2001, p. 432.
106   Ibid.
107   http://encyclopediaofalabama.org, Hugo Black.
108   Tindall and Shi, *America: A Narrative History*, Brief, vol. 2, pp. 739–740.

greatly hindered the black vote. In November of 1910, the state of Oklahoma amended its state constitution by adding this provision,

> *No person shall be registered as an elector of this State or be allowed to vote in any election herein, unless he be able to read and write any section of the constitution of the State of Oklahoma; but no person who was, on January 1, 1866, or at any time prior thereto, entitled to vote under any form of government, or who at that time resided in some foreign nation, and no lineal descendant of such person, shall be denied the right to register and vote because of his inability to so read and write sections of such constitution.*[109]

The Court rather quickly determined that the Oklahoma statute was not acceptable, as it stood in the shadow of the Fifteenth Amendment.

> *We have difficulty in finding words to more clearly demonstrate the conviction we entertain that this standard has the characteristics which the Government attributes to it than does the mere statement of the text. It is true it contains no express words of an exclusion from the standard which it establishes of any person on account of race, color, or previous condition of servitude prohibited by the Fifteenth Amendment, but the standard itself inherently brings that result into existence, since it is based purely upon a period of time before the enactment of the Fifteenth Amendment, but makes that period the controlling and dominant test of the right of suffrage … we must consider the literacy standard established by the suffrage amendment and the possibility of its surviving the determination of the fact that the 1866 standard never took life, since it was void from the beginning because of the operation upon it of the prohibitions of the Fifteenth Amendment.*[110]

It is vital to process this decision from various perspectives. The first is a historical one. As the state of Oklahoma was admitted to the union in 1907, it chose to adopt this form of legalized prejudice that had been embraced by Mississippi and other states in the late 1800s. This act can cause one to wonder how a half century post-Civil War, new states felt confident enough to accept these clearly biased laws as normative standards for their new state. In fact, while the decision appeared to be one that ultimately brought about increased black voting, this was not the case. Although the grandfather clause was voted to be unconstitutional, the state quickly passed new restrictive legislation.

These new statutes provided that, "all persons, except those who voted in 1914, who were qualified to vote in 1916 but who failed to register between April 30 and May 11, 1916, with some exceptions for sick and absent persons who were given additional brief period to register, would be perpetually disenfranchised."[111] In 1939, these new statutes that hindered black voting would themselves be overturned by the High Court. The reality for much of the black community was a lack of the experience and power of voting.

It is the Supreme Court case of *Moore v. Dempsey*, decided in 1923, that in many ways paralleled the *Shipp, Frank,* and *Tallahassee* cases mentioned above. It illustrates, once again,

---

109 http://supreme.justia.com, *Quinn v. United States*, p. 107.
110 Ibid., p. 10.
111 http://answers.com, *Guinn v. United States*, pp. 3–4.

the frighteningly precarious nature of life in America for people of color. The *Moore v. Dempsey* case occurred in Phillips County, Arkansas.

> *On the night of September 30, 1919, a number of colored people assembled in their church were attacked and fired upon by a body of white men, and in the disturbance that followed a white man was killed. The report of the killing caused great excitement and was followed by the hunting down and shooting of many Negroes and also the killing of one Clinton Lee, a white man, for whose murder the petitioners were indicted.*[112]

As a result of this incident, five black men were convicted of first degree murder and sentenced to death by the court of the state of Arkansas. The grounds for their appeal were similar to the *Frank* case. Their attorneys alleged that the possibility of receiving a fair trial and justice for these men was poisoned by the feelings of the locals. Shortly after the arrest of the petitioners, a mob marched to the jail for the purpose of lynching them. The presence of U.S. troops and the promises of some of the town's officials called the Committee of Seven helped restrain the mob. The promise was simple: " ... if the mob would refrain ... they would execute those found guilty in the form of law. This committee made good on their promise by calling colored witnesses and having them whipped and tortured until they received testimony that pointed to the defendants' guilt."[113] Within days, the men had a lawyer appointed to them, and they were placed on trial in front of a jury devoid of black citizens. It was abundantly clear that these men were going to be found guilty. "The Court and neighborhood were thronged with an adverse crowd that threatened the most dangerous circumstances to anyone interfering with the desired result."[114]

The lawyers "defending" the men of color called no witnesses, did not demand a change of venue, and did not put the defendants on the stand. "The trial lasted about three-quarters of an hour and in less than five minutes the jury brought in a verdict of murder in the first degree."[115] It was also noted in the Court's description that, "any prisoner by any chance had been acquitted by a jury he could not have escaped the mob."[116]

As time passed and the date came closer to execute these men, various civic groups, including the American Legion and the Helena Rotary Club, led protests against any commutation of the death sentences with the understanding that justice—i.e., death—would be carried out without any delay. In fact, "In May of the same year, a trial of six other Negroes was coming on and it was represented to the Governor by the white citizens and officials of Phillips County that in all probability those Negroes would be lynched."[117] After reviewing the facts of the case, the High Court found enough issues that troubled them and ordered that the District Court for Eastern Arkansas hear this case.

Even with all the apparent evidence of injustice presented above, two justices dissented from the finding. One, Justice James C. McReynolds, authored their position. In his first paragraph, his position on granting a writ of habeas corpus and finding for the defendants is apparent. "The petition for the writ was supported by affidavits of these five ignorant men whose lives were at stake, the ex parte affidavits of three other negroes who had pleaded guilty and were then confined in the penitentiary under sentences for the same murder, and the affidavits of two

---

112   *Moore v. Dempsey*, U.S. Reports, vol. 261, 1922, p. 87.
113   Ibid., pp. 88–89.
114   Ibid., p. 89.
115   Ibid.
116   Ibid., p. 90.
117   Ibid.

white men—low villains according to their own admissions."[118] Another concern of his is that justice will be delayed if "every man convicted of crime in a state court may thereafter resort to the federal court and by swearing, as advised, that certain allegations of fact tending to impeach his trial are "true to the best of his knowledge and belief," thereby obtain as of right further review, another way has been added to a list already unfortunately long to prevent prompt punishment."[119]

Next, Justice McReynolds reviews evidence and affidavits associated with this case. That includes the following: "To this motion are attached two affidavits, one of Alf Banks, Jr., and another of William Wordlaw who testified to the fact that they were whipped, placed in the electric chair and strangled by something put in their noses to make them testify."[120] Despite such testimony, he concluded, "there was the complete record of the cause in the state courts—trial and Supreme—showing no irregularity."[121]

In his final words, the justice makes clear his opinion of this case.

> *Under the disclosed circumstances I cannot agree that the solemn adjudications by courts of a great State, which this Court has refused to review, can be successfully impeached by the mere ex parte affidavits made upon information and belief of ignorant convicts joined by two white men—confessedly atrocious criminals. The fact that petitioners are poor and ignorant and black naturally arouses sympathy; but that does not release us from enforcing principles which are essential to the orderly operation of our federal system.*[122]

There are positive and negative aspects to the *Moore v. Dempsey* decision. The slim positive perspective is that, in this egregious case of injustice, the Court ruled that the defendants in this case had made a valid argument, and the case was sent back to the lower courts. Eventually, the state of Arkansas freed all the men involved in this case. The negative aspects of this case involved concepts such as race riots, torture, beatings, forced confessions, and the reality of lynching. What is especially depressing are the civic resolutions that local groups generated, which explicitly called for the deaths of individuals outside of the legal system.

Based on Justice McReynolds's brusque comments, it is appropriate to suggest that he, like other justices, reflects the prevailing beliefs in racism and nativism so prevalent at this time. In fact, the prejudice displayed by McReynolds extended to his fellow justices. His animosity also included Jews as well, in addition to blacks. In perhaps the definitive work on Justice Louis Brandeis, authored by Melvin I. Urofsky, McReynolds's racism is detailed.

> *Nor did Brandeis recognize at the time the depth of McReynolds's anti-Semitism. McReynolds detested Brandeis and later Benjamin Cardozo, and there is no official portrait of the Court in 1924 because McReynolds would not sit next to Brandeis as protocol required; when Brandeis retired in 1939, McReynolds refused to sign the traditional letter of farewell. He returned one of Holmes's dissenting opinions with the intimation that Brandeis had made him go wrong and then added a remark that the Lord had tried to make something of the Hebrews for centuries, but finally gave up and turned them out*

---

118   Ibid., p. 92.
119   Ibid., p. 93.
120   Ibid., p. 98.
121   Ibid., p. 96.
122   Ibid., p. 102.

to prey on mankind "like fleas on the dog." Often during conference McReynolds would ostentatiously get up and leave when Brandeis spoke, standing outside until Brandeis had finished and then returning.[123]

From the inner halls of the Supreme Court to the city streets of Louisville, Kentucky, prejudice continued. The various types of prejudice experienced by the black community at this time were only limited to the ever changing nature of the hostility. In the 1914 case of *Buchanan v. Worley*, the Court decided a case involving blatant racism. The city of Louisville, Kentucky, passed an unusual statute in May 1914.

By the first section of the ordinance it is made unlawful for any colored person to move into and occupy as a residence, place of abode, or to establish and maintain as a place of public assembly any house upon any block upon which are occupied as residences, places of abode, or places of public assembly by white people that are occupied as residences, places of abode, or places of public assembly by colored people.

Section 2 provides that it shall be unlawful for any white person to move into and occupy as a residence, place of abode, or to establish and maintain as a place of public assembly any house upon any block upon which a greater number of houses are occupied as residences, places of abode or places of public assembly by colored people than are occupied as residences, places of abode or places of public assembly by white people.

Section 4 provides that nothing in the ordinance shall affect the location of residences, places of abode or places of assembly made previous to its approval; that nothing contained therein shall be construed so as to prevent the occupancy of residences, places of abode or places of assembly by white or colored servants or employees of occupants of such residences, places of abode or places of public assembly on the block on which they are so employed ... [124]

Justice William R. Day, after briefly reviewing the statutes in question, quickly concludes, "This ordinance prevents the occupancy of a lot in the City of Louisville by a person of color in a block where the greater number of residences are occupied by white persons; where such a majority exists colored persons are excluded. This interdiction is based wholly upon color; simply that and nothing more."[125] He references the Thirteenth and Fourteenth amendments in his majority decision,

The statute of 1866 originally passed under sanction of the Thirteenth Amendment, 14 Stat.27, and practically reenacted after the adoption of the Fourteenth Amendment, 16 Stat. 144, expressly provided that all citizens of the United States in any State shall have the same right to purchase property as is enjoyed by white citizens. Colored persons are citizens of the United States and have the right to purchase property and enjoy and use the

---

123 Urofsky, Louis D., *Brandeis*, p. 479.
124 *Buchanan v. Worley*, 1917, pp. 70–71.
125 Ibid., p. 73.

same without laws discriminating against them solely on account of color. Hall v. DeCuir, 95 U.S. 485, 508. These enactments did not deal with the social rights of men, but with those fundamental rights in property which it was intended to secure upon the same terms to citizens of every race and color. Civil Rights cases, 109 U.S. 3, 22. The Fourteenth Amendment and these statutes enacted in furtherance of its purpose operate to qualify and entitle a colored man to acquire property without state legislation discriminating against him solely because of color.[126]

Ultimately, the judgment of the Kentucky Court of Appeals, which had supported the city's plan, was reversed, and the case remanded to that court for further deliberations. It is worthwhile to take one sentence offered by Justice Day and examine it. Above, the Justice wrote, "These enactments did not deal with the social rights of men, but with those fundamental rights in property which it was intended to secure upon the same terms to citizens of every race and color." At first glance, those words may seem positive. Unfortunately, they are not.

The ruling suggests that fundamental legal rights such as buying property are guarded by the Constitution; however, this phrase is a limiting one because it implies that the "rights" to which black citizens are entitled are strictly legal ones. This attitude is reinforced by the phrase that these enactments don't deal with "the social rights of men." This means that while legally, the city of Louisville cannot be so blatant (and almost bizarre) in its enumerating how many black- or white-owned houses there are on a city block, people both black and white are expected not to have neighborly social contacts at all.

The nadir of prejudice and racism of the early 1900s is perhaps best represented by the *Buck v. Bell* case, decided in 1927. As mentioned above, the ideology of eugenics was sweeping across America at this time. Scientists at major universities were proclaiming there was solid scientific evidence that supported contemporary racial theories. The lineage of British, French, and German immigrants had been superior compared to the inferior new immigrants of Slavic groups, Irish, Italians, and Chinese. In fact, people often used terms normally used for animal breeding when discussing the various races. Eventually, proponents of the eugenics movement called for the next logical step: if people are born to inferior races, why not prevent that by the process of enforced sterilization? The state of Virginia, as did a number of other states, passed laws which called for this practice. It was legally challenged and made its way to the U.S. Supreme Court in 1927. Carrie Buck, who lived in the Virginia State Colony of Epileptics and Feeble-Minded, was selected by state authorities to receive an operation leading to her sterilization.

The attorney representing Buck, I. P. Whitehead, makes a compelling argument against the procedure. He contends that it is illegal, "in that it violates her constitutional right of bodily integrity and is therefore repugnant to the due process of law clause of the Fourteenth Amendment."[127] He then goes on to make an argument that is eerily prophetic when one contemplates what the Nazis instituted within a few years.

If this Act be a valid enactment, then the limits of the power of the State (which in the end is nothing more than the faction in control of the government) to rid itself of those citizens deemed undesirable according to its standards, by means of surgical sterilization, have not been set. We will have "established in the state the science of medicine and a corresponding

---

126 Ibid., pp. 78–79.
127 Georgia State University, Digital Archive, *Buck v. Bell*, p. 201.

system of judicature." A reign of doctors will be inaugurated and in the name of science new classes will be added, even races may be brought within the scope of such regulation, and the worst of tyranny practiced.[128]

Aubrey E. Strode represented the state of Virginia. He makes two initial points. First, that the state law did not impose cruel and unusual punishment, and that it does allow for due process of law. He further contends that this action of requiring sterilization was an appropriate exercise of the police power of the state.

An exercise of the police power analogous to that of the statute here in question may be found in the compulsory vaccination statutes; for there, as here, a surgical operation is required for the protection of the individual and of society ... The State may and does confine the feeble-minded, thus depriving them of their liberty. When so confined they are by segregation prohibited from procreation—a further deprivation of liberty that goes unquestioned ... The precise question therefore is whether the state, in its judgment of what is best for the appellant and for society, may through the medium of the operation provided for by the sterilization statute restore her to liberty, freedom and happiness which thereafter she might safely be allowed to find outside of institutional walls.[129]

Justice Oliver Wendell Holmes delivered the finding of the Court in a relatively short summation. After reviewing the facts in the case, the justice finds that the legal grounds for the sterilization procedure did exist.

We have seen more than once that the public welfare may call upon the best citizens for their lives. It would be strange if it could not call upon those who already sap the strength of the State for these lesser sacrifices, often not felt to be such by those concerned, in order to prevent our being swamped with incompetence. It is better for all the world, if instead of waiting to execute degenerate offspring for crime, or to let them starve for their imbecility, society can prevent those who are manifestly unfit from continuing their kind. The principle that sustains compulsory vaccination is broad enough to cover cutting the Fallopian tubes. (Jackson v. Massachusetts, 197 U.S. 11). Three generations of imbeciles are enough.[130]

The judgment of the state of Virginia to proceed with sterilizations was affirmed. Eventually, over the course of decades, between 60,000 and 70,000 people were involuntarily sterilized across America.[131] In fact, the early eugenics movement was embraced by Nazism in its quest to achieve a superior race. Only the tragic realities of concentration camps and crematoriums stopped the onslaught of this pernicious movement in America.

One can suggest that race relations were abysmal in this time period. Not only were there stringent and near-absolute Jim Crow laws and customs in this country that prevented any sort

---

128   Ibid., p. 202.
129   Ibid., pp. 203–204.
130   Ibid., p. 207.
131   http://uvm.edu/eugenics

of racial equality from occurring, there was also an almost palpable distaste and dislike for foreigners, especially the kinds that were coming to America at this time. These decades were categorized by the theme of loss for the black community. Losses were experienced in almost every aspect of life, from job opportunities, to voting rights, in educational possibilities, and more. The right to live, speak, and act freely was denied to blacks. Triumphant Klan marches and movies dedicated to their beliefs certainly intimidated blacks and other minorities. In the end, countless lives were often brutally ended with terror-filled moments at the hands of mobs, as people lost the most basic American beliefs: freedom, liberty, and justice.

While America was completing the decade of the twenties, described by many as the decade of consumerism, awaiting the country in October of 1929—and for a dozen years to follow— was the Great Depression, followed by the Second World War. These events, especially the war, marked the beginning of the end of blatant Jim Crowism and the beginning of a new era in race relations. This postwar period included a high court that reversed the *Plessy* decision and began the slow process, albeit with more violence, sadly, of moving toward greater equality for all citizens.

Discussion Questions

1. Would you vote if you had to pay a poll tax and had to pass an "understanding" clause about your state's constitution?

2. What is your opinion about the *Williams v. Mississippi* case? Did the justices realize that their decision would greatly diminish the black vote?

3. In 1900 in Alabama, the number of eligible black voters was 121,000; however, only 3,000 were registered to vote. What effect did this have on the black community? Are there any contemporary issues that you recognize regarding voting and minorities?

4. In the *Bowman* case, what is your understanding of Section 5507?

5. What were some of the practical negative effects of the *Hodges* case on the black workers of America?

6. How do you react to the words of Justice Brewer, offered in his final paragraph which speaks about "The problem of the emancipated slaves," and "whether this was or was not the wiser way to deal with the great problem [the freed slaves] is not a matter for the courts to decide."

7. What might Ed Johnson have felt and thought when he heard the mob coming to his jail cell?

8. What were the possible thoughts and feelings of the people on the Chattanooga Bridge shooting at Ed Johnson?

9. What are your thoughts about Pickett's work and the reviews that the book received?

10. How did Thomas Watson's writings reflect or affect early 1900s society?

FINALLY, SOME JUSTICE AND VINDICATION

As the country became involved in the Second World War, attitudes toward people of color slowly began to change. The reasons for this change are varied. Over a million black soldiers had served in uniform, and a similar number were represented in the war industries as well. Nearly a half a million people belonged to the NAACP. This well-known organization, supported by eminent lawyers such as Thurgood Marshall, was actively promoting issues of civil rights. In 1944, Marshall argued before the Supreme Court that all-white primaries in the South violated his black client's Fourteenth Amendment right to equal protection. The case, known as *Smith v. Allwright*, was an 8–1 victory for the voting rights of black citizens.[1] (See Figure 6-1.)

During World War Two, the black community had begun a "Double V" campaign, emphasizing victories over the Germans and Japanese, as well as over prejudice and racism at home.[2] Hopefully, the awareness of so many black soldiers serving heroically, despite the reality of segregation, would begin to change the attitudes of some white Americans. Perhaps the change toward equality occurred as the

---

1   http://Authentichistory.com
2   Jones, Wood, Borstelmann, et al., *Created Equal*, p. 788.

Keep us flying!

BUY WAR BONDS

6-1: The dedication and service of a million black soldiers in World War II was a major factor in the unraveling of segregation in America.

actuality of the evilness shown by the Nazis in the Holocaust became known. The soldiers who helped liberate the concentration camps certainly were forever affected by their experiences.

At the same time, the persistence of a new president, Harry Truman, toward a more just society was a factor promoting social change. A new moderation would be shown by the High Court in its postwar findings. Nevertheless, there were some other decisions and episodes of intolerance and brutality that exhibited how destructive the racial climate still remained.

Near the end of the war, the case of *Korematsu v. United States* was decided. This case is rather straightforward. Toyosaburo Korematsu, an American citizen of Japanese descent, was convicted in a federal district for remaining in San Leandro, California. The U.S. Army had directed that, after May 9, 1942, all persons of Japanese ancestry should be excluded from that area.[3] Justice Hugo Black delivered the majority decision of the Court in December of 1944. First, he reviews Executive Order 9066, which subjected all persons of Japanese ancestry in prescribed West Coast military areas to remain in their residences from 8 p.m. through 6 a.m. It Korematsu's attorney argued that, because this order applied only to citizens of Japanese ancestry, it represents a constitutionally prohibited discrimination based solely on race.[4] (Refer to Figure 6-2.)

In the case of the curfew, the Court ruled in the 1943 case of *Hirabayashi v. United States* that the curfew order was within the power of the government to take the necessary steps to prevent espionage and sabotage in an area threatened by Japanese attack. Justice Black continues that, while most citizens of Japanese ancestry were loyal to America, there were an unascertained number of disloyal members of that group that the military had to account for. "Approximately five thousand American citizens of Japanese ancestry refused to swear

---

3 http://caselaw, Findlaw, *Korematsu v. United States*, p. 1.
4 Ibid., p. 2.

unqualified allegiance to the United States and to renounce allegiance to the Japanese Emperor."[5] The decision expresses the idea that the curfew and exclusion edicts would create hardships for those involved, yet,

6-2: Our country offered an apology in the 1980s to the Japanese-Americans who had been interred and had their loyalty questioned during the Second World War.

> *But hardships are part of war, and war is an aggregate of hardships ... Compulsory exclusion of large groups of citizens from their homes, except under circumstances of direst emergency and peril, is inconsistent with our basic governmental institutions. But when under conditions of modern warfare our shores are threatened by hostile forces, the power to protect must be commensurate with the threatened danger.[6]*

Interestingly, the relocation camps that were used for the Japanese Americans were alternatively defined by some as concentration camps, where people were imprisoned. The Court, in its majority decision, addresses this contention: " ... and we deem it unjustifiable to call them concentration camps with all the ugly connotations that term implies—we are dealing with nothing but an exclusion order."[7]

While the majority wrestled with the notion that a whole class of American citizens was removed from their livelihoods, the Court's conclusion is clear.

> *Korematsu was not excluded from the Military Area because of hostility to him or his race. He was excluded because we are at war with the Japanese Empire, because the proper constituted military authorities feared an invasion of our West Coast and felt constrained to take proper security measures, because they decided that the military urgency of the situation demanded that all citizens of Japanese ancestry be segregated from the West Coast temporarily, and finally, because Congress, reposing its confidence in this time of war in our military leaders—as inevitably it must—determined that they should have the power to do this. There was evidence of disloyalty on the part of some, the military authorities considered that the need for action was great, and the time was short. We cannot—by availing ourselves of the calm perspective of hindsight—now say that at that time these actions were unjustified.[8]*

---

5   Ibid., p. 3.
6   Ibid.
7   Ibid., p. 5.
8   Ibid.

After a concurrence from Justice Felix Frankfurter, there are three strongly held dissenting opinions offered. The first is from Justice Owen Roberts. He quickly asserts that this case was not about the temporary exclusion of a citizen from an area for their own safety or that of the community.

> *On the contrary, it is the case of convicting a citizen as a punishment for not submitting to imprisonment in a concentration camp, based on his ancestry, and solely because of his ancestry, without evidence or inquiry concerning his loyalty and good disposition towards the United States ... I need hardly labor the conclusion that Constitutional rights have been violated.*[9]

After further reviewing the details of this case, including the orders for all Japanese citizens to gather at an assembly center, the justice further concludes, "The two conflicting orders, one which commanded him to stay and the other which commanded him to go, were nothing but a cleverly devised trap to accomplish the real purpose of the military authority, which was to lock him up in a concentration camp."[10]

The next dissent is offered by Justice Frank Murphy, whose opening sentence shows his opinion of the majority finding. "This exclusion of 'all persons of Japanese ancestry, both alien and non-alien' from the Pacific Coast area on a plea of military necessity in the absence of martial law ought not to be approved. Such exclusion goes over 'the very brink of constitutional power' and falls into the ugly abyss of racism."[11] He next examines the military's assertions about the Japanese Americans living in the Pacific Coast area. "The Commanding General's Final Report about the Deportation referred to all individuals of Japanese descent as 'subversive' as belonging to 'an enemy race' ... however, no reliable evidence was cited to show that the individuals were disloyal and were a special menace to defense installations or war industries."[12]

Justice Murphy continues in dissent by noting that German Americans and Italian Americans were investigated on an individual basis, whereas the Japanese were condemned as a group. "It seems incredible that under these circumstances it would have been impossible to hold loyalty hearings for the mere 112,000 persons involved—or at least for the 70,000 American citizens—especially when a large number represented children and elderly men and women."[13] His concluding paragraph deserves attention.

> *I dissent, therefore, from this legalization of racism. Racial discrimination in any form and in any degree has no justifiable part whatever in our democratic way of life. It is unattractive in any setting but it is utterly revolting among a free people who have embraced the principles set forth in the Constitution of the United States. All residents of this nation are kin in some way by blood or culture to a foreign land. Yet they are primarily and necessarily a part of the new and distinct civilization of the United States. They must*

---

9   Ibid., p. 6.
10 Ibid., p. 9.
11 Ibid., p. 10.
12 Ibid., p. 11.
13 Ibid., p. 13.

accordingly be treated at all times as the heirs of the American experiment and as entitled to all the rights and freedoms guaranteed by the Constitution.[14]

A third dissent in this 6–3 decided case came from Justice Robert Jackson. In his writing, he posits a strong concern for the future ramifications of this decision.

Much is said of the danger to liberty from the Army program for deporting and detaining these citizens of Japanese extraction. But a judicial construction of the due process clause that will sustain this order is a far more subtle blow to liberty than the promulgation of the order itself. A military order, however constitutional, is not apt to last longer than the military emergency. Even during that period a succeeding commander may revoke it all. But once a judicial opinion rationalizes such an order to show that it conforms to the Constitution, or rather rationalizes the Constitution to show that the Constitution sanctions such an order, the Court for all time had validated the principle of racial discrimination in criminal procedure and of transplanting American citizens.[15]

Justice Jackson is adamant in his criticism of the exclusion order: "I should hold that a civil court cannot be made to enforce an order which violates constitutional limitations even if it is a reasonable exercise of military authority. The courts can exercise only the judicial power, can apply the law, and must abide by the Constitution, or they cease to be civil courts and become instruments of military policy."[16]

Justice Stephen Breyer, currently serving in the Supreme Court, is emphatic about this decision,

Korematsu harmed the Court. It suggested that the Court was unwilling or unable to make an unpopular decision that would protect an unpopular minority ... In general, the Court's ruling in this case has gone down as a judicial failure. Korematsu shows the practical need for the Court to assure constitutional accountability, even of the president and even in time of war or national emergency.[17]

Those forces speaking out against racism accelerated as the war continued and ultimately concluded. In September of 1945, Secretary of War Robert Patterson appointed a board of three general officers to investigate the Army's policy with respect to African Americans. Within a year, this board concluded, "That the Army's future policy should be to eliminate, at the earliest practicable moment, any special consideration based on race."[18]

Unfortunately, at this same time, horrific violence was still suffered by black citizens. In February 1946, a black World War Two veteran, Isaac Woodard (mentioned in the Introduction), was attacked and blinded by policemen in Aiken, South Carolina, in a senseless incident. His story needs to be told. He was a decorated World War Two veteran who had fought bravely

14   Ibid.
15   Ibid., pp.14–15.
16   Ibid.
17   http://trumanlibraray.org, p. 1.
18   http://Authentichistory.com, p. 2.

6-3: Isaac Woodard, shown permanently blinded and disabled as a result of his brutal beating at the hands of law-enforcement individuals.

in the Pacific Theater of war, earning medals for his heroism. He had been discharged a few hours earlier and was on a bus going home. On the way, he had an argument with the bus driver about his ability to use a bathroom during a bus stop.

At the next scheduled stop in Batesburg, South Carolina, the driver contacted the local sheriff, Linwood Shull, who forcibly removed Sergeant Woodard from the bus. He was taken out into an alley and beaten with nightsticks. He was then taken to jail and arrested for disorderly conduct. Overnight, he was beaten repeatedly—so severely that by the morning, he was blind in both eyes and was suffering from partial amnesia. A local judge found Woodard guilty and fined him $50. Eventually, he received some medical attention from a military hospital and was able to return home.[19] (See Figure 6-3.)

President Harry S. Truman heard about this shameful incident and ordered the attorney general to take action. Federal agents collected evidence that was used against Sheriff Shull. In a subsequent trial, Shull was found not guilty of any wrongdoing. At that point, the courtroom erupted in applause. The jury took 30 minutes to reach this verdict. Woodard, who died in 1992, suffered the rest of his life from this attack.[20] A war hero who was not wounded fighting for his country overseas was, however, savagely maimed in his own country while still in uniform! How tremendously sad.

This incident was eclipsed by one in July of 1946 that occurred near Monroe, Georgia. In this depressing event, there had been rumors that George Dorsey, a black Army veteran, had been secretly dating a white woman. Anger was directed toward Roger Malcom, a black citizen, for stabbing a white farmer, Barney Hester. Another white farmer, Loy Harrison, bailed Malcom out of jail and proceeded to drive Dorsey, his wife, and Malcom and his wife outside of town. Near the Moore's Ford Bridge, the group was confronted by a mob of 20 white men, who dragged the passengers from the car, tied them to trees, and fired three volleys of approximately 60 bullets from handguns and shotguns into the couples. One of the victims, Dorothy Malcom, was seven months' pregnant.[21] (Refer to Figure 6-4.)

An outraged President Truman sent the FBI to Monroe, about 45 miles east of Atlanta. But the local community—both blacks and whites—adamantly refused to cooperate in any

---

19 Ibid.
20 http://gcpagenda.org/index. Lynchings at Moore's Ford Bridge.
21 Ibid.

way.[22] After all this time, with most of the participants dead, justice was not served. Imagine the triple horror that this case, bolstered by decades of prejudice, involved. First, George Dorsey was a proud veteran of the Second World War. Second, the two couples had been confronted by vigilantes, as with Ed Johnson, Leo Frank, and thousands of other lynching victims. These mobs knew they almost certainly would not be held responsible. The final indignity was the murder of the wives and the unborn child. The hatred and prejudice born out of "separate but equal" and the countless High Court decisions that held people of color to be lesser citizens—who could easily lose their right to vote or their livelihoods or self-respect—were coming home to roost. Even a proud veteran and his wife were shot like rabid animals.

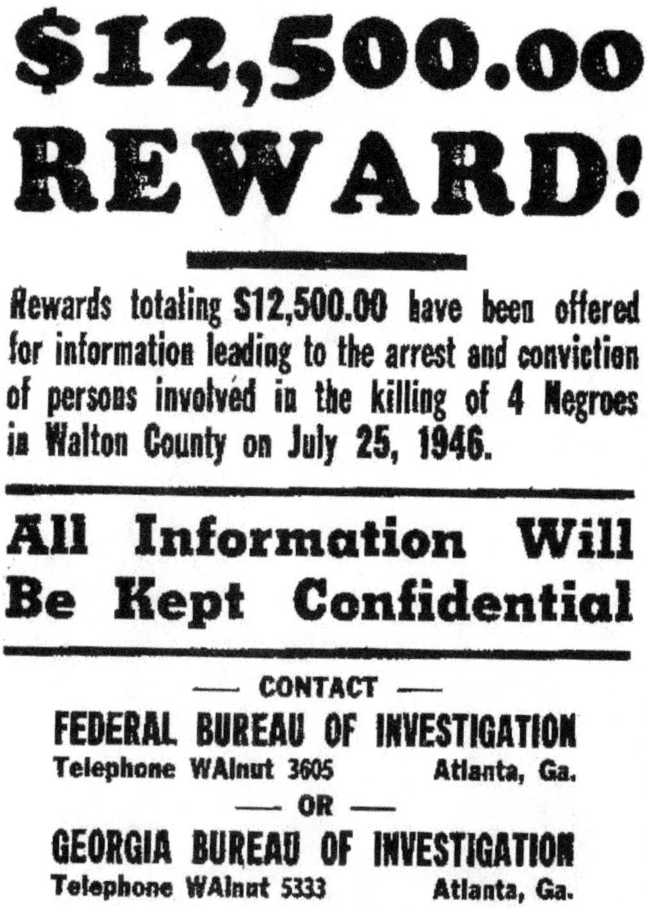

To his credit, President Truman took action to address this racism. In December 1946, he appointed the President's Committee on Civil Rights. Within nine months, this organization issued a straightforward recommendation: " ... legislation and administrative action to end immediately all discrimination and segregation based on race, color, creed or national origin in ... all branches of the Armed Services."[23] By February 1948, Truman announced that he had instructed the secretary of defense to take steps to have the remaining instances of discrimination in the armed services eliminated as rapidly as possible.[24] During the next few months, various black leaders and organizations urged Truman to immediately end segregation in the military. The issue took on national dimensions, when in the 1948 Democratic convention, a plank was offered that called for the desegregation of the armed forces. (Refer to Figure 6-5.)

Indeed, on July 26, 1948, President Truman signed Executive Order 9981, which states, "It is hereby declared to be the policy of the President that there shall be equality of treatment and opportunity for all persons in the armed forces without regard to race, color, religion, or national origin."[25] Within a few years, this policy became the standard in the U.S. military.

The significance of Truman's actions, juxtaposed with the murders at Moore's Ford Bridge, cannot be understated. The stage was being set for a dramatic change in the Supreme Court's

$12,500.00 REWARD!

Rewards totaling $12,500.00 have been offered for information leading to the arrest and conviction of persons involved in the killing of 4 Negroes in Walton County on July 25, 1946.

All Information Will Be Kept Confidential

— CONTACT —

FEDERAL BUREAU OF INVESTIGATION
Telephone WAlnut 3605   Atlanta, Ga.

— OR —

GEORGIA BUREAU OF INVESTIGATION
Telephone WAlnut 5333   Atlanta, Ga.

6-4: Despite offering such large rewards, the local community was silent and has been over the decades regarding these vicious murders at Moore's Ford Bridge.

[handwritten margin note: Not Law, but an executive order]

---

22   http://trumanlibrary, p. 2.
23   Ibid.
24   Ibid., p. 3.
25   http://supreme.justia.com, *Morgan v. Virginia*, pp. 2–3.

6-5: While often recognized for his efforts to successfully conclude World War II, President Truman's actions were crucial in helping create the legal and social foundations for the Civil Rights movements of the 1950s and 1960s.

decision regarding the "separate but equal" finding of *Plessy*. My primary contention in this work is that, while the Court reflected the social beliefs of Americans, it was their role to take a stand for equality for people of color, just as the president was doing. Even though in the past there were numerous opportunities to assist former slaves and free blacks in achieving more political, legal, and social equality, the Court did not avail itself of them. In fact, the justices added to and increased the prejudice toward people of color. As a result, many Americans believed that the rights and lives of people of color were not seen as comparable—by any standard—to their own. (See Figure 6-6.)

Whether it was the war and its horrible examples of concentration camps or death and destruction in general, the excessively brutal attacks against blacks or the actions of President Truman, from 1946 until the *Brown* decision in 1954, the Court began to turn toward fuller equal, legal, and social rights for blacks. The first case in this regard is *Morgan v. Virginia*. Decided almost a decade before Rosa Parks refused to move from her bus seat, this case involves a Virginia statute that required white and black passengers on both interstate and intrastate motor carriers to be separated. While the Supreme Court of Appeals of Virginia affirmed the validity of this code, the Court reversed that decision.

Justice Stanley Reed delivered the majority opinion of the Court in June of 1946. This case is strangely similar to the history-making one of Rosa Parks. A female black passenger on a bus trip from Gloucester County, Virginia, to Baltimore, Maryland, was asked by the driver to move to a back seat in the black section so a white passenger could sit with other whites. Upon refusal to do so, a warrant was obtained, and the female was arrested, tried, and convicted of being in violation of the Virginia code.[26] Quite quickly, the justice offers the rationale for overturning the Virginia code. (Refer to Figure 6-7.)

---

26   Ibid.

The errors of the Court of Appeals that are assigned and relied upon by appellant are, in form, only two. The first is that the decision is repugnant to Clause 3, Section 8, Article I of the Constitution of the United States, and the second the holding that powers reserved to the states by the Tenth Amendment include the power to require an interstate motor passenger to occupy a seat restricted for the use of his race.[27]

Interestingly, the Court delves into some of the practical elements of this type of case. "An interstate passenger must, if necessary, repeatedly, shift seats while moving in Virginia to meet the seating requirements of the changing passenger group. On arrival at the District of Columbia line, the appellant would have had the freedom to occupy any available seat, and so to the end of her journey."[28]

At the conclusion of a fairly brief argument, the majority makes some emphatic points about this case.

As there is no federal act dealing with the separation of races in interstate transportation, we must decide the validity of this Virginia statute on the challenge that it interferes with commerce, as a matter of balance between the exercise of the local police power and the need for national uniformity in the regulations for interstate travel. It seems clear to us that seating arrangements for the different races in interstate motor travel require a single uniform rule to promote and protect national travel. Consequently, we hold the Virginia statute in controversy invalid.[29]

The dissent of Justice Harold Burton raises some interesting historical data. He notes that the laws of ten contiguous states require racial segregation of passengers on motor carriers, while 18 others prohibit racial separation of passengers.[30] The justice even speculates that this finding might invalidate those states where people are segregated by race.

The tempo of social changes was quickening. The President's Committee on Civil Rights recommended the renewal of the Fair Employment Practices Committee and the creation of a permanent civil

6-6: The existence and evil brutality of the Nazi concentration camps might have caused Americans to consider the power an ideology based on the beliefs of stereotyping and prejudice. Pictured here is the Wall of Remembrance at the U.S. National Holocaust Museum in Washington, D.C.

6-7: It was on buses such as this that people of color were humiliated on a daily basis as they were forced to sit in designated seats in the back section of the bus.

---

27   Ibid., p. 5.
28   Ibid., p. 7.
29   Ibid., p. 17.
30   http://Authentichistory.com, p. 2.

6-8: Jackie Robinson's participation and stellar play coupled with President Truman's actions began leading America to an increased awareness about the absurdity of segregation in society.

rights commission to investigate abuses.[31] In the public arena of Major League Baseball, the National League's Brooklyn Dodgers included the first black player to cross the color line, Jackie Robinson.[32] While Robinson was taunted, booed, and spiked and received death threats, by the end of his first season, 1947, he was named rookie of the year. The significance of such developments cannot be overstated. Led by an activist president, Harry Truman, with the knowledge that millions of people of color had served America in World War Two, the country and the men of the Court were coming to grips with a new American reality: all Americans should be treated equally, regardless of race. (Refer to Figure 6-8.)

The pace of favorable cases moving toward the legal and social rights of black Americans continued in 1950. Three major cases, *Shepherd et al. v. Florida*, *Sweatt v. Painter*, and *McLaurin v. Oklahoma State Regents*, were all decided in 1950. In many ways, these decisions make a very strong statement about the changing opinions of the Court concerning the legal rights of black citizens. The first case reflects the harrowing reality that prevailed in the South regarding vigilantism and the lack of fair treatment for blacks. The background to the case is fairly straightforward.

> On the 16th of July, 1949, a seventeen-year-old white girl in Lake County, Florida, reported that she had been raped, at the point of a pistol, by four Negroes (the petitioners). Six days later petitioners were indicted and, beginning September 1, were tried for the offense, convicted without recommendation of mercy, and sentenced to death. The Supreme Court of Florida, in reviewing evidence of guilt, said, "As we study the testimony, the only question presented here is which set of witnesses would the jury believe, that is, the State's witnesses or the testimony given by the defendant-appellants.[33]

Immediately, Justice Robert Jackson shows his skepticism about the case.

> But prejudicial influences outside the courtroom, becoming all too typical of a highly publicized trial, were brought to bear on this jury with such force that the conclusion is inescapable that these defendants were prejudged as guilty and the trial was but a legal gesture to register a verdict already dictated by the press and the public opinion [in] which it was generated.[34]

As part of this rather extraordinary Court case, the justice almost seems to acknowledge the hollow nature of any confessions connected with this case. "Newspapers published as a fact, and attributed the information to the sheriff, that these defendants had confessed ... Witnesses and persons called as jurors said that they had read or heard this statement. However, no confession

---

31 Tindall and Shi, *The Essential America*, vol. II, p. 518.
32 U.S. Reports, vol. 341, 1950, *Shepherd et al. v. Fla.*, pp. 50–51.
33 Ibid.
34 Ibid., p. 51.

was offered at the trial."[35] What is exceptionally powerful about this case is a description in the fourth footnote regarding an alleged confession: "The defense offered, and the court rejected as completely irrelevant and immaterial, evidence of brutal, inhuman beatings by state officers in whose custody they were held."[36] What is incredible is that the Supreme Court of the country is tacitly acknowledging the reality of the routine brutality practiced by police and state officers in the pursuit of racial injustice. In fact, the raw community emotions associated with this incident are also chronicled in detail by the Court in this short review.

> But that is not all. Of course, such a crime stirred deep feeling and was exploited to the limit by the press. These defendants were first taken to the county jail of Lake County. A mob gathered and demanded that defendants be turned over to it. By order of [the] court, they were quickly transferred for safekeeping to the state prison, where they remained until about two weeks before the trial. Meanwhile, a mob burned the home of defendant Shepherd's father and mother and two other Negro houses. Negroes were removed from the community to prevent their being lynched. The National Guard was called out on July 17 and 18 and, on July 19, the 116th Field Artillery was summoned from Tampa. The Negroes of the community abandoned their homes and fled.[37]

The decision continues to offer graphic details about the case, including some of the prejudicial articles and cartoons published, "including a carton published ... picturing four electric chairs and headed, 'No Compromise-Supreme Penalty.'"[38] In the end of its decision to reverse the Florida Supreme Court, the High Court is emphatic. "The case represents one of the best examples of one of the worst menaces to American justice."[39] Interestingly, in this case, the Court finally recognizes the inherent dangers of a mob out of control.

In addition to this case, which clearly reflected miscarriages of justice, two other cases, *Sweatt v. Painter* and *McLaurin v. Oklahoma State Regents* (also decided in 1950), began to crack the educational barriers established under the "separate but equal" rubric. To emphasize the significance of these decisions, both majority findings were delivered by Chief Justice Fred Vinson. In the first case, the petitioner, Sweatt, filed an application for admission to the University of Texas Law School and was rejected because he was black. At that time, 1946, state law mandated that only white students were eligible to attend this school. As a remedy, the state of Texas initiated a separate law school for blacks that it claimed met all legal requirements. Sweatt chose not to attend this new separate school and sued. His case made it up through the Texas Supreme Court, which reaffirmed a lower court's ruling that this new school "offered petitioner privileges, advantages, and opportunities for the study of law substantially equivalent to those offered by the State to white students at the University of Texas."[40]

The Chief Justice made a quick analysis of the faculty, library, and resources of the University of Texas Law School, in contrast with the new one devised for blacks. "The law school which was to have opened in February, 1947, would have had no independent faculty or library ... nor was there any full-time librarian. The school lacked accreditation ... Few students and no

---

35 Ibid.
36 Ibid., p. 53.
37 Ibid.
38 Ibid., p. 55.
39 *Sweatt and Painter et al., Beyond Brown*, p. 2.
40 Ibid., pp. 2–3.

one who has practiced law would choose to study in an academic vacuum, removed from the interplay of ideas and the exchange of views with which the law is concerned."[41] In quick order, the justice determines that the "separate but equal" doctrine as expressed in *Plessy v. Ferguson* did not justify the building of a separate and highly inferior law school. At this time, the justices contend that they

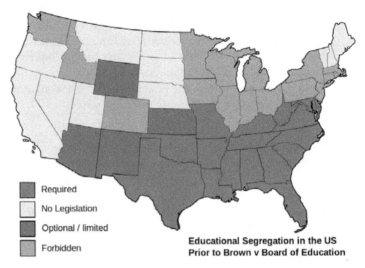

Required

No Legislation

Optional / limited

Forbidden

**Educational Segregation in the US
Prior to Brown v Board of Education**

6-9: This system of definitive segregation ensured that generations of children would grow to adulthood without a black or white friendship or association.

did not "reach petitioner's contention that Plessy v. Ferguson should be reexamined in the light of contemporary knowledge respecting the purposes of the Fourteenth Amendment and the effects of racial segregation."[42] The final decision was an easy one: Sweatt was to be admitted to the University of Texas Law School. (Refer to Figure 6-9.)

The second case, *McLaurin v. Oklahoma State Regents*, also deals with a graduate school program for George McLaurin. He was admitted to graduate school at the University of Oklahoma for a doctorate in education. State law required that blacks in institutions of higher education be taught "upon a segregated basis."[43] Based on a federal court decision, the state was compelled to admit McLaurin to the school. Nevertheless, state authorities set up unusual barriers for McLaurin. "Thus he was required to sit apart at a designated desk in an anteroom adjoining the classroom; to sit at a designated desk on the mezzanine floor in the library, but not to use the desks in the regular reading room, and to sit at a designated table and to eat at a different time from the other students in the school cafeteria."[44] Ironically, the state that originally displayed signs stating, "Reserved for Colored" removed those signs and instituted a system of a more benign segregation such as creating a separate row for black students in the various spaces on campus. The Court accepted none of this milder prejudice. Its reasoning seems to indicate a vastly different approach and methodology.

> *Our society grows increasingly complex, and our need for trained leaders increases correspondingly. Appellant's case represents perhaps the epitome of that need, for he is attempting to obtain an advanced degree in education, to become, by definition, a leader and*

---

41   Ibid., p. 3.

42   http://supremecourt.com, *McLaurin v. Oklahoma State*, p. 1.

43   Ibid., p. 3.

44   Ibid., p. 4.

trainer of others. Those who will come under his guidance and influence must be directly affected by the education he receives. Their own education and development will necessarily suffer to the extent that his training is unequal to that of his classmates. State-imposed restrictions which produce such inequalities cannot be sustained.[45]

During the same period that the above decisions were rendered, the Court was beginning to shine a new judicial light on the various state-sponsored political parties that had been formed with the express goal of excluding blacks from participating in voting. In the 1953 case, *Terry v. Adams*, this disenfranchising process was detailed. In the state of Texas, the Jaybird Association (or Party) was organized in 1889. Its membership had always been limited to white members. This association was run like a political party, with political and administrative expenses. Candidates running in the Democratic primaries needed the endorsement of the organization to win elections. "The party became the dominant political group in the counties and had endorsed every county-wide official elected since 1889. It is apparent that Jaybird activities follow a plan purposefully designed to exclude Negroes from voting and at the same time, to escape the Fifteenth Amendment's command that the right of citizens to vote shall neither be denied nor abridged on account of race."[46]

In fact, as part of the Court's decision, it recorded testimony of the Jaybirds' president:

Q. And then one of the purposes of your organization is for the specific purpose of excluding Negroes from voting, isn't it?"

A. Yes.

Q. And that is your policy?

A. Yes.[47]

Similar organizations existed and functioned in other Southern states. To exempt themselves from any sort of judicial oversight, state legislatures such as in South Carolina voted that these clubs should be entirely "private." The thinking was that the concept of privateness would allow them to operate as they did in the past. The federal courts quickly dispelled this notion. "The Court of Appeals, in invalidating the South Carolina practices, answered these formalistic arguments by holding that no election machinery could be sustained if its purpose or effect was to deny Negroes on account of their race an effective voice in the governmental affairs of their country, state, or community."[48]

What is fascinating is that the continuation of the Court's decision extensively focuses on the Fifteenth Amendment, which in the past had been greatly limited by previous findings, was now touted as the primary legal reasoning against this type of election prejudice.

---

45 http://supreme.justia.com, *Terry v. Adams*, pp. 3–4.
46 Ibid.
47 Ibid., p.5.
48 Ibid., pp. 7–8.

> For a state to permit such a duplication of its election processes is to permit a flagrant abuse of those processes to defeat the purposes of the Fifteenth Amendment. The use of the county-operated primary to ratify the result of the prohibited election merely compounds the offense. It violates the Fifteenth Amendment for a state, by such circumvention, to permit within its borders the use of any device that produces an equivalent of the prohibited election ... The effect of the whole procedure, Jaybird primary plus Democratic election, is to do precisely that which the Fifteenth Amendment forbids—strip Negroes of every vestige of influence in selecting the officials who control the local county matters that intimately touch the daily lives of citizens.[49]

Swiftly, the High Court orders the local district court to determine which provisions are essential to afford black citizens full protection from future discriminatory election practices.

This type of prejudice, as shown above, included Hispanic citizens as well. In the 1954 case of *Hernandez v. Texas*, the Court decided in favor of equal rights for them as well. Hispanics had not been allowed to participate in the legal processes in Texas. The Court quickly found, "The systematic exclusion of persons of Mexican descent from service as jury commissioners, grand jurors, and petit jurors in the Texas county in which petitioner was indicted and tried for murder, although there were a substantial number of such persons in the county fully qualified to serve, deprived petitioner, a person of Mexican descent, of the equal protection of the laws guaranteed by the Fourteenth Amendment, and his conviction in a state court is reversed."[50]

Of course, the major case that people associate with the year 1954 is the *Brown v. Board of Education of Topeka, Kansas*, decision that changed the legal, political, and social landscape of America. The case, known as the *Brown* case, is actually comprised of three separate ones. First, the initial case, followed by *Bolling v. Sharpe*, which dealt with educational issues in the District of Columbia, and then the second *Brown* case, decided in May 1955. This second *Brown* case issued the time frame for initiating the end of "separate but equal" in educational facilities: "with all deliberate speed."[51]

The essence of the *Brown* case is very straightforward: in various states across the country, children of color were often made to travel great distances to attend segregated schools. The situation of Linda Brown from Topeka, Kansas, was indicative of the reality for many. She had to walk one mile through a railroad switchyard to get to her segregated black-only elementary school, even though a school for white children was only seven blocks from her home.[52] The Court consolidated a number of legal challenges, spearheaded by the NAACP, into one major case. It took the Court two years to come to a resolution of the case. Initially, a three-judge federal district court denied relief to the plaintiffs on the so-called "separate but equal" doctrine announced by the High Court in the *Plessy v. Ferguson* decision.[53] In the state of Delaware, that state's high court ordered that the plaintiffs be admitted to the white-only schools because of their superiority to the black-only schools.[54] (See Figure 6-10.)

First, the Court decided to explore the Fourteenth Amendment in its historical context to help them with the *Brown* decision. In the end, the Court found, "This discussion and our own investigation convince us that, although these sources cast some light, it is not enough to resolve

49 http://Supreme.justia.com., *Hernandez v. Texas*, p. 1.
50 Balkin, *What Brown v. Board of Education Should Have Said*, p. 3.
51 http://Watson.org/`lisa/blackhistory, p. 1.
52 http://supreme.justia.com, *Brown v. Board of Education of Topeka, Kansas*, p. 3.
53 Ibid., pp. 2–3.
54 Ibid., p. 3.

the problem [with] which we are faced. At best, they are inconclusive."[55] They next reference the *Plessy* decision made in 1896, although that case is found to be lacking guidance. "We cannot turn the clock back to 1868, when the Amendment was adopted, or even to 1896, when Plessy v. Ferguson was written. We must consider public education in the light of its full development and its present place in American life throughout the Nation."[56] Next, the Court addresses the significance of education in an American context. "In these days, it is doubtful that any child may reasonably be expected to succeed in life if he is denied the opportunity of an education. Such an opportunity, where the state has undertaken to provide it, is a right which must be made available to all on equal terms."[57]

The High Court then quotes from a Kansas court, which, even though it ruled against the black plaintiffs, sounded quite sympathetic to their cause.

> *Segregation of white and colored children in public schools has a detrimental effect upon the colored children. The impact is greater when it has the sanction of the law, for the policy of separating the races is usually interpreted as denoting the inferiority of the Negro race. A sense of inferiority affects the motivation of a child to learn. Segregation with the sanction of law, therefore, has a tendency to [retard] the educational and mental development of Negro children and to deprive them of some of the benefits they would receive in a racially integrated school system. Whatever may have been the extent of psychological knowledge at the time of Plessy v. Ferguson, this finding is amply supported by modern authority. Any language in Plessy v. Ferguson to this finding is rejected.*[58]

It is this paragraph that has generated so much commentary about this decision. This may be the first time the High Court ceded apparent direction and authority for one of their decisions to a new social source: psychology. Nevertheless, it is instructional to appreciate how vastly different the findings were from 1896 to 1954. A different world produced a different outcome.

In fact, immediately following this statement about the psychological effects of a separate education on children of color, the Court makes a clear, emphatic statement.

> *We conclude that, in the field of public education, the doctrine of "separate but equal" has no place. Separate educational facilities are inherently unequal. Therefore, we hold that the plaintiffs and others similarly situated for whom the actions have been brought are, by reason of the segregation complained of, deprived of the equal protection of the laws guaranteed by the Fourteenth Amendment ... We have now announced that such segregation is a denial of the equal protection of the laws.*[59]

In a clear and direct manner, the justices begin the slow process of disassembling the *Plessy* case and its consequences. Consider, for a moment, the decades involved between these two cases. The *Plessy* decision, rendered in 1896, led to almost 60 years of blatant segregation, with segregationist attitudes the norm in America. This opinion, in 1954, began the slow process of

55 Ibid., pp. 4–5.
56 Ibid.
57 Ibid., p. 6.
58 Ibid.
59 Balkin, *What Brown v. Board of Education Should Have Said*, p. 19.

causing Americans to reconsider the underlying premise of race relations that had not been adequately addressed since the end of the Civil War in 1865: Are black and white citizens equal in all ways? This *Brown* case pushed America into that discussion.

As one can imagine, there are various scholarly theories that attempt to explain the motivation of the justices to make this landmark case. As with all these decisions, there is a multitude of plausible determinants. As mentioned above, the groundbreaking work for civil rights undertaken by President Truman must be appreciated. Similarly, the Double-V Campaign that began in the Second World War and the awareness of the evils associated with the Holocaust were certainly factors as well, in terms of possible influences on the justices. There is a foreign policy component at play here as well.

In the postwar era, the Cold War began. The Soviet Union was America's new nemesis. In that regard, the Soviets did not hesitate to point to the existence of Jim Crow laws and practices in America, " ... as proof of the hollowness of American promises of liberty and equality and the moral bankruptcy of the American way of life. These Soviet attacks on Jim Crow were an enormous embarrassment."[60]

This notion—that foreign policy was a factor in the *Brown* case—might be considered with further evidence. The Justice Department, which was dealing with these cases, quoted at length the views of the secretary of state, who emphasized the threat to American interests posed by Jim Crow. "Racial discrimination in the United States remains a source of constant embarrassment to this Government in the day-to-day conduct of its foreign relations; and it jeopardizes the effective maintenance of our moral leadership of the free and democratic nations of the world."[61] In fact, within an hour of Chief Justice Earl Warren's announcement about *Brown*, the Voice of America was broadcasting the finding to Eastern Europe in 34 different languages. The day after the decision, the *New York Times* described *Brown* as a "blow to communism."[62]

Other scholars such as Derrick Bell propose a differing interpretation of the decision. Bell suggests that, "The Supreme Court typically acted to protect the interests of blacks and other racial minorities only when these interests converge with those of whites, and in particular powerful white elites."[63] Michael Klarman argues that the decision had a harmful effect. "The Supreme Court's intervention infuriated a wide range of Southerners and thus gave renewed political power to racists like Bull Connor and political opportunists like George Wallace."[64] Whatever the Court's motivations may have been, the decision was made.

To illustrate the totality and potency of these rulings, the *Bolling v. Sharpe* case should be noted as well. This decision, given at the same time as the *Brown* one, found that, "Racial segregation in the public schools of the District of Columbia is a denial to Negro children of the due process of law guaranteed by the Fifth Amendment."[65] It would have been hypocritical in the utmost for the Supreme Court to find that the states could not maintain separate but equal schools while this practice was continued in the District of Columbia, not a state-led government. This was so stated by the Court: "In view of our decision that the Constitution prohibits the state from maintaining racially segregated schools, it would be unthinkable that the same Constitution would impose a lesser duty on the Federal Government."[66]

---

60 Ibid., p. 20.
61 Ibid.
62 Ibid., p. 21.
63 Ibid., p. 23.
64 http://supreme.justia.com, *Bolling v. Sharpe*, p. 1.
65 Ibid., p. 2.
66 Tindall and Shi, *The Essential America*, p. 552.

The reactions to these cases and the next 60 years comprise the remainder of this work. The immediate response to the *Brown* decision, which included its 1955 opinion that school systems should move forward with desegregation with all deliberate speed, elicited a variety of responses. In the South, widespread hostility was illustrated by the formation of Citizens' Councils. These white supremacist groups were upper-class versions of the Klan. "Instead of physical violence and intimidation, the Councils used economic coercion to discipline blacks who crossed racial boundaries. African-Americans who defied white supremacy would lose their jobs, have their insurance policies canceled, or be denied personal loans or home mortgages."[67]

By the end of 1955, members of Congress began expressing their opposition to the *Brown* decision. In 1956, 101 Southern members of Congress signed a "Southern Manifesto," which denounced the Court's decision as a case of "a clear abuse of judicial power."[68] Yet, the Court's findings galvanized

6-10: Emmitt Till. It is hard to imagine the level of hatred and prejudice that existed when a teenage boy whistles at a woman and forfeits his life in such an inhumane and vicious manner. The men who attacked Till would not treat their animals with such disregard and unimaginable violence.

the black community and set the stage for the modern Civil Rights movement. (Refer to Figure 6-11.)

Sadly, the level of hatred symbolized by lynchings and other forms of brutality manifested itself in the vicious murder of Emmett Till in August of 1955. Till was a 14-year-old Chicago native visiting relatives in Mississippi. While out with cousins and friends, he allegedly made a flirtatious comment to a white woman in a family grocery store.[69] The woman's husband, Roy Bryant, and his half brother, J. W. Milam (and possibly others), kidnapped Till from a relative's home in the middle of the night. They proceeded to beat him viciously, shoot him in the head, and throw his body, tied with barbed wire, to a 75-pound cotton gin into the Tallahatchie River. His mangled body was found three days later, so disfigured that a relative

---

67   Ibid.
68   http://cms.westport.com, k12.
69   http://history.com, p. 2.

6-11: It was my honor to escort Rosa Parks (center) when she visited Naval Air Station, Pensacola, Florida, in 1995. She was inspirational as she and her group related her life story and beliefs to our military personnel and their families.

could only identify him by his ring.[70]

Despite the Court's newfound imperative to end "separate but equal," the violent symptoms within that system still prevailed. At least three generations of Americans had come to believe that segregation was the norm across the country, they were determined to maintain this practice at almost any cost. In 1957 in Little Rock, Arkansas, Governor Orval Faubus called out the National Guard to prevent nine black students from entering Little Rock Central High School under a federal court order. Once the Guard had been removed from the scene by a court order, a hysterical white mob forced the removal of the black students for their own safety. At that point, President Eisenhower, who had said two months earlier that he could not "imagine any set of circumstances that would induce me to send federal troops," quickly changed his mind and ordered one thousand paratroopers to Little Rock to protect the black students, and he placed the Arkansas National Guard on federal service.[71] (Refer to Figure 6-12.)

This same period in the mid-1950s brought to the American consciousness individuals such as Rosa Parks, who in December of 1955 famously refused to give up her seat on a Montgomery, Alabama, bus, sparking a year-long bus boycott, led by the future Nobel Prize–winner, Dr. Martin Luther King Jr. By 1956, the Supreme Court affirmed that, "the separate but equal doctrine can no longer be safely followed as a correct statement of the law."[72] King and his associates organized the Southern Christian Leadership Conference to help coordinate and lead civil rights activities throughout the country. With this push for equality came an equally violent response. In 1957, Dr. King found an unexploded dynamite bomb on his front porch. His response is prophetic,

> *I'm not afraid of anybody this morning. Tell Montgomery they can keep shooting and I'm going to stand up to them; tell Montgomery they can keep bombing and I'm going to stand up to them. If I had to die tomorrow morning I would die happy because I've been to the mountain top and I've seen the promised land and it's going to be here in Montgomery.[73]*

---

70   Tindall and Shi, *America: A Narrative History*, p. 999.
71   Ibid., p. 996.
72   Tindall and Shi, *America: A Narrative History*, p. 997.
73   Ibid., p. 1009.

These violent tactics were not isolated. In 1958, the Temple, a Jewish congregation in Atlanta, Georgia, was bombed in response to the rabbi's sermons in favor of integration. Similarly, in Birmingham, Alabama, in 1963, four black girls were murdered on a Sunday morning prior to church services when the church was bombed. By the early 1960s, the country was engaged in the civil rights movement. Restaurants, churches, public pools, parks—any areas that previously had accepted segregation were now points of integration. Often, this effort, led by black and white college students, was met with violence. "In many communities they were assaulted with clubs, cattle prods, rocks, and fire hoses, verbal abuse and jail time."[74] (See Figure 6-13.)

6-12: This picture typifies the destruction experienced by the Temple in Atlanta, Georgia in 1958 and a church in Birmingham, Alabama in 1963. In both places of worship bombs were exploded.

Dr. King's brilliant and classic "I Have a Dream" speech, delivered in 1963 in the famous march on Washington, D.C., still required much changing of the hearts and minds of many Americans, now a decade or so past the *Brown* decision. In fact, in 1964 and 1965, two major acts were passed that attempted to remedy some of the almost century-old civil rights prejudices still being practiced in America. Under the leadership of President Lyndon B. Johnson, who became president after the assassination of President John F. Kennedy in 1963, the Civil Rights Act of 1964 was passed. This act is considered the most far-reaching civil rights measure ever enacted. "It outlawed racial discrimination in hotels, restaurants, and other public accommodations. In addition, its provisions enabled the attorney general to bring suits to end school desegregation, relieving parents of that painful burden."[75] In the next year, the Voting Rights Act of 1965 was passed. It ensured that all citizens had the right to vote. "In states or counties where fewer than half the adults voted in 1964, the act suspended literacy tests and other devices commonly used to defraud citizens of the vote. By the end of the year, some 250,000 African Americans were newly registered."[76]

To add additional legal force to the Voting Rights Act, the Twenty-fourth Amendment to the Constitution was proposed and ratified by the states in 1964. The intention of the amendment is apparent.

> *The right of citizens of the United States to vote in any primary or other election for President or Vice President, for electors for President or Vice President, or for Senator or*

---

74   Ibid., p. 1022.
75   Ibid.
76   http://supreme.justia.com, *Loving v. Virginia*, p. 8.

Representative in Congress shall not be denied or abridged by the United States or any State by reason of failure to pay any poll tax or other tax.

At this juncture, it is appropriate to examine the dates of the above acts with a historical analysis. As I share with my university students, in many ways, the acts of 1964 and 1965 were sadly not new. The first act forbade discrimination in public places and accommodations. This sort of prejudice was indeed anticipated immediately after the Civil War and certainly was in the minds of the Congress and the country when it ratified the Fourteenth Amendment in 1868, which called for "equal protection of the law." Likewise, the early civil rights acts of 1870 and 1875 specifically called for equal seating aboard all public forms of transportation. Due to the widespread prejudices of most Americans, including the justices of the Court, there existed a gap between the Fourteenth

6-13: Dr. Martin Luther King Jr. (third from left) meets with President John Kennedy (third from right) in August of 1963.

Amendment in 1868 and this act in 1964 of almost a century later. Similarly, the Fifteenth Amendment, ratified in 1870, gave the right to vote to all citizens; yet, over the decades, that right was attacked and effectively removed from much of the black community. It took until the Voting Rights Act of 1965 to get it right on such a fundamental American value as voting. Thus, from 1870 through 1965, almost a full century was squandered in the quest for equality for the long-ago former slaves and their free brothers and sisters.

It is fair to imagine, for a brief moment, how different our country might have been had we not wasted the first hundred years of post–Civil War America. Nevertheless, the country was changing, often slowly, but in the direction of equality for all. In 1967, the country faced a state law that still reflected old fears and old prejudices. The state of Virginia, as well as 15 other states, had laws prohibiting interracial marriage. The Virginia Code was quite explicit.

All marriages between a white person and a colored person shall be absolutely void without any decree of divorce or other legal process ... It shall hereafter be unlawful for any white person in this State to marry any save a white person, or a person with no admixture of blood than white and American Indian. For the purpose of this chapter, the term "white person" shall apply only to such person as has no trace whatever of any blood other than Caucasian; but persons who have one-sixteenth or less of the blood of the American Indian and have no other non-Caucasian blood shall be deemed white persons.[77]

---

77   Ibid., p. 2.

In June of 1958, two residents of Virginia, Mildred Jeter, a black woman, and Richard Loving, a white man, married in the District of Columbia according to its laws. They returned to live in Caroline County, Virginia. In October 1958, a grand jury from that county charged them with violating Virginia's ban on interracial marriage. On January 9, 1959, the Lovings pled guilty to the charge and were sentenced to one year in jail. The trial judge suspended the sentence for a period of 25 years, on the condition that the Lovings leave the state.[78] The words of this judge bear repetition,

> *Almighty God created the races white, black, yellow, malay and red, and he placed them on separate continents. And, but for the interference with his arrangement, there would be no such cause for marriage. The fact that he separated the races shows that he did not intend for the races to mix.*[79]

These words are breathtakingly sad. They reek of prejudice and natavism that seemed far more appropriate for the year 1907, rather than 1967. After a series of legal challenges by the Lovings, the case was heard by Virginia's Supreme Court of Appeals, which upheld the constitutionality of the antimiscegenation statutes. After receiving and reviewing the case, the United States Supreme Court in its 1967 findings quickly held that these laws were in direct contradiction to the Fourteenth Amendment.

> *There is patently no legitimate overriding purpose of invidious racial discrimination which justifies this classification. The fact that Virginia prohibits only interracial marriages involving white persons demonstrates that the racial classifications must stand on their own justification, as measures designed to maintain White Supremacy ... There can be no doubt that restricting the freedom to marry solely because of racial classifications violates the central meaning of the Equal Protection Clause. These statutes also deprive the Lovings of liberty without due process of law in violation of the Due Process Clause of the Fourteenth Amendment. The freedom to marry has long been recognized as one of the vital personal rights essential to the orderly pursuit of happiness of free men.*[80]

Clearly, the country still had a great distance to travel regarding equal rights, as the *Loving* case illustrates. It was also at this time, the mid-1960s, that many of the Northern inner cities—places of poverty, gang activities, drug usage, and violence—are burnt to the ground in summer-long riots. Regrettably, Dr. Martin Luther King and Robert Kennedy were assassinated in 1968. As America moved away from Vietnam in the early 1970s and the Watergate scandal as well, race and racism were constant elements of American society. There would always be people and events to show us how prevalent racism still was. (See Figure 6-14.)

As a historian, it is my task to find proof for any claims regarding the High Court. I believe I have found evidence for these assertions regarding the racism of the Court from an unusual source: the High Court itself. In the 1968 case, *Jones v. Alfred H. Mayer Co.*, Associate Justice William O. Douglas, who served on the Court for 36 years, wrote a powerful concurring opinion

---

78   Ibid.
79   Ibid., p. 7.
80   http:///scholargoogle.com, *Jones et ux. v. Alfred H. Mayer et al.*, p. 1.

6-14: Lyman Trumbull. How amazing that words spoken so eloquently, so long ago, still resonate with us. They cause us to reflect on our country's history of shattered race relations and the way forward.

to the case. The case is straightforward: Joseph L. Jones, a black man, filed a legal complaint that the owners of a home in St. Louis County, Missouri, had refused to sell him their house. A district court and the Court of Appeals for the Eighth Circuit agreed that this complaint should be dismissed. The law in question seems clear enough: "All citizens of the United States shall have the same right, in every State and Territory, as is enjoyed by white citizens thereof to inherit, purchase, lease, sell, hold, and convey real and personal property." (42 U.S.C. 1982) The court argued that this only applied to state action, and not private refusals to sell.[81]

On appeal to the Supreme Court, the judgment of the court of appeals was reversed. The High Court held that this section of law written to enforce the Thirteenth Amendment, "barred **ALL** racial discrimination, private as well as public, in the sale or rental of property, and that the statute, thus construed, is a valid exercise of the power of Congress to enforce the Thirteenth Amendment."[82]

As part of their decision, the justices revert to the history and context of the law. "Section 1982 was part of Section 1 of the Civil Rights Act of 1866."[83] The ensuing deliberations are especially fascinating, as they cause one to reflect on what might have been.

The crucial language for our purposes was that which guaranteed all citizens "the same right, in every State and territory in the United States, … to inherit, purchase, lease, sell, hold, and convey real and personal property … as is enjoyed by white citizens … " To the Congress that passed the Civil Rights Act of 1866, it was clear that the right to do these things might be infringed not only by "State or local law" but also by "custom, or prejudice." Thus, when Congress provided in Section 1 of the Civil Rights Act that the right to purchase and lease property was to be enjoyed equally throughout the United

---

81 Ibid., p. 2.
82 Ibid., p. 4.
83 Ibid.

States by Negro and white citizens alike, it plainly meant to secure that right against interference from any source whatever, whether government or private.[84]

In this paragraph and their conclusions, the justices undo decades of numerous findings such as the 1883 Civil Rights Cases, which decided that, while state governments could not discriminate, individuals could. One can only wonder if the above reasoning had prevailed in the years following the Civil War. In an astonishing bit of historical analysis, the justices referred to the year immediately after the Civil War.

6-15: For me, Justice William O'Douglas's words are classic and prophetic. Study and reflect upon them, feel the emotions that they express, and let them connect with your heart and soul.

That broad language, we are asked to believe, was a mere slip of the legislative pen. We disagree. For the same Congress that wanted to do away with the Black Codes ALSO *had before it an imposing body of evidence pointing to the mistreatment of Negroes by private individuals and unofficial groups, mistreatment unrelated to any hostile state legislation. "Accounts in newspapers North and South, Freedman's Bureau and other official documents, private reports and correspondence were all adduced" to show that "private outrage and atrocity" were daily inflicted on freedmen ... The congressional debates are replete with references to private injustices against Negroes—references to white employers who refused to pay their Negro workers, white planters who agreed among themselves not to hire freed slaves without the permission of their former masters, white citizens who assaulted Negroes or who combined to drive them out of their communities.*[85]

This conversation of the justices is one that I have with my university students, when I suggest that the country "lost" a century, in terms of race relations and civil rights based on the rulings and actions that were taken in the years after the Civil War. It appears that it has taken the High Court a century to gain the insight that they acquired in this case. (Refer to Figure 6-15.)

Interestingly, the justices, in their investigation of the 1866 Civil Rights Act, refer to the congressional debates about the act. They quote the words offered by Senator Lyman Trumbull of Illinois, chairman of the Judiciary Committee and coauthor of the Thirteenth Amendment, who is quite explicit in his January 5, 1866, comments,

That Amendment [Thirteenth] declared that all persons in the United States should be free. This measure is intended to give effect to that declaration and secure to all persons within the United States practical freedom. There is very little importance in the general declaration of abstract truths and principles unless they can be carried into effect, unless

---

84   Ibid.
85   Ibid., p. 5.

the persons who are to be affected by them have some means of availing themselves of their benefits.

The trumpet of freedom that we have been blowing throughout the land has given an "uncertain sound." And the promised freedom is a delusion. Such was not the intention of Congress, which proposed the constitutional amendment, nor is such the fair meaning of the amendment itself. … I have no doubt that under this provision … we may destroy these discriminations in civil rights against the black man; and if we cannot, our constitutional amendment amounts to nothing. It was for that purpose that the second clause of that amendment was adopted, which says that Congress shall have authority by appropriate legislation, to carry into effect the article prohibiting slavery. Who is to decide what that appropriate legislation is to be? The c=Congress of the Unites States; and it is for Congress to adopt such appropriate legislation as it may think proper, so that it be a means to accomplish the end."[86]

[handwritten margin note: Uncertainty in freedom]

[handwritten margin note: not Practicing freedom if bad and racist things are still happening]

The entire context of these paragraphs is so superb, as previous generations of justices apparently had little concern for the thoughts and possible original motivations that the congressional authors of such amendments had in mind. In fact, the justices in 1968 quote once again Senator Trumbull, that the bill would "break down **ALL** discrimination between black men and white men."[87] In addition to referencing the original sponsors in the Senate, the Court researched the original House sponsors of the Civil Rights Act as well. They quote the words of Representative Wilson of Iowa, who served as the floor manager for the 1866 act. "The end is the maintenance of freedom … A man who enjoys the civil rights mentioned in this bill cannot be reduced to slavery … This settles the appropriateness of this measure, and that settles its constitutionality."[88]

Justice William O. Douglas, one of the Court's longest-serving justices, added an extraordinary concurring opinion to this 1968 *Jones v. Alfred H. Mayer Co.* case. I find his words quite revealing, somewhat apologetic, historically instructive, and personally powerful in terms of what he acknowledges.

The true curse of slavery is not what it did to the black man, but what it has done to the white man. For the existence of the institution produced the notion that the white man was of superior character, intelligence, and morality. The blacks were little more than livestock—to be fed and fattened for the economic benefits they could bestow through their labors, and to be subjected to authority, often with cruelty, to make clear who was master and who slave."[89]

At this stage in his opinion, the justice writes something unbelievable. I offer it below verbatim.

MR. JUSTICE DOUGLAS, concurring.

---

86 Ibid., p. 6.
87 Ibid., p. 9.
88 Ibid.
89 Ibid.

Some badges of slavery remain today. While the institution has been outlawed, it has remained in the minds and hearts of many white men. Cases which have come to this Court depict a spectacle of slavery unwilling to die. We have seen contrivances by States designed to thwart Negro voting, e.g, Lane v. Wilson, 307 U.S. 268. Negroes have been excluded over and again from juries solely on account of their race, e.g, Strauder v. West Virginia, 100 U.S. 303, or have been forced to sit in segregated seats in courtrooms, Johnson v. Virginia, 373 U.S. 61. They have been made to attend segregated and inferior schools, e.g, Brown v. Board of Education, 347 U.S. 483, or been denied entrance to colleges or graduate schools because of their color, e.g, Pennsylvania v. Board of Trusts, 353 U.S. 230; Sweatt v. Painter, 339 U.S. 629. Negroes have been prosecuted for marrying whites, e.g, Loving v. Virginia, 388 U.S. 1. They have been forced to live in segregated residential districts, Buchanan v. Warley, 245 U.S. 60, and residents of white neighborhoods have denied them entrance, e.g, Shelley v. Kraemer, 334 U.S. 1. Negroes have been forced to use segregated facilities in going about their daily lives, having been excluded from railway coaches, Plessy v. Ferguson, 163 U.S. 537; public parks, New Orleans Park Improvement Assn. v. Detiege, 358 U.S. 54; restaurants, Lombard v. Louisiana, 373 U.S. 267; public beaches, Mayor of Baltimore v. Dawson, 350 U.S. 877; municipal [p446] golf courses, Holmes v. City of Atlanta, 350 U.S. 879; amusement parks, Griffin v. Maryland, 378 U.S. 130; buses, Gayle v. Browder, 352 U.S. 903; public libraries, Brown v. Louisiana, 383 U.S. 131. A state court judge in Alabama convicted a Negro woman of contempt of court because she refused to answer him when he addressed her as "Mary," although she had made the simple request to be called "Miss Hamilton." Hamilton v. Alabama, 376 U.S. 650.[90]

[handwritten margin note: Cases that were unfair / All cases were not Practical Freedom]

What is truly astounding about this list is the initial assertion it makes: The "badges of slavery" supposedly outlawed by the Thirteenth Amendment, have manifested themselves in numerous legal ways over the century, between 1865 and 1968. The justice's list is a fairly obvious acknowledgment of the role that the Court failed to play in the long series of cases over the decades after the Civil War, some of which have been explored by this work. When Justice Douglas writes, "Cases which have come to this Court depict a spectacle of slavery unwilling to die," I feel that he is admitting, indirectly, the role of the Court in not working to attain fuller social, economic, political, and personal equality for people of color over time. When he further notes, "While this institution [slavery] has been outlawed, it has remained in the minds and hearts of many white men," I believe that some of the white men mentioned above were members of the High Court itself.

The fact that the justice proceeds to record those prior cases is an admission of the multi-leveled degrees of prejudice experienced by people of color, with very little assistance in fighting that intolerance from the nation's highest court. In my opinion, Douglas is expressing notions of a very personal and emotional level. This is certainly verified by his next quotation. Justice Douglas quotes from a recognized American leader and icon, Frederick Douglass (1817–1895), who wrote the following in the 19th century.

Of all the races and varieties of men which have suffered from this feeling, the colored people of this country have endured most. They can resort to no disguises which will enable them to escape its deadly aim. They carry in front the evidence which marks them

---

90 Ibid., pp. 9–10.

for persecution. They stand at the extreme point of difference from the Caucasian race, and their African origin can be instantly recognized, though they may be several removes from the typical African race. They may remonstrate like Shylock—

Hath not a Jew eyes? hath not a Jew hands, organs, dimensions, senses, affections, passions? fed with the same food, hurt with the same weapons, subject to the same diseases, healed by the same means, warmed and cooled by the same summer and winter, as a Christian is?—but such eloquence is unavailing. They are Negroes—and that is enough, in the eye of this unreasoning prejudice, to justify indignity and violence. In nearly every department of American life, they are confronted by this insidious influence. It fills the air. It meets them at the workshop and factory, when they apply for work. It meets them at the church, at the hotel, at the [p447] ballot box, and, worst of all, it meets them in the jury box. Without crime or offense against law or gospel, the colored man is the Jean Valjean of American society. He has escaped from the galleys, and hence all presumptions are against him. The workshop denies him work, and the inn denies him shelter; the ballot box a fair vote, and the jury box a fair trial. He has ceased to be the slave of an individual, but has, in some sense, become the slave of society. He may not now be bought and sold like a beast in the market, but he is the trammeled victim of a prejudice, well calculated to repress his manly ambition, paralyze his energies, and make him a dejected and spiritless man, if not a sullen enemy to society, fit to prey upon life and property and to make trouble generally. [n2]

Today the black is protected by a host of civil rights laws. But the forces of discrimination are still strong.[91]

What is truly incredible about the above quote is that the sentiment that William Douglas, via Frederick Douglass, via William Shakespeare refers to is one that we can relate to: The feelings we experience when others attack a part of our person which is different from theirs, be that ethnic, religious, sexual, economic, or more! When we are made to feel lesser than others, without provocation, we feel hurt, degraded and ashamed. One sentence is especially powerful to me: "He has ceased to be the slave of an individual, but has, in some sense, become the slave of society."

To finish this quite stirring "confessional," the justice continues with contemporary prejudices, as he laments,

A member of his race, duly elected by the people to a state legislature, is barred from that assembly because of his views on the Vietnam war. Bond v. Floyd, 385 U.S. 116.

Real estate agents use artifice to avoid selling "white property" to the blacks. [n3] The blacks who travel the country, though entitled by law to the facilities for sleeping and dining that are offered all tourists, Heart of Atlanta Motel v. United States, 379 U.S. 241, may well learn that the "vacancy" sign does not mean what it says, especially if the motel has a swimming pool.

---

91 Ibid., p. 10.

On entering a half-empty restaurant, they may find "reserved" signs on all unoccupied tables. [p448]

The black is often barred from a labor union because of his race. [n4]

He learns that the order directing admission of his children into white schools has not been obeyed "with all deliberate speed," Brown v. Board of Education, 349 U.S. 294, 301, but has been delayed by numerous stratagems and devices. [n5] *State laws, at times, have even encouraged [p449] discrimination in housing. Reitman v. Mulkey, 387 U.S. 369. This recital is enough to show how prejudices, once part and parcel of slavery, still persist.* [92]

In many ways, the words of Justice Douglas provide a terminal point for this work. In an eerie and poetic manner, this 1968 case refers to 1866 and reviews an entire century of cases, many of which were decided against the rights and freedoms of the black community.

It is gratifying to see Justice Douglas offer his apologies for the past. I don't know if it changed anything, but as a person who has experienced prejudice, an apology is a good beginning.

---

92 http://southcentralhistory.com, p. 1.

6-16: President Barack Obama.

Final Thoughts

Justice Douglas's words about prejudice being a part and parcel of our society are quite accurate. As the 20th century came to a close, two major events infused with racism shook America and illustrated how raw and ever present the racial divide is. Both events in the early 1990s center around two vastly different people and situations. On March 3, 1991, Rodney King, fleeing from the police at high speeds due to his concern over a possible violation of his parole, was beaten by Los Angeles police officers. The police maintained that he was resisting arrest and on drugs as well. The entire situation was being filmed by a citizen, who gave the video to a local TV news station, which began repeatedly showing the film.[93] Four white officers, deemed to be the major participants in this arrest, were brought to trial for the use of excessive force.

On April 29, 1992, the mostly white jury in this case against the officers found them not guilty. Combined with negative feelings about the shooting previously of a young girl by a Korean store owner, the streets of South Central Los Angeles quickly dissolved into a major riot. "The riots happened very quickly. Liquor stores, fast-food places, and white people were the main targets of looting fire and violence … Reginald Denny, a white truck driver, was pulled from his car and severely beaten on his head. He barely survived this incident. In the end, 53 people were killed; mostly rioters or innocent victims and over one billion dollars of damages were suffered."[94] Riots also occurred in other towns across America as well. It is an easy assertion to make that race was a major aspect of the Rodney King situation.

A similar conclusion can be reached in the 1994–1995 trial of O. J. Simpson for the murders of his ex-wife, Nicole Brown Simpson, and her friend, Ronald L. Goldman. While the case should have been about that murder and all its forensic details, race became a major component of this trial. "By the end of the criminal trial, national surveys showed dramatic differences in the assessment of Simpson's guilt between most blacks and whites."[95] One of the primary detectives, Mark Fuhrman, denied that he was a racist or that he had used derogatory terms when defining black people. In a later court proceeding, the defense played audio tapes of Fuhrman repeatedly using crass racial terms regarding people of color. These tapes brought his integrity and testimony into question.[96] Due to such evidence and the approach of the various attorneys, the case became one about race in America, not the murder of innocent victims. Ultimately, a majority of whites felt that Simpson was guilty, while an equal number of blacks felt that he was innocent. "Whatever the exact nature of the 'racial divide,' to this very day, the Simpson case

---

93 Ibid.
94 http://Wikipedia.org, Shooting of Trayvon Martin, p. 1.
95 Ibid., p. 12.
96 Ibid., p. 21.

continues to be assessed through the lens of race with most white people believing Simpson to have committed the murders, while most black people believe the opposite."[97]

The election of Barack Obama to the presidency in 2008 and 2012 was, for some people, the possible fulfillment of Dr. King's dreams for America. Another factor to consider is the sad events of September 11, 2001, and more recently, the attacks at the Boston marathon in April of 2013. These are abrupt reminders that

6-17: Here I sit with Supreme Court Justice Stephen Breyer (left), discussing my research and conclusions.

there are groups of people in this world who are opposed to us because we are Westerners and promoters of democracy. When the country faces such vicious and evil actions, it is clear that the differences among us, most often manufactured by ourselves, are minor in scope, when compared with terrorists who wish to obliterate our society.

And yet, prior to congratulating ourselves about the possible demise or diminution of prejudice, two additional points must be made and considered. First is the writing of the late Professor Derrick Bell. In his work, *Faces at the Bottom of the Well*, he makes the following assertion.

> *I want to set forth this proposition, which will be easier to reject than refute: Black people will never gain full equality in this country. Even those herculean efforts we hail as successful will produce no more than temporary "peaks of progress," short-lived victories that slide into irrelevance as racial patterns adapt in ways that maintain white dominance. This is a hard-to-accept fact that all history verifies. We must acknowledge it, not as a sign of submission, but as an act of ultimate defiance.* [98]

Bell emphatically states that racism is a permanent component of American life.

At the very least, these statements deserve our analysis and considerations. As a corollary to this notion of America being in a permanent state of racism, I suggest that we examine our contemporary society for clues about the way we feel and think about race. The fatal shooting of Trayvon Martin by George Zimmerman in Sanford, Florida, took place on February 26, 2012. While the incident might have centered on vigilantism and the use of inappropriate force, it has become another symbol of our ongoing struggle with race. Following is a fairly typical way that the incident is described: "Martin was an unarmed African American. George Zimmerman, a 28-year-old multiracial Hispanic American, was the appointed neighborhood

---

97   Bell, *Faces at the Bottom of the Well*, pp. 12–13.
98   www.wikipedia.org, Shooting of Trayvon Martin, p. 1.

6-18: Congressman John Lewis (right) is an icon of the Civil Rights Movement. We discussed how to educate future generations about the history of race relations in America.

watch coordinator where Martin was temporarily staying and where the shooting took place."[99]

In mid-July 2013, Zimmerman was found not guilty of the murder of Trayvon Martin. The response to this verdict was intense, including remarks by President Barack Obama. In a White House briefing on July 19, the president made his comments personal when he reflected on this case. He said that the slain black teenager " … could have been me 35 years ago."[100] In fact, as the briefing continued, the president made comments that are consistent with the premise of this work. "I think it's important to recognize that the African-American community is looking at this issue through a set of experiences and a history that doesn't go away."[101] The history that wouldn't go away is what this work represents.

A somewhat parallel case to the Zimmerman case occurred in Jacksonville, Florida, on November 23, 2012. A group of four black teenagers pulled up to a convenience store at the same time as Michael Dunn, a white man. After asking them to turn down their loud music, which they did, then apparently put on again, an argument took place. According to prosecutors, Dunn saw the loud teenagers as "gangsters" playing "thug music."[102] Within a few moments, Dunn went to his vehicle, retrieved a gun, and fired off ten rounds at the car as it was pulling away. One teenager, Jordan Davis, was shot and killed.

In February 2014, Dunn was found guilty of three charges of attempted murder; the jury deadlocked on a count of premeditated murder, for which he will be tried in the months ahead. At the conclusion of that trial, Dunn will receive his punishment for the various guilty offenses. Certainly, that will include decades' worth of prison time. One can only wonder if the four young men had been white and not "thugs" playing rap music, would the incident have evolved the way it did?

---

99   *Atlanta Journal-Constitution*, July 20, 2013, front page.

100   Ibid., p. 9.

101   *New York Times*, National Edition, February 17, 2014, pp. 910.

102   *New York Times*, National Edition, March 19, 2014, p. 17.

The reach of prejudice and racism does indeed have deep roots in our society. Two contemporary events indicate the tenaciousness of such concepts. The *New York Times* edition of March 19, 2014, reported that the New York City Fire Department agreed to a number of reforms whose goal is to increase the number of black and Hispanic firefighters. The paper details this agreement: "On Tuesday, that long fight to diversify the overwhelmingly white department came to an end with an agreement to settle the case and pay nearly $100 million in back pay and benefits to minorities whose efforts to join the department were thwarted by what courts have ruled were institutional biases."[103]

A second, even more poignant, article regarding prejudice was reported in the same issue of the *Times*. Based on a 2001 law, the Department of Defense was ordered to review records from World War Two and the Korean and Vietnam wars to determine if any black, Hispanic, or Jewish men, who had been nominated for a Medal of Honor, were unfairly downgraded to receive a Distinguished Service Cross instead. The findings were definitive—24 service members had been unfairly denied the Medal of Honor. These men were honored by the White House on March 18, 2014. Unfortunately, only three heroes were still alive. Family members accepted the medal on behalf of those who had passed on. President Obama's comments at this occasion fit well into this work: "No nation is perfect. But here in America, we confront our imperfections and face a sometimes painful past, including the truth that some of these soldiers fought and died for a country that did not always see them as equal."[104]

I don't think that society will ever be totally free of intolerance and prejudice. Nevertheless, we, as individuals and as a civilization, can make personal decisions and actions that make this a more likely and possible scenario. We owe it to the Ed Johnsons, the Leo Franks, the Isaac Woodards, the Dorseys, the Malcolms, and the generations who were treated unfairly in a distinctly un-American way. I fervently believe that everyone should read the words of the justices and make their own judgments about their motivations, and yes, prejudices. These nine individuals have an essential role in our government. The more we are familiar with them and their beliefs, the better it is for our democracy. Imagine how our country would be if we were able to transform the negative energy of the past into positive deeds. The overwhelming power of history is the deep personal insights we can gain from it, coupled with present-day actions.

In this instance, knowledge about the Court's prejudicial findings in prior centuries should help us as we confront and begin to resolve our contemporary racial and social issues. The words that greet people as they come into the Supreme Court Building are "Equal Justice Under Law." They are quite profound. In some cases, for a large part of our history, those words were not fully realized. Our task is to help ensure that every American, moving forward into a new century, lives, experiences, and achieves that lofty goal.

---

103   Ibid., p. 15.
104   Ibid.

Discussion Questions

1. What effect did the presence of a million black soldiers in World War Two have on race relations?

2. What must Sergeant Isaac Woodard have been thinking and experiencing as he was being relentlessly beaten by sheriff's deputies within a few hours of being discharged from the Army?

3. Review the incident at Moore's Ford Bridge. Why were the white citizens so hateful that they shot innocent people, including a pregnant woman?

4. What motivated President Truman to take the actions he did regarding civil rights?

5. What impact did Jackie Robinson's joining professional baseball have on America's race relations?

6. How much time did it take for the country to fully accept the *Brown* decision?

7. Why would someone feel compelled to plant bombs at houses of worship?

8. What caused the state of Virginia to pass laws prohibiting white and black citizens from marrying?

9. What are your thoughts about the *Jones v. Alfred H. Mayer Co.* decision, especially its reference to Senator Trumbull and the original intent of the 1866 Civil Rights Act?

10. What is the future of race relations in America?

Bibliography

Primary Sources: Supreme Court Cases

United States v. the Amistad, January 1841

Groves v. Slaughter, January 1841

Prigg v. Commonwealth of Pennsylvania, January 1842

Jones v. Van Zandt, 1847

Strader v. Graham, 1850

Dred Scott v. Sanford, December 1856

Ableman v. Booth and *United States v. Booth*, December 1858

Blyew et al. v. United States, December 1871

Slaughterhouse Cases, December 1872

United States v. Cruikshank et al., October 1875

United States v. Reese et al., October 1875

Hall v. DeCuir, October 1877

Ex Parte Virginia, 1879

Strauder v. West Virginia, October 1879

Virginia v. Rives, 1880

United States v. Harris, January 1883

Chae Chan Ping v. United States, May 1889

Louisville, New Orleans & Texas Ry. Co. v. Mississippi, March 1890

Civil Rights Cases, October 1883

Fong Yue Ting v. United States, Wong Quan v. United States, Lee Joe v. United States, May 1893

Plessy v. Ferguson, October 1895

Williams v. Mississippi, October 1897

Cumming v. Richmond County Board of Education, October 1899

Giles v. Harris, April 1903

James v. Bowman, May 1903

Giles v. Teasley, February 1904

Clyatt v. United States, March 1905

Hodges v. United States, October 1906

United States v. Shipp, December 1906

Guinn v. United States, June 1915

Frank v. Mangum, April 1915

United States v. Mosley, June 1915

Buchanan v. Warley, October 1917

Moore v. Dempsey, October 1923

Buck v. Bell, October 1926

Gong Lum et al. v. Rice et al., November 1927

Ozie Powell, Willie Roberson, Andy Wright, and Olen Montgomery v. Alabama, Haywood Patterson v. Same and *Charley Weems and Clarence Norris v. Same*, November 1932

Nixon v. Condon et al., May 1932

Chambers v. Florida, February 1940
Toyosaburo Korematsu v. United States, December 1944
Akins v. Texas, June 1945
Morgan v. Virginia, June 1946
Sweatt v. Painter et al., June 1950
McLaurin v. Oklahoma State Regents, June 1950
Shepherd et al. v. Florida, April 1951
Terry v. Adams, May 1953
Hernandez v. Texas, May 1954
Bolling v. Sharpe, May 1954
Brown v. Board of Education, May 1954
Bell v. Maryland, June 1964
United States v. Guest, March 1966
Loving v. Virginia, June 1967
Jones et ux. V. Alfred H. Mayer Co. et al., June 1968

Note: In traditional sources for Supreme Court Cases, two numbers follow the case. These represent the volume number and page of the "United States Reports" which functioned as the official repository of the Court's findings. With the advent of the internet and web-based sources, I have not put in the traditional citations, but rather, the month and year of the decision. This will allow full access for those who desire to read the case and assist students as they place these decisions in their historical context.

Roberts v. Boston, Massachusetts Supreme Judicial Court, November 1849

United States Court of Appeals:

Gary L. Penick et al. v. Columbus Board of Education et al., United States Court of Appeals, Sixth Circuit, July 1948

Periodicals:

Ebony Magazine, Special Issue, August 1975.
Atlanta Journal-Constitution, December 19, 2013. Let Us Bury Desire to Use a Self-Denigrating Word. Leonard Pitts.
New York Times, November 20, 2013. Safer Cities? Try Telling This Neighborhood, John Eligon.
New York Times, February 27, 2013. Voting Act Challenge Hinges on a Formula. Adam Liptak.
New York Times, April 3, 2012. From Striking Symbol of Segregation to Victim of Golf's Success. Karen Crouse.
Atlanta Journal-Constitution, January 27, 2005. Eliminating "Jim Crow" Laws. Nancy Badertscher.
Atlanta Journal-Constitution, March 18, 2013. Suspect in 1964 Klan Slayings Dies. Associated Press.
Marietta Daily Journal, September 15, 2013, Congressional Black Caucus Remembers Girls Killed in Alabama. Jay Reeves.
Atlanta Journal-Constitution, May 3, 2005. Dolls Proved Toll of Racism. Drew Jubera.
New York Times, September 27, 2005. Using History as a Guide but Skipping the Details. Janet Maslin.

Atlanta Journal-Constitution, December 3, 2005. Florida Links 4 Klansman to 1951 Civil Rights Killing. Laurin Sellers.

New York Times, March 15, 2012. This Was Bull Connor's Town. John Hanc.

Atlanta Journal-Constitution, April 28, 2013. Waiving Our Civil Rights Is Rarely Necessary or Wise. George Will.

Atlanta Journal—Constitution, January 5, 2003. The Unfinished story of Emmett Till. Bob Longino.

New York Times Book Review, February 16, 2003. Jim Crow's Last War, review of David P. Colley's book, *Blood for Dignity*, Ann Banks.

Atlanta Journal-Constitution, July 16, 2013. As Race Card Was Played, Justice Was Undermined. Thomas Sowell.

Articles:

American Historical Review, "Book Review, Maltz, Earl M. The Fourteenth Amendment and the Law of the Constitution." (vol. 109, April 2005).

American Historical Review, "Book Review of Labbe, Ronald M., Lurie, Jonathan. The Slaughterhouse Cases: Regulation, Reconstruction and the Fourteenth Amendment." (vol. 110, June 2005).

American Historical Review, "Book Review of Klarman, Michael L. From Jim Crow to Civil Rights: The Supreme Court and the Struggle for Racial Equality." (vol. 110, June 2005).

Bogen, David S. "Why the Supreme Court Lied in Plessy." Villanova Law Review (September 2007).

Dinnerstein, Leonard. "The Supreme Court and the Rights of Aliens." Reprinted from *This Constitution: A Bicentennial Chronicle*. Fall 1975. Published by Project '87 of the American Political Science Association and American Historical Association.

Drobak, John N. "Political Economy Working Paper: The Courts and Slavery in the United States." Box 1208, St. Louis: Washington University (1992).

Federal Bureau of Investigation. Routine report on Moore's Ford Bridge Incident (April 2006).

Killian, Johnny H. "The Constitution of the United States of America." Washington, DC: U.S. Government Printing Office (1987).

Patton, Randall L. "Managing Desegregation: The First African-American Supervisor at Lockheed-Georgia, 1952–1961." Kennesaw State University, Presentation to History Department (2012).

Ross, Michael A. "Justice Miller's Reconstruction: The Slaughter Houses Cases, Health Codes, and Civil Rights in New Orleans, 1861–1873." *Journal of Southern History* (November 1998): 649–676.

Schweninger, Loren. "Prosperous Blacks in the South." *American Historical Review* 95 (February 1990): 31:56.

Scott, Rebecca. "Public Rights, Social Equality, and the Conceptual Roots of the Plessy Challenge." *Michigan Law Review* (March 2008), vol. 106.

Books:

Andrews, William L., and Henry Louis Gates Jr. *Slave Narratives*. New York: Literary Classics of the United States, 2000.

Arnesen, Eric. *Black Protest and the Great Migration*. Boston: Bedford/St. Martin's, 2003.

Bibliography

Ayers, Edward l., Lewis L. Gould, David M. Oshinsky, and Jean R. Soderlund. *American Passages*. Belmont, CA: Wadsworth, 2003.

Balkin, Jack M. *What "Brown v. Board of Education" Should Have Said*. New York: New York University Press, 2002.

Barrett Jr., Edward L., and William Cohen. *Constitutional Law*. Mineola, NY: Foundation Press, Inc., 1981.

Bartholomew, Paul C. *Summaries of Leading Cases of the Constitution*. Totowa, NJ: Littlefield, Adams & Co., 1974.

Bell, Derrick. *Faces at the Bottom of the Well*. New York: Basic Books, 1992.

Black, Henry C. *Black's Law Dictionary*. St. Paul: West Publishing Co., 1951.

Blight, David W. *Narrative of the Life of Frederick Douglass, an American Slave, Written by Himself*. Boston: Bedford/St. Martin's, 2003.

Botkin, B. A., Ed. *Lay My Burden Down: A Folk History of Slavery*. Chicago: University of Chicago Press, 1945.

Brinkley, Alan. *The Unfinished Nation*. Boston: McGraw Hill, 2004.

Brundage, W. Fitzhugh. *Up from Slavery* by Booker T. Washington. Boston: Bedford/St. Martin's, 2003.

Carnes, Mark C. and John A. Garraty. *American Destiny*. New York: Pearson Education, Inc., 2003.

Coco, Al. *Finding the Law*. Denver: University of Denver, 1982.

Corbett, P. Scott, and Ronald C. Naugle. *Documents in American History*, vol. I. Boston: McGraw Hill, 2004.

Currie, Stephen. *Life of a Slave on a Southern Plantation*. San Diego: Lucent Books, 2000.

Curtis, Michael K. *No State Shall Abridge The Fourteenth Amendment and the Bill of Rights*. Durham: Duke University Press, 1986.

Cushman, Robert F., and Susan P. Koniak. *Cases in Constitutional Law*. New Jersey: Prentice Hall, 1994.

Dernbach, John C., and Richard V. Singleton II. *A Practical Guide to Legal Writing and Legal Method*. Littleton, CO: Fred B. Rothman & Co., 1981.

DeSantis, Vincent P. *The Shaping of Modern America: 1877–1916*. Notre Dame, IN: Forum Press, 1973.

Faragher, John, Mari Jo Buhle, Daniel Czitrom, and Susan H. Armitage. *Out of Many: A History of the American People*. Upper Saddle River, NJ: Pearson Education Inc., 2006.

Fehrenbacher, Don E. *The Dred Scott Case*. Oxford, UK: Oxford University Press, 1978.

Findlay, Bruce, and Esther Findlay. *Your Rugged Constitution*. Stanford, CA: Stanford University Press, 1952.

Finkelman, Paul. *An Imperfect Union*. Chapel Hill: University of North Carolina Press, 1981.

Fleischner, Jennifer, Ed. *Incidents in the Life of a Slave Girl*. Boston: Bedford/St. Martin's, 2010.

Foner, Eric. *Give Me Liberty! An American History*. London: W. W. Norton & Company, 2012.

Foster, James C., and Susan M. Leeson. *Constitutional Law*. Upper Saddle River, NJ: Prentice Hall, 1998.

Friedman, Leon, and Fred L. Israel, Eds. *The Justices of the United States Supreme Court*, volumes I, II, and III. New York: Chelsea House Publishers, 1997.

Gifis, Steven. H. *Barron's History of Legal Terms*. Hauppauge, NY: Barron's Educational Services, 1998.

Grant, Donald L. *The Anti-Lynching Movement: 1883–1932*. San Francisco: Fort Valley State College, 1975.

Gunther, Gerald. *Constitutional Law*. New York: Foundation, 1991.

Hall, Kermit l., William W. Wiecek, and Paul Finkelman. *American Legal History Cases and Materials*. Oxford, UK: Oxford University Press, 1991.

Hall, Kermit l., Ed., *Race Relations and the Law of American Slavery*. New York: Garland Publishing, 1987.

Henretta, James A., and David Brody. *America: A Concise History*. Boston: Bedford/St. Martin's, 2010.

Higham, John. *Strangers in the Land*. New York: Atheneum, 1963.

Hirshson, Stanley P. *Farewell to the Bloody Shirt*. Gloucester: Peter Smith, 1968.

Hopkins, Vincent C. *Dred Scott's Case*. New York: Atheneum, 1967.

Howard-Pitney, David. *Martin Luther King Jr., Malcolm X, and the Civil Rights Struggle of the 1950s and 1960s*. Boston: Bedford/St. Martin's, 2004.

Hurmence, Belinda, Ed. *Before Freedom*. Winston-Salem, NC: John F. Blair, Publisher, 2007.

Irons, Peter. *A People's History of the Supreme Court*. New York: Penguin Books, 1999.

Jones, Jacqueline, Peter H. Wood, Thomas Borstelmann, Elaine Tyler May, and Vicki L. Ruiz. *Created Equal*. New York: Pearson Education, Inc., 2003.

Kaczorowski, Robert J. *The Politics of Judicial Interpretations: The Federal Courts, Department of Justice and Civil Rights, 1866–1876*. New York: Oceana Publications, 1985.

Kauffman, Blair., Collier, Bonnie, Law in America. China: Beaux Arts Editions, 2001.

Kelly, Alfred H., and Winfred A. Harbison. *The American Constitution*. New York: W. W. Norton & Company Inc., 1963.

Klarman, Michael J. *From Jim Crow to Civil Rights*. New York: Oxford University Press, 2004.

Kull, Andrew. *The Color-Blind Constitution*. Cambridge, MA: Harvard University Press, 1992.

Labbe, Ronald M., and Jonathan Lurie. *The Slaughterhouse Cases. Regulation, Reconstruction, and the Fourteenth Amendment*. Lawrence: University Press of Kansas, 2003.

Lawson, Steven F., Ed. *To Secure These Rights*. Boston: Bedford/St. Martin's, 2004.

Lewis, John. *Walking with the Wind*. New York: Simon & Schuster, 1998.

Link, Arthur S. *American Epoch*. New York: Alfred A. Knopf, 1956.

Litwack, Leon F. *North of Slavery*. Chicago: University of Chicago Press, 1961.

Lockhart, William B., Yale Kamisar, Jesse H. Choper, and Steven H. Shiffrin. *Constitutional Rights and Liberties*. St. Paul, MN: West Publishing Company, 1991.

Maltz, Earl M. *The Fourteenth Amendment and the Law of the Constitution*. Durham: North Carolina Academic Press, 2003.

Martin Jr., Waldo E. *Brown v. Board of Education*. Boston: Bedford/St. Martin's, 1998.

McGovern, James R. *Anatomy of a Lynching*. Baton Rouge: Louisiana State University Press, 1982.

Medley, Keith W. *We as Freemen: Plessy v. Ferguson*. Gretna: Pelican Publishing Company, 2003.

Mitau, Theodore G. *Decade of Decision*. New York: Charles Scribner's Sons, 1967.

Nash, Gary B., and Julie R. Jeffrey. *The American People*. New York: Addison-Wesley Educational Publishers Inc., 2003.

Nieman, Donald G. *Black Southerners and the Law*. New York: Garland Publishing, Inc., 1994.

Oakes, James, Michael McGerr, Jan Ellen Lewis, Nick Cullather, and Jeanne Boydston. *Of the People: A History of the United States*. Oxford, UK: Oxford University Press, 2011.

O'Brien, David M. *Constitutional Law and Politics*. New York: W. W. Norton & Company, 1995.

Paul, Arnold M. *Conservative Crisis and the Rule of Law: Attitudes of Bar and Bench, 1887–1895*. Gloucester: Peter Smith, 1976.

Pfeifer, Michael J. *Rough Justice: Lynching and American Society, 1874–1947*. Urbana: University of Illinois Press, 2004.

Pickett, William P. *The Negro Problem*. New York: G. P. Putnam's Sons, 1909.

Roark, James L., Michael P. Johnson, Patricia C. Cohen, Sarah Stage, Alan Lawson, and Sarah M. Hartmann, Eds. *The American Promise*. Boston: Bedford/St. Martin's, 2002.

Redlich, Norman, John Attanasio, and Joel K. Goldstein. *Understanding Constitutional Law*. New York: Matthew Bender & Company, 1999.

Rehnquist, William H. *The Supreme Court*. New York: Alfred A. Knopf, 2001.

Rosen, Robert. *A Short History of Charleston*. San Francisco: Lexikos, 1982.

Royster, Jacqueline J., Ed. *Southern Horrors and Other Writings*. Boston: Bedford/St. Martin's, 1997.

Stockett, Kathryn. *The Help*. New York: Berkley Books, 2009.

Tindall, George B., and David E. Shi, *America: A Narrative History*. New York: W. W. Norton & Company, 2010,

Tindall, George B., David E. Shi, and Thomas L. Pearcy. *The Essential America*. New York: W. W. Norton & Company, 2001.

Tribe, Laurence. *American Constitutional Law*. New York: Foundation Press, 2000.

Twombly, Robert C. *Blacks in White America Since 1865*. New York: David McKay Company, Inc., 1971.

Unger, Irwin. *These United States*. New Jersey: Prentice Hall, 2003.

Urofsky, Melvin I. *Louis Brandeis: A Life*. New York: Pantheon Books, 2009.

Van Dervolt, Thomas R. *Equal Justice Under the Law: An Introduction to American Law and the Legal System*. New York: West Publishing Company, 1994.

Van Geel, T. R. *Understanding Supreme Court Decisions*, 4th ed. New York: Pearson Education Inc., 2005.

Vorenberg, Michael. *The Emancipation Proclamation*. Boston: Bedford/St. Martin's, 2010.

Warren, Charles. *The Supreme Court in United States History*. Toronto: Little, Brown, and Company, 1926.

Waters, Andrew, Ed. *I Was Born in Slavery*. Winston-Salem.NC: John F. Blair, Publisher, 2003.

Williams, Horace R., Ed. *Weren't No Good Times*. Winston-Salem. NC: John F. Blair, Publisher, 2004.

Wilson, Kirk H. *The Reconstruction Desegregation Debate: The Politics of Equality and the Rhetoric of Place, 1870–1875*. East Lansing: Michigan State University Press, 2002.

Woodward, C. Vann. *American Counterpoint*. Boston: Little, Brown and Company, 1964.

Online Sources:

The Lynching of Leo Frank
http://trutv.com/library
This day in History—Birth of a Nation
http://thomaswatsonmust go.org
Habeas Corpus: Rethinking the Great Writ of Liberty
http://gvpt.umd.edu
The Birth of a Nation and Black Protest
http://Chnm.gmu.edu.
History of Leo Frank
http://Georgiaencyclopedia.org
Birth of a Nation/Summary
http://sparknoted.com
Fusion Tickets
http://dailykos.com/story

Academic Book Reviews of *The Negro Problem* by W. P. Pickett
http://jstor.org
Poll Tax in the United States
http://Wikipedia.org
A Black History Moment The Blinding of Isaac Woodard Jr.
http://theobamacrat.com
Exhibits—Hall Timeline
http://Visitthecapital.gov/exhibits-hall timeline
Slavery and Identity among the Cherokee
http://nativeamericanhistory.about.com/od
The Federalist No. 78
http://Constitution.org
Speech on the Reception of Abolition Petitions—John C. Calhoun 1837
http://utk.edu.com
Commonwealth v. Aves, 1836
http://law.jrank.org/pages
Adams's Arguments in *Amistad* Case
http://history.com
Thomas Jefferson to John Holmes
http://loc.gov/exhibits
Cohens v. Virginia
http://oyez.org/cases
Slavery in New Jersey
http://slavenorth.com
The Three-Fifths Compromise
http://digitalhistory.uh.edu.
The Stono Rebellion
http://pbs.org/wgbh
The Cotton Gin and Eli Whitney
http://history.com/topics
The *Amistad* Case
http://npg.si.edu
The Thirteenth Amendment
http://13thamendment.harpweek.com
The Dred Scott Decision
http://gilderlehrman.org
United States v. Ortega
http://press-pubs.uchicago.edu
Civil Rights Act of 1866
http://wikisource.org
Ku Klux Klan Act
http://education.harpweek.com
A Supreme Case of Contempt
http://abajournal.com/magazine
Guinn v. United States
http://answers.com/topic
Review of Eric Freedman's Book, *Habeas Corpus: Rethinking the Great Writ of Liberty*
http://gvpt.umd.edu

Bibliography

Justice Hugo Black
http://encyclopediaofalabama.org
Geary Act
http://Wikipedia.org
Los Angeles Riots
http://southcentralhistory.com
Heart of Atlanta Motel v. United States
http://oyez.org/cases
Commerce Clause
http://law.cornell.edu
Rebecca Felton
http://georgiaencyclopedia.org
O. J. Simpson Murder Trial
http://Wikipedia.org
The Case of Emmett Till
http://history.com
Emmett case
http://cms.westport.K12.ct.us
1946 Lynchings at Moore's Ford Bridge
http://gcpagenda.org/index
Desegregation of the Armed Forces
http://trumanlibrary.org
Civil Rights, 1946
http://authentichistory.com/1946

CPSIA information can be obtained
at www.ICGtesting.com
Printed in the USA
BVHW07s2101270818
525643BV00008B/361/P